Exam Ref SC-100
Microsoft Cybersecurity
Architect

Yuri Diogenes
Sarah Young
Mark Simos
Gladys Rodriguez

Exam Ref SC-100 Microsoft Cybersecurity Architect

Published with the authorization of Microsoft Corporation by:
Pearson Education, Inc.

ISBN-13: 978-0-13-799730-5
ISBN-10: 0-13-799730-2

Library of Congress Control Number: 2022950836

ScoutAutomatedPrintCode

TRADEMARKS

WARNING AND DISCLAIMER

SPECIAL SALES

For information about buying this title in bulk quantities, or for special sales opportunities (which may include electronic versions; custom cover designs; and content particular to your business, training goals, marketing focus, or branding interests), please contact our corporate sales department at corp-sales@pearsoned.com or (800) 382-3419.

For government sales inquiries, please contact governmentsales@pearsoned.com.

For questions about sales outside the U.S., please contact intlcs@pearson.com.

Printed in Great Britain by Ashford Colour Press Ltd.

CREDITS

EDITOR-IN-CHIEF
Brett Bartow

EXECUTIVE EDITOR
Loretta Yates

SPONSORING EDITOR
Charvi Arora

DEVELOPMENT EDITOR
Rick Kughen

MANAGING EDITOR
Sandra Schroeder

SENIOR PROJECT EDITOR
Tracey Croom

COPY EDITOR
Rick Kughen

INDEXER
Erika Millen

PROOFREADER
Donna Mulder

TECHNICAL EDITOR
Mike Martin

EDITORIAL ASSISTANT
Cindy Teeters

COVER DESIGNER
Twist Creative, Seattle

COMPOSITOR
codeMantra

GRAPHICS
codeMantra

Pearson's Commitment to Diversity, Equity, and Inclusion

Pearson is dedicated to creating bias-free content that reflects the diversity of all learners. We embrace the many dimensions of diversity, including but not limited to race, ethnicity, gender, socioeconomic status, ability, age, sexual orientation, and religious or political beliefs.

Education is a powerful force for equity and change in our world. It has the potential to deliver opportunities that improve lives and enable economic mobility. As we work with authors to create content for every product and service, we acknowledge our responsibility to demonstrate inclusivity and incorporate diverse scholarship so that everyone can achieve their potential through learning. As the world's leading learning company, we have a duty to help drive change and live up to our purpose to help more people create a better life for themselves and to create a better world.

Our ambition is to purposefully contribute to a world where:

- Everyone has an equitable and lifelong opportunity to succeed through learning.
- Our educational products and services are inclusive and represent the rich diversity of learners.
- Our educational content accurately reflects the histories and experiences of the learners we serve.
- Our educational content prompts deeper discussions with learners and motivates them to expand their own learning (and worldview).

While we work hard to present unbiased content, we want to hear from you about any concerns or needs with this Pearson product so that we can investigate and address them.

- Please contact us with concerns about any potential bias at https://www.pearson.com/report-bias.html.

Contents at a glance

Contents

Chapter 6 Design a strategy for securing server and client endpoints   159

Introduction

The SC-100 exam measures your ability to accomplish the following technical tasks: design a Zero Trust strategy and architecture; evaluate Governance Risk Compliance (GRC) technical strategies and security operations strategies; design security for infrastructure; and design a strategy for data and applications.

Candidates for this exam should have advanced experience and knowledge in a wide range of security engineering areas, including identity and access, platform protection, security operations, securing data, and securing applications. They should also have experience with hybrid and cloud implementations.

Responsibilities for a Microsoft Cybersecurity Architect include designing and evolving the cybersecurity strategy to protect an organization's mission and business processes across all aspects of the enterprise architecture. The cybersecurity architect designs a Zero Trust strategy and architecture, including security strategies for data, applications, access management, identity, and infrastructure. The cybersecurity architect also evaluates Governance Risk Compliance (GRC) technical strategies and security operations strategies. The cybersecurity architect continuously collaborates with leaders and practitioners in IT security, privacy, and other roles across an organization to plan and implement a cybersecurity strategy that meets the business needs of an organization.

This book covers every major topic area found on the exam but does not cover every exam question. Only the Microsoft exam team has access to the exam questions, and Microsoft regularly adds new questions to the exam, making it impossible to cover specific questions. You should consider this book a supplement to your relevant real-world experience and other study materials. If you encounter a topic in this book that you do not feel completely comfortable with, use the "Need more review?" links you'll find in the text to find more information and take the time to research and study the topic. Great information is available at *docs.microsoft.com*, MS Learn, and blogs and forums.

Organization of this book

This book is organized by the "Skills measured" list published for the exam. The "Skills measured" list is available for each exam on the Microsoft Learn website: *microsoft.com/learn*. Each chapter in this book corresponds to a major topic area in the list, and the technical tasks in each topic area determine a chapter's organization. If an exam covers six major topic areas, for example, the book will contain six chapters.

Preparing for the exam

Microsoft certification exams are a great way to build your resume and let the world know about your level of expertise. Certification exams validate your on-the-job experience and product knowledge. Although there is no substitute for on-the-job experience, preparation through study and hands-on practice can help you prepare for the exam. This book is *not* designed to teach you new skills.

We recommend that you augment your exam preparation plan by using a combination of available study materials and courses. For example, you might use the *Exam Ref* and another study guide for your at-home preparation and take a Microsoft Official Curriculum course for the classroom experience. Choose the combination that you think works best for you. Learn more about available classroom training, online courses, and live events at *microsoft.com/learn*.

Note that this *Exam Ref* is based on publicly available information about the exam and the author's experience. To safeguard the integrity of the exam, authors do not have access to the live exam.

Microsoft certifications

Microsoft certifications distinguish you by proving your command of a broad set of skills and experience with current Microsoft products and technologies. The exams and corresponding certifications are developed to validate your mastery of critical competencies as you design and develop, or implement and support, solutions with Microsoft products and technologies both on-premises and in the cloud. Certification brings a variety of benefits to the individual and to employers and organizations.

> **MORE INFO** **ALL MICROSOFT CERTIFICATIONS**
>
> For information about Microsoft certifications, including a full list of available certifications, go to *microsoft.com/learn*.

Quick access to online references

Throughout this book are addresses to webpages that the author has recommended you visit for more information. Some of these links can be very long and painstaking to type, so we've shortened them for you to make them easier to visit. We've also compiled them into a single list that readers of the print edition can refer to while they read.

Download the list at *MicrosoftPressStore.com/ExamRefSC100/downloads*

The URLs are organized by chapter and heading. Every time you come across a URL in the book, find the hyperlink in the list to go directly to the webpage.

Errata, updates, & book support

We've made every effort to ensure the accuracy of this book and its companion content. You can access updates to this book—in the form of a list of submitted errata and their related corrections—at:

MicrosoftPressStore.com/ExamRefSC100/errata

If you discover an error that is not already listed, please submit it to us at the same page.

For additional book support and information, please visit *MicrosoftPressStore.com/Support*.

Please note that product support for Microsoft software and hardware is not offered through the previous addresses. For help with Microsoft software or hardware, go to *support.microsoft.com*.

Stay in touch

Let's keep the conversation going! We're on Twitter: *twitter.com/MicrosoftPress*.

Acknowledgments

The authors would like to thank Loretta Yates and the entire Microsoft Press/Pearson team for their support in this project. We would also like to thank Mike Martin for reviewing this book, Hassan Rasheed for the assistance with the exam topics, and Rick Kughen for the editorial review.

Yuri would also like to thank: my wife and daughters for their endless support; my great God for giving me strength and guiding my path on each step of the way; my co-authors Mark, Sarah and Gladys for the amazing partnership on this project and for their friendship.

Mark would also like to thank: my wonderful wife and children for their patience, support, and love; my many mentors for their patience in answering my questions and teaching me; the Security and IT professionals on the front lines for sacrificing more than you should for the safety of our organizations, society, and economy; and Yuri, Sarah, and Gladys for your partnership on this book and your friendship.

Sarah would also like to thank my parents for their unwavering support throughout my life; my awesome co-authors Mark, Yuri and Gladys; a shout out to my many Microsoft colleagues who have supported me through challenging times: Pen, Shelly, Gary, Michael, Naomi, Orin and Matt; and finally, Grayson, Minako and Shion who did nothing to help write this book. Grayson, please stop breaking your teeth because the vet bills are extortionate.

Gladys would also like to thank my husband and children for their understanding and support, my parents and sisters being there for me when needed and the many colleagues and mentors that have helped me learn and grow both technically and professionally including Yuri, Mark, Sarah, Michael, Lora, Paul, Marialina, and Roger.

About the authors

YURI DIOGENES, MSC Master of science in cybersecurity intelligence and forensics investigation from UTICA College, currently working on his PhD in Cybersecurity Leadership from Capitol Technology University. Yuri has been working at Microsoft since 2006, and currently he is a Principal PM Manager for the CxE Microsoft Defender for Cloud Team. Yuri has published a total of 29 books, mostly around information security and Microsoft technologies. Yuri is also a Professor at EC-Council University where he teaches at the Bachelor in Cybersecurity Program. Yuri also has an MBA and many IT/Security industry certifications, such as CISSP, MITRE ATT&CK® Cyber Threat Intelligence Certified, E|CND, E|CEH, E|CSA, E|CHFI, CompTIA Security+, CySA+, Network+, CASP and CyberSec First Responder. You can follow Yuri on Twitter at @ yuridiogenes.

MARK SIMOS Mark Simos is Lead Cybersecurity Architect for Microsoft where he leads the development of cybersecurity reference architectures, best practices, reference strategies, prescriptive roadmaps, CISO workshops, and other guidance to help organizations meet cybersecurity and digital transformation goals. Mark is co-host of the Azure Security Podcast and actively contributes to open standards and other publications such as the Zero Trust Commandments, The Open Group Zero Trust Core Principles, NIST Guide for Cybersecurity Event Recovery (800-184), NIST Guide to Enterprise Patch Management (800-40), Microsoft Digital Defense Report, and Microsoft Security blogs. Mark also co-chairs the Zero Trust Architecture (ZTA) working group at The Open Group and has presented numerous conferences including Black Hat USA, RSA Conference, Gartner Security & Risk Management, Microsoft BlueHat, Microsoft Ignite, and Financial Executives International.

SARAH YOUNG Sarah Young is a Senior Cloud Security Advocate at Microsoft and a CNCF Ambassador with over a decade of experience in security across Europe, the US and Asia. Sarah is an experienced public speaker and has presented on a range of IT security and technology topics at industry events and holds numerous industry qualifications including CISSP, CCSP, CISM and Azure Solutions Architect and has previously co-authored Microsoft Press technical books. She is also a co-host of the Azure Security Podcast. Sarah has also won the Security Champion award at the Australian Women in Security Awards. She is an active supporter of both local and international security and cloud native communities. You can follow Sarah on Twitter @_sarahyo, although expect many dog pictures alongside security content.

GLADYS RODRIGUEZ Gladys Rodriguez is Principal Cybersecurity Engineer with over 25 years in the Information Technology field. As part of the Mission Engineering team, Gladys has helped embed existing security capabilities within Microsoft developed products/services. She has also helped create new security functionality for customers to enable zero trust in their environment. Recently, Gladys has been involved in helping develop zero trust strategies for Operational Technology used in Critical Infrastructure with special focus in aerospace solutions. Gladys is co-host of the Azure Security Podcast for both English and Spanish version. She has also contributed to publications such as the Microsoft Zero Trust publications, NIST SP 800-207, Zero Trust Architecture, Microsoft Exam SC-100: Microsoft Cybersecurity Architect and others. Gladys also spends a lot of time mentoring and sharing her knowledge with others to help them get more involved in the cybersecurity space.

CHAPTER 1

Build an overall security strategy and architecture

Building an end-to-end technical strategy and architecture is a foundational skill for cybersecurity architects. Cybersecurity architects (also known as security architects) are responsible for aligning and integrating the security architecture with existing enterprise, technical, and business architectures and strategies. Security architects are critically important for ensuring that the security team's capabilities and work are aligned with the business goals and reduce business risk. The skills described in this chapter will help you successfully architect security solutions and integrate capabilities into a security architecture.

Most organizations are on a Zero Trust transformation journey (even if they don't call it that) to modernize their security to keep up with continually evolving attacks while migrating to cloud services and adapting to rapidly changing business processes. This Zero Trust transformation is comparable in size and scope to cloud transformation in IT and digital transformation in the larger organization, shifting the core philosophy of security into an asset-centric, data-centric, and business-aligned function.

Security architecture is critical to this security transformation, aligning technical teams and capabilities with business and technology needs. Security architecture also connects and integrates security teams and capabilities with a coherent technical vision that helps everyone get on the same page, helping avoid and resolve technical conflicts. Architects translate the strategy and principles into actionable plans and designs that enable technical teams to move forward, often influencing or helping shape an organization's security strategy in the process.

This chapter introduces some core concepts, terminology, and skill sets of a cybersecurity architect.

Skills covered in this chapter:

- Skill 1-1: Identify the integration points in a security architecture by using Microsoft Cybersecurity Reference Architectures (MCRA)
- Skill 1-2: Translate business goals into security requirements
- Skill 1-3: Translate security requirements into technical capabilities, including security services, security products, and security processes
- Skill 1-4: Design security for a resiliency strategy
- Skill 1-5: Integrate a hybrid or multi-tenant environment into a security strategy
- Skill 1-6: Develop a technical governance strategy for security

Security architecture

Security architecture identifies, documents, and rationalizes all security and technical components, bringing them together into diagrams and documents to ensure they all fit together and meet the business and other external requirements. This technical discipline was modeled after how architecture works in building construction. Because security helps mitigate organizational risk, a security architect's job encompasses aspects of security, technical, and software architecture.

One of the most important aspects of security architecture is the translation of strategy into technical components and capabilities, similar to the role of an enterprise architect (see Figure 1-1).

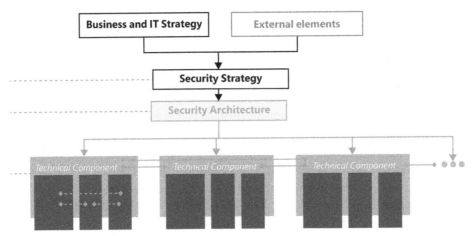

FIGURE 1-1 Security architecture diagram

Security architecture aligns with the security strategy and translates it into specific technical capabilities and relationships, providing clear technical guidance across all technical initiatives and security disciplines. Following are several key outcomes provided by security architecture:

- **Alignment** Security architecture is composed of artifacts that describe the end state for security, providing a unifying vision that makes the security strategy real by identifying the specific technical capabilities and components that implement it in the technical estate. This security architecture is a unifying force that connects security elements and guides the work and priorities of technical teams. Without this alignment, teams might work on lower-priority projects that have limited or zero impact on reducing organizational risk. Security architecture should also influence security strategy as architects learn what is (and isn't) possible with current security capabilities and the technical estate.

- **Integration** A good technical architecture clearly captures the major technical components (sometimes called *architectural building blocks*), their key relationships and dependencies, and how they integrate. Without this clarity and coordination, teams often work in isolation, creating gaps and conflicts. Often, attackers can find and successfully exploit these conflicts, creating organizational risk. By creating diagrams that outline the connections and relationships of all relevant components, many problems and conflicts can be discovered early and resolved while it's still easy and inexpensive to do so, rather than finding them in production when they are hard and/or expensive to change.

- **Continuous improvement** Security architectures are not perfect documents stored in an ivory tower; instead, they are living documents that are reviewed and updated regularly as requirements and capabilities change. Security architecture must help the technical teams document, track, and adjust to changing security, business, and IT strategies, threat trends, compliance requirements, cloud capability changes, and so on.

TIP

The technical estate is the total of an organization's technology and supporting elements, including devices, networks, applications, identities, and more. Before Zero Trust, this was often referred to casually as "the network," which is no longer an accurate description.

Security architecture is a connecting function and unifying force. This function helps ensure the time, effort, and money spent on security are focused on the most important and effective actions while reducing the occurrence of common internal coordination, integration, and alignment problems.

Security architects

Security architects build and maintain the artifacts that contain the technical vision for security and help security teams work with each other and other teams.

Security architects look at the technical estate and security program from strategic and tactical perspectives. They are always hunting for opportunities to be more effective at reducing security and organizational risks. Security architects also play a significant role in helping prioritize technical teams' work to ensure they focus on the most important risks, the most effective mitigations, and the easiest implementations.

IMPORTANT Architects are more than just technical experts! While architects must have some technical expertise in security disciplines, their focus and daily activities are very different from those of a technical expert. Technical experts focus on building and applying deep specialized knowledge in a particular security discipline, whereas architects focus on the big picture across all these disciplines and capabilities. Architects help ensure they all fit together into a coherent whole and support business and security strategies. Many security architects start as technical experts, but a security architect requires a different mindset (big picture and organizational risk–centric thinking) and additional skill sets (communication skills, business strategy, organizational dynamics, and more).

Figure 1-2 builds on Figure 1-1, adding the key responsibilities of a security architect:

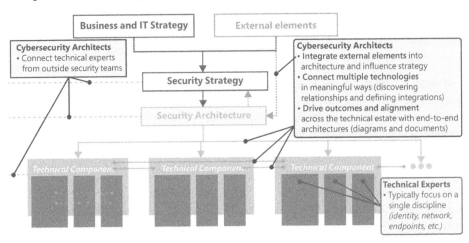

FIGURE 1-2 Security architect responsibilities

Through the course of their daily work, security architects are expected to do the following:

- Connect multiple technologies in meaningful ways to
    - Discover relationships between the technologies and technical teams.
    - Identify dependencies and hidden requirements in those relationships.
    - Identify opportunities from the connection of those technologies (for example, requiring healthy endpoint security before allowing users on those endpoints to access resources).
- Drive outcomes and alignment across teams to ensure technical work is coordinated and compatible. This helps reduce the constant stream of conflicting changes and other challenges when teams operate in isolated "silos" and don't communicate enough with each other.
- Integrate external elements into architecture (which can also directly influence security strategy), such as the threat environment, new cloud capabilities, new security capabilities (for instance, tools that could automate a manual process like XDR), and more.
- Connect technical experts in the IT and business units to ensure alignment with current goals, capabilities, and initiatives (the right security monitoring is applied to key business workloads, such as migrating to the cloud).

Collectively, these tasks keep the security architecture current, connect security teams to each other, and connect security to the larger organization.

Architects work across teams and roles

Security architects often work across many teams and with many roles at different levels within the organization. Figure 1-3 depicts how architects typically work in an organization.

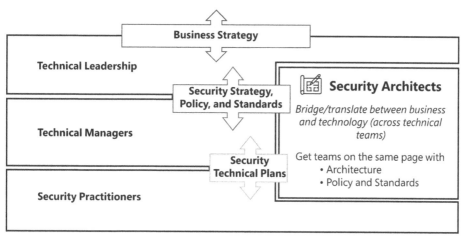

FIGURE 1-3 Security architect interactions

Architects engage in various leadership roles with teams, technical managers, and technical experts on the ground. This helps the architect understand the organization and ensures the technical vision and strategy are consistently understood and executed throughout the organization. This also helps ensure that feedback on technical constraints is accurately reflected in the strategy and planning process to avoid breaking expectations.

Zero Trust transformation and security architects

Security architects today operate in the context of a Zero Trust security transformation and are critical to its success. Zero Trust is the security component of a digital business strategy and is comparable in size and scope to the digital business and cloud technology transformation. This transformation is fundamentally shifting the assumptions of how information security operates—from protecting assets by securing the network to protecting assets wherever they are in the world. The technical drivers for this transformation are depicted in Figure 1-4.

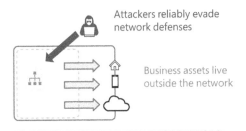

Attackers reliably evade
network defenses

Business assets live
outside the network

Zero Trust assumes _an open network_ where
trust must be _explicitly validated_

FIGURE 1-4 Zero Trust technical drivers

As the organization moves to digital business models and cloud platforms, they quickly find that classic network security strategies, such as the ones shown below, aren't enough to keep assets safe.

- A security perimeter approach will not protect assets outside the traditional network and firewall boundary (on cloud services and mobile devices, working from home, and so on).

- Network controls are ineffective at defending many other attack vectors (email/ phishing, endpoint, identity attacks like password spray, and so on).

Also, organizations find that rigid processes will not keep up with the rapid changes and demands of cloud platforms, business requirements, and rapidly evolving threats. Zero Trust is based on the following three principles:

- **Assume-breach (or assume compromise)** Assume-breach shifts the overall thinking, strategy, and architectures from creating a safe network to protecting assets anywhere, including those on an open network. This mindset shift helps you see the technical estate as a graph of connected nodes—like attackers do—making security planning more effective.

- **Verify explicitly** Reduces the attack surface of each asset.

- **Least-privilege access** Reduces the blast radius of compromises.

Zero Trust brings incredible benefits to your security posture and productivity while reducing the friction between internal teams in organizations. However, Zero Trust is disruptive because it changes many aspects of an organization's operations, shifting technology architectures, technical capabilities, and people's assumptions and mindsets about security.

Security architects are critical to Zero Trust

Security architecture plays a significant role in helping enable and support this Zero Trust security transformation. The clarity provided by the architecture and architects helps security and technical teams quickly understand what needs to be done and the order in which it should be done. This helps security teams effectively protect the organization's assets wherever they are instead of trying to apply old models that aren't effective or efficient in the age of cloud and dynamic threats.

Skill 1-1: Identify the integration points in an architecture by using Microsoft Cybersecurity Reference Architectures (MCRA)

The Microsoft Cybersecurity Reference Architectures (MCRA) is a key tool that helps security architects understand this journey and guide their teams through it. The MCRA is a set of modern security reference architectures focused on the needs of the current threat environment, cloud capabilities, and the Zero Trust security transformation.

> **NOTE** These reference architectures (in PowerPoint format) can be downloaded from *https://aka.ms/MCRA* and include detailed slide notes and links to Microsoft technical documentation. Videos are also available at *https://aka.ms/mcra-videos*.

MCRA and Cloud Adoption Framework Secure Methodology

The MCRA's technical architectures are complemented by the program and strategy guidance in the Cloud Adoption Framework (CAF) Secure Methodology. CAF Secure and MCRA provide guidance for modernizing security for Zero Trust. MCRA focuses on the technology aspects, while CAF Secure focuses on strategy and program elements. The CAF Secure methodology is described later in this book. Figures 1-5 and 1-6 show the two main menus of the MCRA that visually illustrate the contents of the MCRA.

Microsoft Cybersecurity Reference Architectures (MCRA)

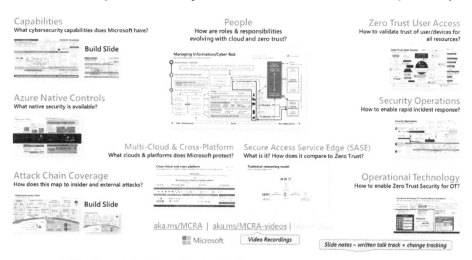

FIGURE 1-5 MCRA PowerPoint Zoom thumbnails of technical and other diagrams

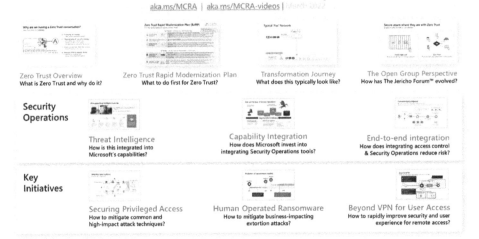

FIGURE 1-6 MCRA Main Menu Slide #2 with PowerPoint Zoom thumbnails of several sections on Zero Trust and other topics

The MCRA has a number of different perspectives on cybersecurity that currently includes the following:

- **Capabilities** This diagram describes Microsoft's overall cybersecurity capabilities, including a static slide and an animated build slide that introduces capabilities in small groups.

- **People diagram** This diagram describes key learnings on the current state of security roles and responsibilities.

- **Multi-cloud and cross-platform diagram** This section highlights the Microsoft cybersecurity capabilities that can help secure assets across multiple clouds.

- **Multi-cloud and cross-platform** Some people may incorrectly believe that Microsoft security only protects Microsoft products, but Microsoft security technology is multi-cloud and cross-platform, meaning its security capabilities are designed to protect all of an organization's assets across

  - Amazon Web Services (AWS)

  - Google Cloud Platform (GCP)

  - Third-party Software as a Service (SaaS) apps like ServiceNow and salesforce

  - On-premises datacenters

  - Linux, Windows, Mac, iOS, and Android

  - Various IoT and OT platforms

  - Microsoft platforms and applications

- **Attack chain coverage** This diagram illustrates common kill chain steps and maps in Microsoft capabilities to show how to get full end-to-end visibility and coverage across IT, IoT, and OT assets.

- **Technical reference diagrams** These diagrams illustrate how to address specific problem spaces in security (including technology integration points), including the following:

  - **Zero Trust user access** This diagram describes the components that provide secure access to workloads, explicitly validating user and device risk/trustworthiness using high-quality signals.

  - **Secure Access Service Edge (SASE)** This section describes this architectural approach and how Microsoft capabilities map to it.

  - **Security operations** This diagram describes the human-centric approach to security operations and how Microsoft capabilities help enable it, including

    i. Microsoft Defender (Extended Detection and Response – XDR)

    ii. Microsoft Sentinel (Security Information and Event Management – SIEM)

    iii. Supporting technologies in Defender and Sentinel, such as Security, Orchestration, Automation, and Response (SOAR), machine learning (ML), and User and Entity Behavior Analytics (UEBA)

- **Azure native controls** This diagram describes the Microsoft cybersecurity capabilities that provide visibility and control to help secure Azure environments and workloads, many of which are cloud-native and built into Microsoft Azure.

- **Operational technology (OT)** This diagram describes the challenges of securing industrial control systems (ICS) and how Microsoft Defender for IoT and Microsoft Sentinel help meet these challenges.

Zero Trust sections describe several aspects of Zero Trust, including the following:

- **Overview of Zero Trust** This section summarizes why Zero Trust is important, its principles, and other key elements.

- **Zero Trust Rapid Modernization Plan (RaMP)** This section describes a prioritized set of quick options for rapidly adopting Zero Trust approaches.

- **Transformation journey** This section contains a sequence of visual diagrams that use PowerPoint morphing transitions to show the evolution of a technical estate from a traditional flat network to a fully modern Zero Trust adaptive access approach.

- **The Open Group Perspective** This section shows an independent, third-party perspective on Zero Trust from The Open Group, which hosted the original Jericho Forum that pioneered the de-perimeterization concept in the early 2000s.

Additional security perspectives, including the following:

- **Beyond VPN** This section describes how to increase the security of virtual private networks (VPNs) and then move beyond this technology to more secure and user-friendly remote access solutions.

- **Ransomware** This section describes the attack patterns for highly damaging ransomware/extortion attacks and key mitigations.

- **Securing privileged access** This section describes privileged access attacks that greatly expand the damage and impact of an incident and a summary of Microsoft recommendations to mitigate them.

- **Security operations integration** This section describes how important and difficult it is to integrate security operation tools and Microsoft investments to solve these challenges.

- **Threat intelligence** This section describes the value of applying Threat Intelligence effectively and how Microsoft approaches this area.

TIP

Don't miss the details in the MCRA. This reference architecture includes detailed slide notes with a talk track describing each slide (broken down by each click for animated slides). Most of the product-capability boxes in the MCRA also have links to the associated document type and a ScreenTip with a short description of the capability.

How to use the MCRA to identify integration points

The MCRA can be used for many purposes, including as a starting point for creating a security architecture, as a comparison for an existing security architecture, or as a learning or teaching tool. One of the most useful aspects of the MCRA for architects is that it can help identify technical integration points. The MCRA provides the following information about integration points:

- Modern technical security architectures for identity and access, security operations, cloud platforms, and more

- The technical capabilities available from Microsoft

- How these technical solutions relate to and integrate with each other

- How these solutions integrate with existing technology (across clouds and platforms)

- How the technologies relate to the overall technical strategy of a Zero Trust transformation

- How threat intelligence works and is integrated into Microsoft capabilities (often saving you the trouble of significant manual integration work)

- How to prioritize the implementation of capabilities to get the highest-impact quick wins using the Zero Trust RaMP

- What the overall Zero Trust implementation journey looks like architecturally

Security architects can use the MCRA to guide their journey through security modernization and Zero Trust. These modern security reference architectures allow you to

- Identify key integration points
- Learn about security and Microsoft capabilities
- Accelerate the development and maturity of your security architecture

Skill 1-2: Translate business goals into security requirements

One of the core responsibilities of a cybersecurity architect is to help translate business goals into security requirements that clearly articulate the desired outcomes and their success criteria. This is critically important because it keeps security efforts aligned with important business strategies and risks, avoiding wasted security resources, time, and effort on lower-impact activities.

This translation to security requirements is often done in partnership with security leaders and other stakeholders that also play a role in bridging interests between the larger organization and security teams.

> **IMPORTANT** This activity is similar in many ways to the enterprise architect's responsibility to translate business requirements into technology capability requirements. You can learn more about enterprise architecture from sources like the TOGAF standard at *https://www.opengroup.org/togaf*.

Following are some examples of business goals and risks that need to be translated into security requirements:

- **Business-critical assets** An organization has business-critical assets required for its mission.
  - **Intellectual property** Intellectual property is used to maintain a competitive advantage (and/or to ensure customers don't get pricing leverage on the organization's core business).
  - **Critical systems** Critical systems are used to generate a large amount of money while online that will be lost if they are offline.
- **Digital transformation** The organization is undertaking a new digital initiative that can't fail or be taken offline by ransomware/extortion or other attacks. (For example, a brick-and-mortar retailer might add digital capabilities to adopt an omnichannel approach critical to its strategy.)
- **Expanding to new market(s)** The organization is entering a new market or country and is focused on quickly capturing market share before its competitors do. This market or country has strict security and privacy regulations that must be met before operating the business.

Translation process

Translating these business priorities, goals, and risks into actionable security outcomes and requirements is an iterative process that typically includes these activities:

- **Discover and capture the business goals, risks, insights, and requirements.** This can be sourced directly from the business stakeholders or indirectly via stakeholders that work directly with those business leaders (security leaders, enterprise architects, and so on).

- **Identify and document the security requirements that are required to meet these goals.** These should reflect a clear and coherent set of security outcomes and the success criteria to measure whether you have achieved them. Sometimes the security requirements are explicitly called out in the business context. Sometimes, they are only implied by these requirements and would need to be validated with business stakeholders.

Some examples from the above list are

- Protecting business-critical assets could include protecting intellectual property from theft and protecting critical systems from ransomware or extortion attacks.

- Expanding to new markets in the European Union or Brazil would require demonstrating compliance with local privacy and security regulations in order to do business.

This discovery and analysis may be a formal, deep process or quick and informal steps depending on the scope and urgency of the situation (a large project with extensive planning, urgent learnings from an active security incident, digital transformation project, smaller agile workstreams within it, and so on). Regardless of this process's level of formality, the results must always be documented and shared with stakeholders for validation.

- **Align to and influence the security strategy** As security architects go through this, they should ensure the approach they are taking is aligned with the security strategy (which is, ideally, the security component of the digital business and/or cloud technology strategy). This translating activity should influence that strategy (or trigger the creation of a strategy), particularly for organizations earlier in the Zero Trust journey without a formal documented strategy or formal integration of security strategy into business or cloud strategy. Additional reading on security strategy may be found at *https://aka.ms/securitystrategy*.

  Because the business environment, goals, and risks are constantly changing, this process will need to be run iteratively as needed to ensure the security requirements reflect the current needs of the business. For example, the business may face business or regulatory challenges trying to enter a market and delay or cancel that expansion in favor of another country, market, or another business initiative altogether.

- **Build a dialog and relationship with business counterparts** When interacting with their business counterparts, security architects (and other team members) should listen carefully and ask clarifying questions in business language. This can help start up a productive (and ongoing) two-way dialog and relationship with business leaders and team members. This relationship can benefit everyone and create increased trust and sharing of relevant insights and feedback to help everyone avoid surprise problems and internal friction.

Skill 1-3: Translate security requirements into technical capabilities, including security services, security products, and security processes

Architects also help with the next step of translating those security requirements into specific technical solutions and capabilities. Architects work with technical teams across security and IT (and sometimes business teams) to ensure the solutions and technical capabilities are designed and implemented to meet those requirements.

Translating security requirements into technical solutions and capabilities is an iterative process focused on continuous improvement, so security architects should expect to do this task regularly as they build and refine solutions. This is because business requirements change (as described in Skill 1-2) and also because technology changes as cloud applications, platforms, and internal technical teams update them. Additionally, the available security capabilities on the market and security threats also change frequently, which may require updates to security solutions and capabilities. Architects should adopt and advocate for a continuous improvement approach that makes incremental progress.

The translation of security requirements into technical capabilities focuses on two types of activities:

1. **Plan technical architectures and solutions** These architectures and solutions will achieve the requirements' desired outcomes and success criteria. Typically, this involves these tasks:

    - **Identify the risks and threats to the assets** This includes the security assurances for assets that are required to protect them against those threats. This can be done through a formal threat-modeling exercise or informal expertise and knowledge of an attack. The main security assurances are confidentiality, integrity, and availability, though safety and other physical considerations can become important with Internet of Things (IoT) and Operational Technology (IT) / Industrial Control Systems (ICS).

    - **Identify and evaluate security controls** These controls should provide the desired security assurances and mitigate the risks to the assets. You can use the MCRA to help identify the applicable technology you can use for these scenarios. For example, you might find that a business-critical solution is composed of containers hosted in Azure, servers, SQL databases (on-premises and in AWS), and Azure

Storage. For designing controls to detect and respond to anomalous activities, refer to the MCRA Security Operations and Azure Native Controls diagrams. These show how to use a combination of Defender for Cloud (for the underlying infrastructure components) and Microsoft Sentinel (for custom logging/alerting and detecting application layer anomalies). Because this is a custom application, you can also use threat modeling tools to help identify specific controls for the application's design and components.

> **NOTE** Depending on the asset's value, you should also include additional defense-in-depth provisions that assume a breach will occur (such as assuming a determined adversary will find a way to work around one or more controls). Ensure the fallback controls are different than the primary controls to ensure that the adversary cannot use the same workaround again (such as not using a firewall as a backup control in case another firewall fails).

- **Identify integration points**   Once you have identified the controls you need, you need to ensure these controls will be integrated with other processes and other parts of the technical estate, including existing security capabilities. For example, ensure the business-critical application's security alerts will appear as high-priority alerts in an alert queue monitored by security operations analysts. Also, ensure the analysts are educated on interpreting alerts and initiating escalation processes.
- **Continuously improve architecture documentation**   You should do this as requirements and capabilities change (or as your understanding of them improves).

2. **Support detailed technical planning and implementation by security and technical teams**   Depending on the culture, size, and responsibilities of your organization, security architects may lead these activities or simply act in a review and oversight capacity.

- **Develop the technical design and plan**   Define the detailed technical end state identified in the previous step and the technical implementation plan to get there. This hands-on activity often includes learning and testing in a technical lab (or test cloud tenant) before production implementation. It also includes capturing that procedure in automation or documentation with enough detail to rapidly rebuild if a disaster such as a ransomware/extortion attack occurs.
- **Use MCRA as a design reference**   This is another place where the MCRA is a critically important asset for leveraging the work, wisdom, and learnings from other experts. The MCRA technical architectures can act as a starting point for your design or for comparison with an existing design. Additionally, technical security documentation from Microsoft can also help. (See *https://aka.ms/securitydocs*.)
- **Continuously improve documentation and implementation**   As requirements and capabilities change (or as your understanding of them improves), you should continuously improve your documentation and implementation.

This planning process is an iterative and ongoing problem-solving process that benefits from having diverse perspectives, experiences, and expertise applied to it. Successful architects follow these principles in this problem-solving process:

- **Make it a collaborative partnership** among technical teams, rather than the architects designing it in isolation or having each technical team design their part in separate silos. While there is always individual work to do, a collaborative and integrated approach helps avoid conflicting assumptions and gaps, allowing you to find and resolve issues quickly before they derail projects. Effective security outcomes must span the traditional technical silos of network, identity, apps, data, and so on. Different experts must work together to resolve issues.

- **Think completely about the change** Architects should take a big picture view to do the following:

  - **Identify downstream effects** Understand the impact on other systems from the planned solutions. Architects and technical teams should ask and answer the questions like "What impacts does this change have on other systems? What could it enable? What could it break?"

  - **Evaluate for the lifecycle** Understand the full lifetime of systems, how they will be used, and plan for that. For example, many organizations fall into the "collection is not detection" trap and adopt log collection and analysis tools without any plan for who will be creating the alerts, who will be monitoring and responding to them, not wasting time on false-positive alerts, and so on.

- **Always document** You should always capture the key outcomes and reasoning for decisions in architectural documents and diagrams to make sure the solution is understood by the teams implementing, operating, or modifying it later.

- **Make it an iterative/creative process** This problem-solving often requires experimentation, design, and other creative skills to find the best way to approach a technical problem and communicate with others. Teams should constantly question their definition of the problem and their solution. They should focus on learning, improving, forming and proving/disproving hypotheses, and continuously incorporating feedback. Sometimes, you need to refine a solution, sometimes, you need to abandon an approach, and sometimes, you need to add a completely new approach.

Following are some illustrative examples of applying these techniques to security requirements:

Requirement: Mitigate compromise of accounts using password spray and other credential compromise

This is a common attack that is used against both privileged and standard user accounts (which could come from threat intelligence reports, analysis of previous attacks on the organization, or other sources):

- **Primary security controls** Azure AD Identity Protection, Azure AD Conditional Access, Microsoft Defender for Identity

- **Primary MCRA section(s)** Zero Trust User Access, Securing Privileged Access
- **Primary security disciplines** Access Control, Security Governance

Requirement: Shorten response times to attacks across resources in the environment

This is a common requirement across organizations and business requirements.

- **Primary security controls** These vary by asset types that need to be monitored and the maturity of the organization's processes and skill sets. Architectural considerations for meeting this requirement should focus on common attacker entry points of endpoint, identity, email, and other application attacks. Microsoft Defender 365 capabilities function both as a detection and threat-hunting capacity. As the organization migrates workloads to cloud providers like Azure, AWS, and GCP, this can include using Microsoft Defender for Cloud to monitor the underlying infrastructure and workloads and Microsoft Sentinel to provide custom alerting on application anomalies. As Security Operations processes and skill sets mature, this can include requiring custom analytics for detection and threat hunting, leveraging Microsoft Sentinel.
- **Primary MCRA diagrams** Security operations.
- **Primary security disciplines** Security operations, innovation security, and security governance.

Requirement: Integrate network security into Infrastructure as Code (IaC) automation

This is a common requirement for organizations adopting IaC approaches to mature infrastructure management using Azure Resource Manager (ARM) templates, Bicep language, Terraform automation, and similar technologies.

- **Primary security controls** Azure Firewall, Microsoft Defender for Cloud, Azure Web Application Firewall (WAF) capabilities in Application Gateway and Front Door
- **Primary MCRA diagram** Azure native controls
- **Primary security disciplines** Asset Protection, Innovation Security, and Security Governance

Requirement: Enable eDiscovery processes for Office 365 data

This is a common requirement for organizations adopting Office 365 that must meet legal requirements for identifying and delivering electronic information that can be used as evidence in legal cases.

- **Primary security controls** Microsoft Purview eDiscovery solutions
- **Primary MCRA diagrams** Azure native controls
- **Primary security disciplines** Security Governance

In summary, architects help translate security requirements into specific technical solutions and capabilities, working across teams to drive consistent and coherent outcomes that meet those requirements.

Skill 1-4: Design security for a resiliency strategy

The daily work of architects must always be done in the context of increasing organizational resilience. Resilience is the ability to resist the impact of damage and recover quickly, which is critical as all types of organizations today face non-step disruptive forces from business, technology, and security sources. Security threats such as extortion and ransomware are increasingly focused on monetizing the disruption of business operations (by threatening to shut down operations or threatening not to enable the restoration of operations). Therefore, ensuring the security strategy and architectures are focused on business resilience as a top priority is critical.

Architects are responsible for ensuring the security strategy, architecture, and technical plans will support the organization's resiliency.

Reducing risk by reducing critical security events

Security resiliency focuses on reducing organizational risk by reducing the number and severity of business-impacting security events. As described by the assume breach (assume compromise) principle in Zero Trust, there is no such thing as perfection in security. You must always assume the attackers will achieve at least some degree of success and plan your defenses accordingly. (This concept is sometimes referred to as "defense in depth.")

Achieving resiliency in cybersecurity requires balancing investments across the lifecycle, which is shown in Figure 1-7.

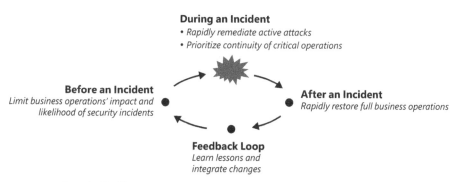

FIGURE 1-7 Security Resilience

Cybersecurity architects should balance their focus and investments across these areas:

- **Before an incident** Focuses on setting up preventive controls that block attack techniques, contain potential adversary activity, detections that allow security operations to quickly learn about an active attacker, and additional telemetry to support investigations. This is also a good time to prepare teams to rapidly recover from attacks with attack simulations, tabletop exercises, red/purple teaming, and similar activities.

- **During an incident**   Focuses on the accuracy, impact, and speed of an investigation to reduce organizational risk by reducing the time attackers have access to resources (dwell time). Security Operations must be able to rapidly detect an attack, investigate it to understand the nature and extent of the attack, and coordinate with IT Operations and DevOps teams to remove the attackers' access to the organization's assets (response/recovery).

- **After an incident**   Focuses on rapidly recovering any lost business capabilities and functionalities, such as technical elements like restoring data and rebuilding systems. It can also include helping implement temporary workarounds and planning replacement systems. Depending on the attack, this may also require sustaining and repairing customer trust and the organization's reputation (which often starts during the incident).

- **Feedback loop**   Focuses on making sure past attacks don't work again tomorrow by performing a root-cause analysis on high-impact and new/novel incidents that help the organization learn how to better block, detect, or respond to future similar incidents. Security architects help with this root-cause analysis (often leading it) and ensure they are integrated into the technical architectures and processes of the organization.

- **Potential for overlapping stages**   In some organizations, different teams may perform these focus areas simultaneously. Larger organizations often have different specialized teams and often manage multiple smaller incidents simultaneously (and sometimes larger incidents from multiple advanced adversaries). Security architects help ensure that investments are balanced across these phases and the organization is not neglecting any one of them. The consequences of an off-balance strategy create unnecessary organizational risk. Some examples include:

  - **Neglect detection and response by focusing only on preventive controls**   This situation leaves organizations unable to detect and respond to attacks until most (or all) of the damage is already done.

  - **Neglect prevention by focusing too heavily on detection and response**   This situation can cause the organization to experience more avoidable incidents and increase the severity of all incidents because they cannot block or slow the attackers' progress with preventive controls.

  - **Neglect the feedback loop**   This situation causes the organization to experience the same types of incidents repeatedly because they haven't performed a root-cause analysis to learn from previous instances.

Resilience requires shifting from a network-centric to an asset- and data-centric mindset

Security architects can help increase resilience by helping shift the strategies, architectures, and technical teams' mindsets from network-centric security approaches to focusing on business-critical data and systems. Many existing security programs and controls are myopically focused on protecting the network (assuming anything in it will be safe). This creates a weak (and non-resilient) security posture because security has limited visibility or control over non-network attacks (like phishing and password spray). This includes anything that doesn't cross the network boundary, such as lateral traversal attacks, mobile devices accessing cloud services, and so on.

Protecting business assets in today's threat environment requires shifting from this generic network protection strategy to tailoring and prioritizing security for the most important assets and using a full multi-technology architecture based on Zero Trust principles. Part of an architect's job is to help mature the security architecture and teams. As part of this maturation process, the architect transitions them from a network defense approach into an asset-centric approach that focuses on the business-critical data and systems that have the most impact on the organization's goals and risks.

The architectures and tools described in the MCRA and throughout this book will help you plan and implement security controls that balance investments across all these phases, shift to an asset-centric and data-centric approach, and increase your organization's resilience to cyberattacks.

Skill 1-5: Integrate a hybrid or multi-tenant environment into a security strategy

Another key challenge faced by security architects today is adapting to the "hybrid of every-thing" technical estate that often includes

- Traditional on-premises IT systems (traditional user devices and applications, servers and datacenters, server and web applications, and so on)
- Operational technology (OT) and industrial control systems (ICS)
- Internet of Things (IoT)
- Software as a Service (SaaS) applications
- A workload hosted on multiple cloud vendors (often referred to as *multi-cloud*) for Infrastructure as a Service (IaaS) and Platform as a Service (PaaS) services such as Micro-soft Azure, Amazon Web Services (AWS), or Google Cloud Platform (GCP)

Security architects must ensure that technical capabilities are designed for all these technical estate elements. Doing so efficiently and effectively requires the following two principles:

- **Embrace cloud-native solutions** These solutions are built for the cloud (unlike legacy on-premises solutions that pre-date the cloud). This prevents the team from manually adapting the tooling to the cloud or particular cloud provider(s). These solutions are also often delivered using a cloud SaaS model that speeds up adoption and reduces ongoing overhead to maintain the solution (compared to on-premises solutions that require infrastructure installation and management).
- **Embrace multi-cloud and hybrid solutions** These solutions help drive a consistent outcome across the various cloud providers and provide common management portals,

reports and analytics, application programming interfaces (APIs), and more. This simplifies your processes and helps avoid the need for multiple tools that provide similar information and controls that must be reconciled and integrated (which takes time and resources away from much more important tasks like designing a profound of controls and responding to threats).

Following the above principles will ensure the organization has effective and efficient technical solutions. Usually, solutions will embrace both of these principles (like Microsoft Defender for Cloud), but sometimes, solutions are built for a single cloud provider only. This creates a choice for security architects and technical teams, who must balance each option's benefits.

Adapting security technical capabilities and processes to a shared responsibility is another critical aspect of securing cloud resources. For cloud-hosted workloads, cloud providers are responsible for many tasks that security and IT teams typically do for on-premises datacenters. However, cloud providers don't handle all security concerns, nor can you monitor their internal networks and servers that also host other customers. That means it's critical to understand who does what. Architects help technical teams and leaders understand what cloud providers do and don't do for security, enabling the organization to focus on what must be done.

Cloud providers' responsibility varies by their individual capabilities, but generally, they are responsible for SaaS applications, PaaS platforms, and IaaS platforms, as shown in Figure 1-8.

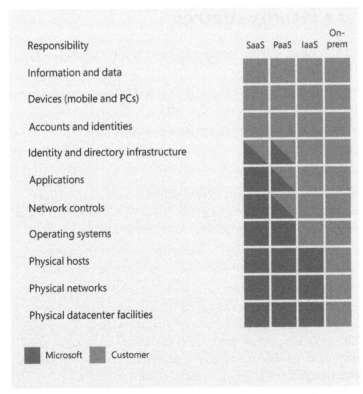

FIGURE 1-8 Shared responsibility model

NOTE You can read more about the shared responsibility model at *https://aka.ms/ sharedresponsibility*.

Integrating a hybrid or multi-tenant environment into a security strategy requires updating how the organization executes the identify, protect, detect, respond, and recover security lifecycle. This includes adopting cloud-native and multi-cloud capabilities and updating the organization's processes and skills accordingly. This also includes educating teams on the shared responsibility model and adapting the organization's processes to that model.

Skill 1-6: Develop a technical governance strategy for security

Another key responsibility of architects is developing a technical governance strategy that supports the overall security governance strategy—the overall security strategy and larger business strategy. Governance helps ensure that the planned security controls and assurances are implemented consistently across the technical state and processes of the organization. Without governance, security assurances and controls often rapidly drift as other priorities cause them to be neglected, resulting in a degraded security posture and a false sense of security.

Architects are instrumental in developing the technical governance strategy that includes elements like these:

- **Advising on security governance tooling** This includes cloud security posture management solutions (CSPM) like Microsoft Defender for Cloud and threat and vulnerability management (TVM) capabilities like those included in Microsoft Defender for Endpoint (MDE).

- **Providing technical advice** Architects provide security leaders and managers as they establish and mature new governance functions like security posture management teams.

- **Advising on regulatory compliance** Architects help evaluate and interpret requirements, review draft compliance reports, and evaluate the effectiveness and accuracy of methods and processes to report compliance.

- **Technical consistency and completeness** Ensuring that security architecture and implementation address all technology types and provide end-to-end consistency. The key focus areas are

  - **Balanced multi-technology strategy** Ensuring the organization has a complete and balanced approach for visibility and control across identity, application, devices, data, network, and infrastructure (not just classic network security perimeter controls).

- **Consistent execution** Ensuring the organization executes a policy effectively within a technology layer. For example, ensuring the device/endpoint strategy doesn't have long-term or permanent exceptions that increase organizational risk, such as devices without endpoint detection and response (EDR) agents, devices with local users as local administrators, and so on.

- **Inter-team process monitoring** Ensuring governance teams can monitor processes between teams to make sure they are consistently executed, including

  - **External threat intelligence** Architects ensure that the right stakeholders analyze external threat reports from different teams, and the actionable learnings are documented and shared across teams. For example, an architect would design detections for a new attack type and initiate threat-hunting activity for any attacks that slipped past the detections before they knew about it.

  - **Internal threat intelligence** Architects make sure posture management and other teams are being informed of attack trends in security operations, such as increasing or decreasing instances of phishing, exploiting unpatched vulnerabilities, or exploiting zero-day vulnerabilities.

  - **Root-cause analysis** Architects ensure a root cause is initiated for novel and major incidents.

These technical elements enable an effective and efficient security governance process, helping reduce avoidable organizational risk and a false sense of security.

Thought experiment

In this thought experiment, demonstrate your skills and knowledge of the topics covered in this chapter. You can find answers to this thought experiment in the next section.

Tailoring security technology to different business scenarios

Fabrikam is a company that manufactures premium high-tech auto parts, sells these products at its retail stores, and licenses its retail business model and brand to franchisees. After one of Fabrikam's competitors was hit by a ransomware/extortion attack and couldn't manufacture or sell parts for over two months, cybersecurity became a top business priority at Fabrikam.

You are the lead cybersecurity architect at Fabrikam and are working closely with the chief information security officer (CISO) of Fabrikam to "make sure this never happens to us." Business leaders from the key business units involved in creating revenue (manufacturing, retail store/franchise management) have provided a list of top business assets and capabilities to protect and recover if a business outage occurs. The IT and OT teams have identified the technical systems associated with critical business assets on the list, and you are tasked with prioritizing and helping design protections for them.

The retail store/franchise management business leaders have identified their business priorities as follows:

- **Franchisee and customer trust** Show customers and franchisees that Fabrikam will continue providing them with quality products when needed (to meet their customer and financial demands)

- **Franchisee and customer communications** The ability to communicate among themselves and with franchisees, including during an IT system crisis

Manufacturing leaders have identified their business priorities as:

- **Manufacturing line uptime** Ensure that manufacturing lines can continue operating and making products, even during a cyberattack.

- **Manufacturing line quality** Ensure that manufacturing processes haven't been tampered with, which could cause customer safety or liability issues.

With this information in mind, answer the following questions:

1. What are the security requirements for the retail store/franchise management business priorities?

2. What MCRA diagrams and technical solutions would you use to meet these requirements?

3. What are the security requirements for the manufacturing division's business priorities?

4. What MCRA diagrams and technical solutions would you use to meet these requirements?

Thought experiment answers

This section contains the solution to the thought experiment. Each answer explains why the answer choice is correct.

1. The retail store/franchise management business priorities include one explicit security requirement and raise the possibility of several implicit requirements:

   - The explicit requirement is to protect the availability of internal and customer communication systems (email with Office 365 and chat/phone/conference services using Microsoft Teams).

   - Some implicit requirements that are likely to be desired by business stakeholders are the confidentiality of sensitive communications (so they aren't disclosed and used against the organization) and the integrity of these communications to ensure they aren't tampered with.

2. Because business stakeholders would be accountable for any negative business impact of an attack, all explicit and implicit requirements should be articulated, documented, and discussed with business stakeholders to confirm and correct them as needed. Because security resources are always limited, these requirements discussions should also prioritize the importance of these requirements based on business needs.

3. The Zero Trust User Access diagram and Securing Privileged Access section of the MCRA are the primary diagrams you would use to meet the retail store/franchise management security requirements. Using the Shared Responsibility Model, the architect can identify that Microsoft Teams and Office 365 are SaaS services where Microsoft has most of the responsibility for service availability. The Fabrikam security responsibility attack surface they need to secure includes the user and administrator accounts and workstations where these accounts log into (which are addressed by these sections in the MCRA).

4. The manufacturing business priorities include two explicit security requirements and raise the possibility of an implicit requirement:

   - The explicit requirement to protect the availability (uptime) of manufacturing line operations.

   - The explicit requirement to protect the integrity of the process (quality).

   - A potential implicit requirement is the confidentiality of the unique designs of Fabrikam's products. Business stakeholders may be concerned that product designs, proprietary manufacturing processes, or other intellectual property could be stolen and provided to a competitor that could produce an identical or similar item. Because this wasn't explicitly called out, you should ask business stakeholders if this is an important consideration or if there are other business risk mitigations in place (patents for products/processes, competitors don't have advanced metallurgical skills required to effectively copy the processes, and so on).

> **NOTE** This prioritization of requirements (with confidentiality last) is unusual for IT systems but very common for operational technology (OT) systems.

The Operational Technology (OT) diagram is the primary MCRA diagram you would use to meet the manufacturing security requirements. This diagram describes the use of Defender for IoT to monitor OT systems and common approaches to isolation (such as the hard boundary of physical disconnection, soft(ware) boundary, and internal segmentation). Security architects must work with security technologies and OT teams to identify and plan the best controls for these systems.

Based on the MCRA guidance, the technical capabilities and solutions that may be applicable include

- **Defender for IoT** This is a high-likelihood component because it is non-intrusive to business operations because it is based on passive network packet capture.

- **Isolation boundaries** Security architects will have to work with OT teams to determine whether this solution would be feasible based on a deeper analysis of Fabrikam technical systems and processes. A hard boundary would not be feasible if the production lines require connectivity to IT networks or the cloud for control consoles, business analytics, or other functions. Any soft boundary would have to be carefully planned with OT teams to consider people, process, and technology aspects across all scenarios in the asset lifecycle. For example, external vendors who maintain the OT systems must be able to maintain the equipment (often using vendor-managed laptops) but shouldn't be able to introduce malware, worms, and other security risks in the process.

- **Security updates and patches**   Security architects will have to work with OT teams to determine whether these mitigations would be feasible based on a deeper analysis of technical systems, processes, and vendor support contracts. Most manufacturing line systems are based on Windows and Linux, but the versions are frequently outdated. The OT teams have expressed concerns that they may be unable to update this software because of stability issues, such as older hardware, support contract restrictions, and safety regulations (which certified the whole system, including the software).

Chapter summary

Security architecture plays a critical role in helping security teams reduce organizational risk by providing

- Alignment is the process of providing diagrams and documents that describe the end state for security, defining the unifying technical vision that aligns with the business strategy, and making these real with specific technical capabilities and components.

- Integration is the process of showing how the major technical components integrate, including key relationships and dependencies.

- Continuous improvement is the process of providing living documents that are updated regularly to meet evolving requirements and capabilities.

- Cybersecurity architects are critically important to the success of the security strategy of the organization. They build, maintain, and evangelize the security architecture, help integrate new requirements and capabilities, and help drive team outcomes and alignment.

- Architects help the organization adapt to continuous changes from external forces like threat evolution, business strategy shifts, technical platform changes, and new security capabilities.

- Cybersecurity architects are different than technical experts. While architects require technical acumen and some technical expertise, they are fundamentally different from technical specialists and experts. Architects use different thought processes and communication patterns as they engage across different technical and business teams daily and spend more time asking questions than answering them.

- The Microsoft Cybersecurity Reference Architectures (MCRA) documentation at *https://aka.ms/MCRA | https://aka.ms/MCRA-videos* is a key resource for cybersecurity architects. This documentation provides references that can be used as a starting point for new architectures, as a comparison point for existing security architectures, and as a learning resource. The MCRA helps you build a clear technical end state and identify key integration points in an architecture.

- Cybersecurity architects' key responsibility and skill is translating business goals into security requirements. These security requirements clearly articulate the outcomes and success criteria for achieving those outcomes. These security requirements should always be documented and validated with business and other stakeholders.

- Security architects help technical teams translate those security requirements into technical capabilities, including security services, products, and processes. Architects take a collaborative and holistic approach where security architects partner with technical teams and others to design and validate the capabilities and solutions that meet the security requirements over a full lifecycle. Architects use iterative approaches where these solutions and capabilities are continuously and incrementally improved over time.

  - Security architects design security for a resiliency strategy that ensures the organization can limit the impact of damage from attacks and recover quickly from them.

  - Security architects help the organization adapt to the "hybrid of everything" technical estate that spans traditional IT, OT, and IoT resources. This includes helping the organization adopt a hybrid and multi-cloud approach for infrastructure and development security to provide consistent security controls across multiple IaaS and PaaS providers.

  - Architects also support a technical governance strategy for security that supports and enables the security governance strategy, providing technical tooling and technical advice and helping ensure sound practices are followed for compliance reporting, technical design, and inter-team processes.

CHAPTER 2

Design a security operations strategy

Security operations are often thought of as the "cool" bit of security. Aside from the stereotype of people in black hoodies hunched over their keyboards, it is often the next thing that comes to mind when both the public and non-security stakeholders think about IT security. The general security operations stereotype is of many dedicated security operations center (SOC) analysts in an operations room with a big screen, a la *War Games*, where attacks are stopped in their tracks.

While aspects of this stereotype are indeed based on reality, crafting a modern security operations strategy ideally starts long before you hire a single SOC analyst. Before you can detect attacks, you need to be able to define the events you need to collect in your environment, select the right tooling, and so on.

Skills covered in this chapter:

- Skill 2-1: Design a logging and auditing strategy to support security operations
- Skill 2-2: Develop security operations to support a hybrid or multi-cloud environment
- Skill 2-3: Design a strategy for SIEM and SOAR
- Skill 2-4: Evaluate security workflows
- Skill 2-5: Evaluate a security operations strategy for the incident management lifecycle
- Skill 2-6: Evaluate a security operations strategy for sharing technical threat intelligence

Skill 2-1: Design a logging and auditing strategy to support security operations

From a top-down IT organizational view, logging and auditing isn't an activity that is necessarily exclusive to the security domain. Many other IT functions need logs from the IT environment; most commonly, this is the IT operations and internal audit function within an organization. However, the logs these functions require are unlikely to be the same as those required for a security operations function (although there is often some overlap). This section of the chapter covers the skills necessary to design a logging and auditing strategy to support security operations according to the Exam SC-100 outline.

Centralizing log collection

In the past, it wasn't unusual to have logs collected in several different stores throughout an organization's IT environment because having a central place to store logs could be costly and complicated to set up. With the advent of cloud services, those challenges have largely dissipated, so you should aim to have logs collected in one central store: this makes management and querying of the logs more straightforward and efficient. In global organizations, local regulatory requirements may exist to keep log data within a certain jurisdiction. If this is the case, endeavor to minimize the number of log stores required to keep the log collection architecture as simple as possible.

Deciding which logs have security value

Security operations always start with logs. Without logs, we can have no visibility into what is happening in the IT environment. However, while most components of an IT environment create logs—whether they be user accounts, applications, virtual machines (VMs), or firewalls—not all logs have security value. Logging and storing logs for the sake of logging and storing logs is an unsustainable practice, albeit one that has been used countless times in the past. The disadvantages to this approach are many, but the three key downsides are:

- **Cost and management of log storage**   The more logs you have, the more storage you need to have available to store said logs. As all good architects are aware cost is king. Most stakeholders who hold the purse strings will need justification as to why the spend on log storage is necessary, so it is important to be able to demonstrate that the logs you are collecting and storing are actively being used in security operations. In Log Analytics (the underlying log storage mechanism for Microsoft Sentinel), the cost of the platform is based on the number of logs ingested into a workspace and how long they are retained.

> **NOTE**   Logging isn't just a security function, and discussions will need to be had with other parts of an IT organization—operations and development—to decide how and what is logged and who is paying for it.

- **Performance impact of log searches**   The more logs your query must search through, the slower the query may become. The impact on the query performance will depend on the log-searching tool you use. For example, if you use a cloud-based security information and event management (SIEM) tool such as Microsoft Sentinel that can increase its compute power as required, the performance hit will be less than if you were using something that was on-premises and had a fixed compute capability. However, it is still something to consider when designing your logging and auditing strategy. Even Microsoft Sentinel queries using Kusto Query Language (KQL) can time out if the query is taking too long to run.

- **Complexity of queries** With more logs to search through, the complexity of queries and detections being run as part of the security operations function may increase, which can put more overheads on SOC analysts and the general management of your SOC.

But how do you decide which logs have value in the context of security operations? This is a question that security architects have long been plagued by, and sadly there is no one-size-fits-all answer that can be applied to every organization. However, a rule of thumb is if a log isn't going to be used for reactive security operations (such as detections) and If it isn't going to be used for proactive security operations (such as hunting), then, as a security architect, you need to seriously question whether that log needs to be collected. If you can't demonstrate a tangible security use for a log type, then it probably shouldn't be collected by your SOC.

Too often, this step is overlooked. Rather than questioning what a log will be used for when connecting or activating a new device in the environment, a security engineer will just select all of them rather than evaluating each log, as shown in Figure 2-1.

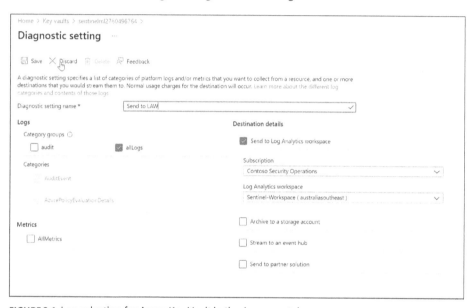

FIGURE 2-1 Log selection for Azure Key Vault in the Azure portal

Designing security operations use cases

The most effective method for creating an effective logging and auditing strategy is to know your organization's security operations use cases. Having a range of use cases from different parts of your organization allows you to work back from the use case and determine which logs and audit trails are required to allow said use case to be realized in your security operations.

For example, let's say the accounting department needs the security operations team to take action and investigate if any privilege escalation occurs in their SAP system that handles payment of expenses and employee salaries. This is a high-priority issue because it could disrupt the payment of employee salaries. A malicious actor could start changing the bank accounts that are paid. Because this issue is so sensitive, the accounting team wants any account involved in such an incident to be disabled immediately. There are three questions we need to ask:

1. The first question we need to ask is this: What logs do we need to be able to create a detection for this in our SIEM? In this case, we will need the audit logs from SAP, and if it's SAP on Azure, we might also require the Azure AD sign-in and audit logs to get more detail about user actions.

2. After we have determined what logs we need, the second step is to create a detection that will pick up on this activity. In Microsoft Sentinel, we would create an analytics rule with the appropriate KQL to determine this in the logs. At this stage, we would also need to determine how frequently the analytics rule would need to run. Because it's a high priority, it will likely be running more frequently (maybe every 10 minutes), and the SOC team needs to be alerted quickly and be able to take action if an incident is raised.

3. Thirdly, we can now design automation to go along with this incident: The accounts team has asked that any user account in such an incident be blocked. We can create remediation automation in Azure Logic Apps to immediately trigger an account block if an incident is raised.

No doubt, creating security operations use cases takes time and effort, but it allows security architects to have full traceability of the whys when questioned about a logging and auditing strategy.

> **NOTE** It can also be helpful to use industry-standard frameworks such as MITRE ATT&CK to determine your organization's coverage of their Tactics and Techniques. You can read more about this at *https://attack.mitre.org/*.

The MITRE ATT&CK coverage screen in Microsoft Sentinel is shown in Figure 2-2.

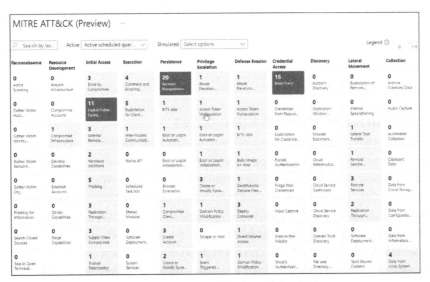

FIGURE 2-2 Mapping MITRE ATT&CK coverage in Microsoft Sentinel

Determining log retention periods

The rule of thumb and determining your use cases for security operations discussed in the previous section is a great starting point for deciding which logs have security value. Still, even within the logs with value, not all logs are created equal. Many organizations split their security logs into:

- **Low fidelity** Logs that are noisy and high-volume but provide less useful signals to be used in security operations (for example, Azure Firewall logs)
- **High fidelity** Consolidated alerts from specialized security tools that have already analyzed the raw logs (such as Microsoft Defender for Cloud alerts)

In that same vein, not all logs collected for use in security operations need to be retained for the same period. Determining the exact retention periods required for the security and audit logs for your organization will come down to several factors, which may include:

- Use cases
- Budget
- An organization's internal IT standards
- External regulatory IT standards

Remember that not all logs need to be retained for the same period. For example, in Log Analytics, you can configure retention periods on a per-table basis and thus can keep some tables for longer than others as required, as seen in the screenshot below.

> **NOTE** The default (and free) retention setting for logs in Log Analytics is 30 days. If Microsoft Sentinel has been activated on a Log Analytics workspace, then logs can be retained in that workspace at no cost for up to 90 days. Make sure you take advantage of this if you are using Microsoft Sentinel.

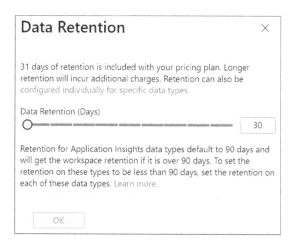

FIGURE 2-3 Configuring Data Retention settings in Log Analytics

Azure Data Explorer (ADX) and Blob Storage are other options for the long-term storage of logs.

NOTE You can read more about integrating Log Analytics/Microsoft Sentinel into ADX at *https:// docs.microsoft.com/azure/sentinel/store-logs-in-azure-data-explorer?tabs=adx-event-hub*.

Skill 2-2: Develop security operations to support a hybrid or multi-cloud environment

It may seem obvious, but security operations need to cover an organization's entire IT environment, end to end. Malicious actors look for blind spots and gaps in monitoring and remediation that they can use in order to evade detection. Of course, having security operations cover your entire environment—which has always been challenging—has become even more difficult since an organization's IT environment stopped being solely in an organization's datacenter. This section of the chapter covers the skills necessary to develop security operations to support a hybrid or multi-cloud environment according to the Exam SC-100 outline.

Cross-platform log collection

As discussed in Skill 2-1, log collection is a key foundation of a strong security operations function. In modern environments, this has become even more challenging. Not only do you have to decide what logs you need to collect that have security value, but those logs need to be extracted from a wide variety of places ranging from your own on-premises datacenter to a public cloud (or clouds) to a SaaS platform and collected into a centralized SIEM function. It is also rare/impossible that the logs will all be collected in the same manner, so you need to use tooling that can support log collection in different formats.

In a modern cloud-based SIEM like Microsoft Sentinel, collecting logs from multiple sources was considered when building the product. Hundreds of sources are provided for out-of-the-box solutions—including other public clouds such as AWS and GCP—that can be deployed at the click of a button through the Content Hub, as shown in Figure 2-4.

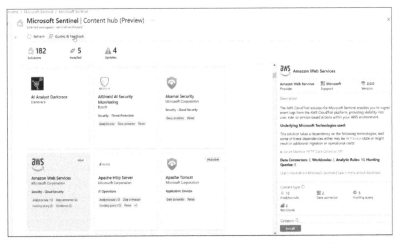

FIGURE 2-4 Searching for solutions in the Microsoft Sentinel Content Hub

Even Microsoft can't provide solutions to every potential data source out there, so Microsoft Sentinel includes several generic methods of data collection to cover data sources that may not have an out-of-the-box solution:

- **Log Analytics agent (LA agent) for Windows** This agent can collect Windows Security Events and send them to a Log Analytics workspace from any machine on which it is installed, whether on-premises or in the cloud.

- **Log Analytics agent for Linux (also known as the OMS agent)** This agent can centralize syslog and Common Event Format (CEF) logs from any host that generates them and send them to a Log Analytics workspace, whether on-premises or in the cloud.

- **Azure Monitor Agent (AMA)** This is the latest version of Microsoft's log collection agent and is available for both Windows and Linux. Eventually, it will completely replace the LA agent. AMA supports the same log collection methods as the LA agent and provides enhanced capabilities for filtering logs before they are sent into a Log Analytics/Microsoft Sentinel workspace.

> **MORE INFO** You can read more about the differences between the LA Agent, OMS Agent, and the AMA at *https://docs.microsoft.com/azure/sentinel/ama-migrate*.

- **Codeless connector platform (CCP)** This platform allows partners and developers to create custom data connectors for Microsoft Sentinel using an API connection. Connectors made using CCP are fully SaaS-based.

Many options and methods are available for bringing logs into a SIEM from all corners of your environment for effective detection and response.

> **NOTE** This section has discussed some features found within Microsoft Sentinel, Microsoft's cloud-based SIEM solution. If your organization uses another SIEM tool, we recommend that you choose a cloud-based one so that it can safely handle the large amounts of telemetry that modern IT environments generate and can use machine learning and AI to process the anomalies without human intervention.

Cloud security posture management (CSPM)

Although it has "cloud" in the title of its name, CSPM isn't just for cloud-based entities. CSPM tools are tools that monitor the security posture of an entity and will give recommendations based on best practices and industry standards about how to increase the security posture of said entity.

It may not sound particularly exciting or sexy, but research shows that misconfiguration is one of the leading—if not *the leading*—causes of breaches. Malicious actors look for misconfigurations to exploit—and they often find them. Typically, a misconfiguration is a minor and easy-to-fix problem that has been previously overlooked for some reason. For example, a virtual machine (VM) with port 23—Telnet—left open to the Internet will be found within seconds by port scanners that malicious actors are constantly running. If anyone in your organization tries to log in to that machine via Telnet, it is easy to intercept the username and password. Those credentials could subsequently be used elsewhere in your environment. This might seem like a basic example, but the reality is that misconfiguration happens all the time, whether it be intentional, accidental, or through a lack of knowledge. And it causes breaches.

Microsoft's CSPM tool is Defender for Cloud (previously known as Azure Security Center) and covers both Infrastructure as a Service (IaaS) and Platform as a Service (PaaS). For VMs, it can be installed on hosts in Azure, AWS, GCP, and on-premises. Even if you have legacy VMs on-premises, it doesn't mean they can't benefit from the tooling now powered by the cloud. Defender for Cloud security posture feature provides a grouped list of security posture improvement recommendations, as shown in Figure 2-5.

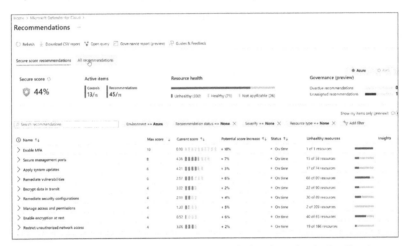

FIGURE 2-5 Checking security posture recommendations in Defender for Cloud

You can drill into these recommendations to see each individual recommended change, as shown Figure 2-6.

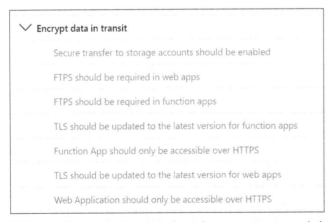

FIGURE 2-6 Drilling into the grouped security posture recommendations in Defender for Cloud

These recommendations can be automatically remediated or manually actioned by your SOC team (or whatever team takes responsibility for this). Sometimes, configuration changes will be actioned outside the SOC. By enabling CSPM across your entire IT environment, you can ensure that configurations stay consistent and secure and reduce your risk of a misconfiguration causing a breach. Alerts from a CSPM tool can also be integrated into a SIEM so the SOC team can act if a high-risk misconfiguration is detected. We discuss posture management using Defender for Cloud in more depth in Chapter 5.

Focus on identity

You may have already heard the phrase "identity is the new perimeter" when discussing cloud and hybrid IT environments. In modern IT environments, identity is our perimeter rather than the traditional network. The most effective way to modernize your security operations and enable identity across different clouds and platforms is to focus on prevention, detection, and response for identities rather than networks. Network-based detections can't pick up on devices not connected to your internal network. Especially in this post-COVID-19 era, think about how many devices are connected to your internal network versus an external one. Most of you reading this will likely agree that there are far more external than internal!

Identities are the most effective way to track user activity across multiple platforms, clouds, and hybrid environments. Several Microsoft security tools can assist with monitoring identities:

- **Microsoft Entra**   This suite of products includes Azure Active Directory, Microsoft Entra Permissions Management, and Microsoft Entra Verified ID. Entra Permissions Management is a cloud infrastructure entitlement management (CIEM) solution that facilitates the management and monitoring of permissions entitlement across different cloud platforms.

> **NOTE**   You can read more about Microsoft Entra Permissions Management at *https:// aka.ms/PermissionsManagement.*

- **Microsoft Identity Protection**   This tool incorporates all of Microsoft's identity risk learnings gathered from all the cloud platforms that Microsoft runs (Azure, Xbox, and so on) and uses this information to highlight risks in your identity setup. It can automatically remediate these risks and export the alerts to a SIEM for correlation with other data sources.
- **Azure AD sign-in logs and audit logs**   If I was asked to provide a top ten list of the logs that I recommended that people ingested into their SIEM, this would be at the top. It's critical that you can correlate sign-in and audit logs with other data sources to flush out anomalies and—assuming that you have a centralized identity provider—this is how SOC analysts can track activity that is likely to be tied to one user, even if they are moving across clouds and different platforms.

Internet of Things (IoT) / Operational Technology (OT) coverage

IoT/OT environments can be quite different in how they can be monitored compared to the rest of an IT environment, so it's worth calling this out as part of multi-platform, modern security operations. Traditionally, IoT/OT environments were not monitored or sparingly monitored. There were a few reasons for this:

- **Inability to install monitoring on IoT devices** Many IoT devices run rudimentary OSs that cannot have additional software or functionality installed on them, which can severely hinder monitoring efforts.

- **Proprietary protocols** Many IoT/OT technologies use proprietary protocols that cannot talk to a standard IT environment, so they are often left alone from a monitoring perspective because it is too hard and/or not worth the effort to integrate them into the wider security operations function.

- **Air-gapped environments** Some IoT/OT environments are completely air-gapped, which makes monitoring challenging or impossible with older monitoring technologies.

- **Limited use of IoT/OT outside specialized industries** About ten years ago, IoT/OT environments only existed for certain industry verticals such as manufacturing.

Many of these challenges still exist with regard to monitoring an IoT/OT environment. The explosion of IoT technologies and several high-profile breaches of IoT/OT environments have made it harder for organizations to simply ignore the IoT environment.

Because of these challenges, specialized security tools for IoT/OT environments are necessary for managing and monitoring devices in these environments. Defender for IoT is a unified security solution for identifying IoT and OT devices, vulnerabilities, and threats and managing them through a central interface. As with all good security tools, the alerts it generates can be exported to a SIEM solution to gain further correlation and visibility across your entire IT environment.

MORE INFO You can read more about Defender for IoT at *https://docs.microsoft.com/azure/ defender-for-iot/*.

Skill 2-3: Design a strategy for SIEM and SOAR

At the heart of a SOC is a SIEM and—at least in more recent times—a security orchestration, automation, and response (SOAR) tool. These tools provide a central hub for the SOC and SOC analytics to conduct their security operations function from. Sometimes, a SIEM and SOAR are separate tools, and sometimes—as is the case with Microsoft Sentinel—the SIEM and SOAR functions are combined into one product.

This suite of capabilities allows SOC analysts to centralize logs and detect, analyze, and respond to threats in your organization's environment. Thus, designing an effective strategy for your SIEM and SOAR use is critical for fit-for-purpose security operations. This section discusses the skills necessary to design a strategy for SIEM and SOAR according to the Exam SC-100 outline.

Microsoft Security Operations Reference Architecture

Microsoft has its own reference architecture for security operations, as shown in Figure 2-7.

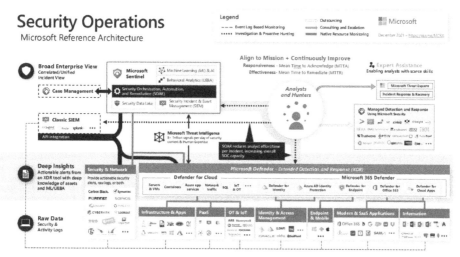

FIGURE 2-7 The Microsoft Security Operations Reference Architecture

Figure 2-7 is complicated, and while you don't need to memorize the information shown here for the SC-100 exam, it is important to be familiar with the principles of this architecture.

> **MORE INFO** You can read more about the Microsoft Security Operations Reference Architecture at *https://aka.ms/mcra*.

Ingest logs into your SIEM

Earlier in this chapter, we discussed determining which logs have security value as part of a logging and auditing strategy. You already know what logs help your security operations team need to detect things in your environment: great! In years gone by, the next step would be to connect all those logs directly into your SIEM. However, a modern approach is to consider whether any of the specialized security tooling in your environment is already analyzing those logs and creating consolidated, "high-fidelity" alerts.

For example, Microsoft Defender for Endpoint (DfE) collects and analyzes the activity on the endpoint devices it is installed on. The DfE product will analyze those logs and create alerts if malicious behavior patterns are detected on that device. Microsoft as a vendor provides regular updates to the DfE product based on new threat intelligence so it can detect new types of attacks or patterns of suspicious behavior. So, as an architect or SOC engineer, you have a choice: You can ingest the consolidated alerts from DfE and write detections based on those alerts (and others) coming in from the rest of your IT environment, or you can ingest the raw logs and write all the detections (including the ones that Microsoft manages for you in DfE) yourself. I know which one sounds easier to me! This is just an example, but this principle holds true for any specialized security tooling that analyzes a subset of your environment's logs and creates alerts. In the Microsoft security tool environment, these tools would be:

- Microsoft Defender for Cloud Apps
- Microsoft Defender for Cloud
- Microsoft Defender for IoT
- Microsoft Defender for Endpoint
- Microsoft Defender for Identity
- Microsoft Defender for Office 365
- Azure Active Directory Identity Protection

There are many advantages to using this approach in your SIEM:

- **Reduce the volume of raw logs being ingested into the SIEM**   Especially if you are using a cloud-based SIEM, reducing the volume of logs ingested into your SIEM will reduce your operating costs of the tool.

- **Reduce the complexity of detections in the SIEM**   Taking advantage of the specialized detections that are being written and updated by your vendor means that you can write simpler detections at the SIEM level.

- **Reduce false positives**   Using high-fidelity signals that have gone through additional layers of analysis reduces the likelihood that an incident could be a false-positive, which can waste a SOC analyst's time. (An analyst's time is something that is precious and in short supply!)

This is not to say that this approach can be taken for every log you need to collect. Realistically, there will be some raw logs in your environment for which you don't have specialized tooling, and that's OK. Figure 2-8 shows how a combination of raw logs and consolidated alerts can be ingested into a SIEM.

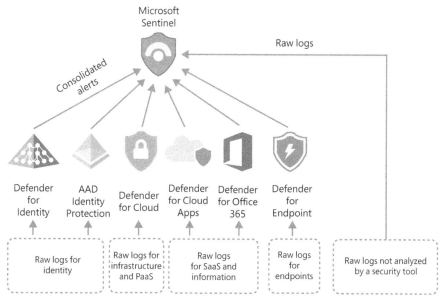

FIGURE 2-8 Ingesting raw logs into specialized security tools and ingesting consolidated alerts into a SIEM (where possible)

Automate, automate, automate

It's a well-known fact—even in the most mature SOC—that SOC analysts have too much to do and too little time to do it. Research shows that 44 percent of SOC alerts never get investigated by an analyst. That's a lot of alerts that are never looked at or action taken on them, and any one of those alerts has the potential to be a serious breach that isn't stopped before damage is done. So, how do we minimize the number of alerts within the SOC that aren't investigated? Well, you could look to hire more SOC analysts, but there are challenges with this approach:

- There is a worldwide shortage of SOC analysts (and has been for many years).
- SOC analysts are expensive to hire and retain due to their niche and in-demand skillset.
- Signals and alerts from modern IT environments are exploding exponentially, and the rate of signal and alert increase is much faster than the rate any organization can hire SOC analysts.

So, hiring more SOC analysts and throwing more people at the problem isn't the answer; what is? Automation! Automation can take people out of the equation when responding to incidents, and unlike people, automation allows for fast, consistent responses to alerts and incidents. Some specialized security tools (like the ones mentioned earlier in this section) can remediate alerts they generate before sending them to a SIEM. Still, in some circumstances, you will need an overarching SOAR capability to take action after a SIEM tool has done the correlation across the whole IT environment and detected that action needs to be taken. Sometimes, a SOAR is a separate tool from a SIEM, but Microsoft Sentinel is both a SIEM and SOAR product combined: Sentinel uses playbooks within Azure Logic Apps to automate actions in response to an incident, as shown in Figure 2-9.

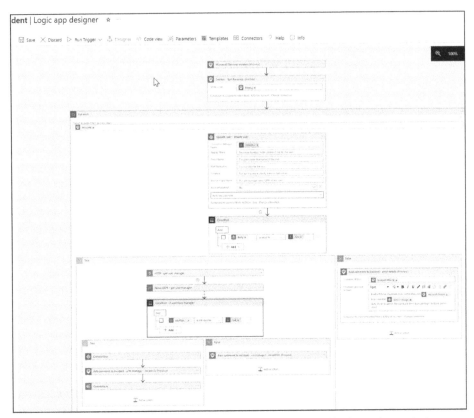

FIGURE 2-9 Designing a playbook for automation in Microsoft Sentinel in the Logic app designer

Automation can be used to remediate, notify, and sync to another third-party product, such as a ticketing system) Also, automation can be used to perform enrichment, such as taking the IP address(es) from an incident and calling a third-party API like VirusTotal to see if that IP is known to be malicious. Essentially, automation should—insofar as possible—minimize the number of time-consuming, repetitive tasks that SOC analysts would do manually. This frees up their time to look at more complex incidents (maybe that have never been seen before) that require a real person to look at them. We often hear in the media that automation is a way of reducing the number of people who need to be employed as automation is free and that by using automation, some people will be automated out of a job. This is certainly not the case in security operations. Using automation effectively frees SOC analysts from the burden of repetitive tasks and allows them to concentrate on complex security incidents.

Skill 2-4: Evaluate security workflows

When a security incident takes place—exactly like when a normal IT incident takes place—organizations need to have workflows that list the processes that need to take place, who needs to do them, and in what order. Typically these workflows can include processes such as triage, opening a ticket, taking remediation action, notifying relevant stakeholders, and so on. This section of the chapter covers the skills necessary to evaluate security workflows according to the Exam SC-100 outline.

General incident response workflow

Although not specifically part of the SC-100 exam outline, it's helpful to look at some industry standards here. The NIST Cybersecurity Framework Core Functions lists five overarching functions that should be performed continuously as part of an organization's operational environment to reduce cybersecurity risk. These functions are shown below in Figure 2-10.

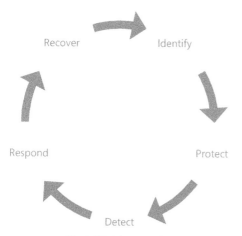

FIGURE 2-10 The NIST Cybersecurity Framework Core Functions

In this section, we will be focusing on activities that would come under:

- Respond
- Recover

But before we dive more into the details of security workflows, it is important to appreciate that these activities should exist as part of a bigger circle that plugs into and aligns with an organization's wider cybersecurity processes. Indeed, we have already touched on the Identify, Protect, and Detect parts of this flow earlier in the chapter, and will discuss them again later on.

> **NOTE** You can read more about the NIST Cybersecurity Framework at *https://www.nist.gov/ cybersecurity.*

Evaluating responses to incidents Incidents need to be evaluated from both a technical and operational perspective.

Technical response to incidents

On the technical side, there can be several goals (depending on your organization's security posture and risk tolerance), but there are two key goals that every incident response should aim to address from a technical perspective. The first is identifying the scope of the attack: malicious actors won't have breached a single endpoint, VM, user account, and so on.

Usually, attackers will move laterally through an environment and take over various assets in the IT environment until they find something of value to them. It is imperative to try and understand how widespread a breach is in your environment, as it will determine the exact recovery response, and if the attackers aren't removed from the entire environment effectively, they may persist and reinitiate the attack on your environment when things have "settled down."

In Microsoft Sentinel, the investigation graph is an example of using a SIEM to understand the full scope of an incident and all the entities and parts of the IT environment that may have been touched by this, as can be seen in Figure 2-11.

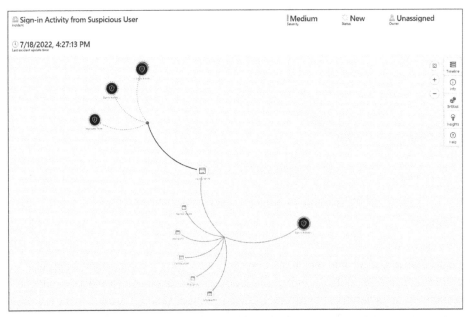

FIGURE 2-11 Using the Microsoft Sentinel investigation graph to understand the scope of an incident

Secondly, it can be helpful to attempt to identify the objective of an attack. The reasons that malicious actors target certain systems over others vary enormously, but they can usually be grouped into three broad buckets:

- Monetary gain
- State-sponsored
- Activism

The one that applies to your organization most likely depends on the industry vertical, geography, political landscape, and so on. It's helpful to know why you have been attacked because that knowledge will indicate whether attackers are likely to try again and maybe stay in your environment. For example, state-sponsored attackers are much more likely to try to maintain a foothold in an environment they are targeting, as there will be a specific reason they are doing so. Conversely, criminal gangs who are looking for "low-hanging fruit" organizations that can easily be breached by ransomware (making the attackers money) are less likely to spend time and resources trying to maintain a foothold in a specific organization because it will be easier and less time consuming to find the next easy-to-breach target.

Operational response to incidents

As with technical incidents, you should define several goals for an operational response. These will vary depending on your organization. However, following are a few that should be part of every incident response:

- **Clear roles and responsibilities for incident response**   Without these, who does what and when can become unclear and, worst case, mean key activities in the workflow aren't executed.

- **Stay business-focused**   This can be hard for the more technical folks out there, but it's important to keep in mind the business impact of both the attack and the response actions. Pull the plug to your organization's Internet connection to block the attackers from doing any further damage? Great, but that will take out all other operational systems and may lose the organization even more money and cause even more disruption. Sometimes compromises need to be made in the "ideal" security response to keep the business running as optimally as possible during the incident. Keep the lines of communication open with key stakeholders!

- **Evaluating recovery from incidents**   Evaluating the recovery from an incident can also be split into technical and operational, just like responses. As with technical incidents, several goals should be defined here that will vary depending on your organization:

  - **Keep focused on restoring the pre-incident environment**   Keep the recovery laser-focused on exactly what needs to be done to recover from the incident and to restore the environment how it was before the incident occurred. Teams may try to use this opportunity to get some technical debt fixed or upgrade a security tool now that they have an additional business justification. This isn't part of incident recovery and should be discussed another time as part of a wider security uplift.

- **Operational recovery from incidents**   As with technical incidents, there should be several goals defined here that will vary depending on your organization:

  - **Strong communication plan for both internal and external stakeholders**   I'm sure that everyone reading this has received an email from an organization at some point in their lives that says something along the lines of, "We've had a breach; here's what you need to know." Clear lines of communication must be established for internal and external stakeholders, so the right updates are given to the right people at the right time.

  - **Don't allow recovery scope-creep**   This is relevant to the operational side of recovery as well: make a recovery plan and stick to it unless new information comes to light.

NOTE Microsoft also publishes its own advice on incident response and incident response playbooks at *https://learn.microsoft.com/en-us/security/compass/incident-response-overview*.

Automation, automation, automation (again)

It's already been discussed in some detail earlier in this chapter, but it's worth calling out again how critical automation is to security workflows. The more steps that can be automated, the more quickly and more reliably actions can be taken. The following are tools that can be used within the Azure platform to create automation:

- **Azure Logic Apps**   Covered in detail earlier in the chapter.
- **Microsoft Sentinel**   As well as using playbooks provided by Azure Logic Apps, Microsoft Sentinel also has automation rules that allow for straightforward automations to take place in response to an incident (such as changing the status of an incident, assigning an owner, and so on). They can trigger playbooks for more advanced automation to take place. Figure 2-12 shows a new automation rule being created in Microsoft Sentinel.

FIGURE 2-12 Creating a new automation rule in Microsoft Sentinel

- **Microsoft Defender for Cloud**   DfC's workflow automation feature can trigger playbooks from Azure Logic apps to run in response to DfC alerts and recommendations, as shown in Figure 2-13.

FIGURE 2-13   Creating workflow automation in Microsoft Defender for Cloud

- **Microsoft 365 Defender automated investigation and response (AIR)**   This feature in M365 Defender can take remediation actions immediately or after approval by a nominated operations team. It can also help lessen the load of SOC analysts by recommending (and taking) other actions and determining whether a threat needs any action taken against it.

Skill 2-5: Evaluate a security operations strategy for the incident management lifecycle

This chapter has drawn many analogies with traditional IT operations. The incident management lifecycle is something you might be familiar with from standard IT operations and support, so let's look at how to approach this strategically from a security operations point of view, as there are both similarities and differences.

Just like in IT operations, security incidents should be responded to and contained as soon as possible to protect data, IT assets, and critical business processes. An effective incident response strategy will contain details about quickly and efficiently preparing, investigating, containing, and recovering from security threats to minimize business impact. This section covers the skills necessary to evaluate a security operations strategy for the incident management lifecycle according to the Exam SC-100 outline.

Microsoft's approach to security incident management

As you know—we hope anyway!—the SC-100 exam is a Microsoft exam. Therefore, it is helpful to look at how Microsoft handles security incident management using the NIST 800-61 response management phases, as shown in Figure 2-14.

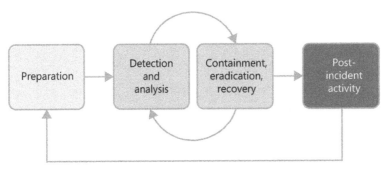

FIGURE 2-14 Microsoft's approach to security incident management

Microsoft's combined security teams and operational teams work side-by-side and use the same process when there is a security incident, just as you are recommended to do in your organization:

- **Preparation**   This is the preparedness work that an organization needs to do before a security incident occurs. Activities falling under this phase include readiness and staff training, security operations processes, and security tooling.

- **Detection and analysis**   This is when activities to detect a security incident in an organization's environment occur. This phase is also where the incident analysis takes place to confirm whether it is indeed a security incident (such as the eradication of false-positives and how much of the environment has been breached).

- **Containment, eradication, and recovery**   This refers to the actions taken to contain, eradicate, and recover from the security incident after it has been confirmed as a true-positive. Figure 2-14 shows more analysis may be required before recovery can be completed and the incident considered closed; it often isn't a one-step, linear process.

- **Post-incident activity**   When an incident has been closed and fully recovered, this phase is where the security incident's post-mortem happens, unlike a root-cause analysis from traditional IT operations. In this phase, the organization will look at why the security incident happened and what can be done to lower the risk of it happening again (the preparation phase). The post-mortem should also look at the effectiveness of the next four phases (detection and analysis and containment, eradication, recovery) to see if anything can be done better next time.

> **MORE INFO**   You can read more about Microsoft's approach to security incident management at *https://docs.microsoft.com/en-us/compliance/assurance/assurance-security-incident-management*.

Preparation

Many activities come under the umbrella of preparation: It's not just preparing for a security incident; it can also be activities that can prevent an incident from happening in the first place. All employees of an organization should receive training on security incidents and what to do if they suspect a security incident is occurring or has occurred.

Think about when you joined your current organization, academic institution, and so on. Did you have to take some mandatory security training as part of your onboarding procedure? Do you have to do refresher training yearly or even more frequently?

All employees who are granted access to IT systems (which is everyone nowadays) must understand the following:

- What a security incident is.
- How to report a potential security incident.
- How security incidents are responded to by the SOC.
- Where to find escalation contacts for security incidents.
- Any special security concerns relevant to that organization (these will often be privacy related because many jurisdictions have strict privacy laws and more and more jurisdictions have privacy breach reporting requirements).
- Some employees with special or privileged access to IT systems may require additional specialized training.

> **NOTE** We recommend that employees have an annual security incident training refresher.

Detection and analysis

We've mentioned earlier in this chapter that logging should be centralized (insofar as possible for your organization) to make detecting anomalies or suspicious activity straightforward. See Skill 2-1 earlier in this chapter if you need a refresher.

When an incident is detected, a severity rating should be assigned based on the triggered detection type. In Figure 2-15, you can see the configuration of an analytics rule in Microsoft Sentinel where the user decides on the initial severity rating of an incident that the analytics rule will create if triggered.

When an incident is raised, it should be triaged by the security response team, who will conduct additional analysis and use threat intelligence to ascertain whether the incident raised is a true-positive. If so, the security response time will confirm or adjust the incident's severity level so it is treated according to the organization's security operations processes.

From the moment a security incident is raised—just like in a normal IT incident— the security operations team needs to record all actions taken and relevant information gathered. This information gathering is necessary to ensure that everyone working on the incident knows who is doing what; what actions have already been taken; and what will be required for the post-incident analysis.

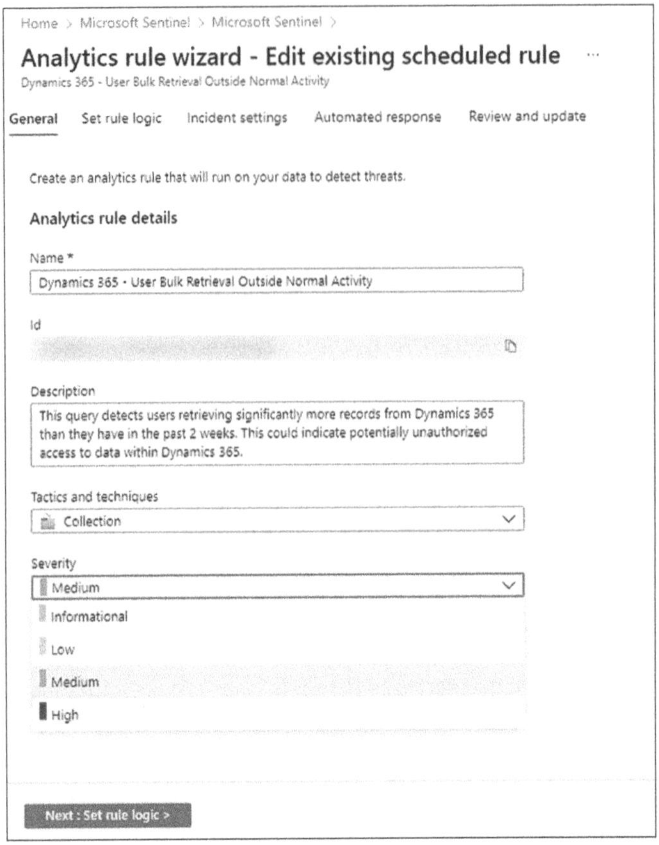

FIGURE 2-15 Setting the severity of a Microsoft Sentinel analytics rule

Containment

After the incident analysis is complete, containment is the next step. Containment stops malicious actors from moving any further through the IT environment. Also, this limits and/or prevents damage to the systems and data that have already been compromised.

It's important not to rush to contain an incident without fully completing the analysis stage of incident response. Rushing could lead to the containment activity not actually containing everything that has been compromised. Attackers can be sneaky. They might try to hide some of their tracks so that they can stay in your environment, wait for things to quiet down, and then restart their attack later. There have been breaches where attackers have "gone quiet" for years, sitting dormant in an organization's environment before relaunching their attack. This may sound far-fetched, but it happens quite frequently.

Eradication

As the name suggests, this is the process of removing an attacker(s) from the environment and mitigating any vulnerabilities that allowed the attacker into the environment in the first place.

For example, if the incident analysis showed that compromised credentials had started an incident without multifactor authentication (MFA), then part of the eradication process would be to have the credentials reset and turn on MFA for that account. (But you already have MFA on all your user accounts, right?) Containment must be fully completed before eradication occurs so that—as already discussed—attackers can't slip through the net and keep a foothold in your environment.

Recovery

When both containment and eradication have been completed, it's time to recover and restore business processes (and the underlying systems that support those processes) back to the state they were in before the incident started. This will involve identifying when the last known good state of an affected system was and may involve using backups to restore the system (this is often the case if the incident involves ransomware).

The security team will need to confirm that the restored state mitigates any identified vulnerabilities that contributed to the incident, so further changes might need to be made to a system that has been restored from a backup before the recovery can be considered complete. For example, if the incident was caused by an unpatched vulnerability, that patch should be applied as part of the recovery process.

We recommend that the security team apply enhanced monitoring controls to all parts of the IT environment that were affected by an incident to ensure that the attackers have been eradicated and don't try to re-enter the environment.

Post-incident activity

When everyone collectively breathes a sigh of relief because the incident is over and things are back to normal, that isn't quite the end of the process. A post-mortem of the incident should take place to identify:

- Firstly, and most importantly, is the root-cause analysis.
- Based on the root cause, are there improvements to the IT environment's security or to the security incident response process that can be undertaken?
- Can detections be improved in the SOC to detect a similar breach more quickly in the future?
- Can automation be used to mitigate a similar incident in the future, speeding up response times?
- Are there any follow-ups with other stakeholders or business units that need to take place because of this incident?

Any action items and lessons learned from the incident should be documented and disseminated to the appropriate teams and added as work items (or similar) so that these actions are traceable and will be implemented.

Post-incident activities are often the most neglected part of the incident response process. Still, they are critical for improving an organization's overall security posture and the effectiveness of its security operations. Think about how airline incidents are handled. When a bad airplane accident happens, there is always a detailed investigation into what happened, what went wrong, and what should be done to prevent it from happening again.

That's why airline travel is the safest mode of transportation: the industry constantly learns from its mistakes. Would you feel as comfortable getting on a plane if the airline industry shrugged its shoulders every time an accident happened and said, "Oh well, we're sure it won't happen again"? Didn't think so! Make sure you apply the same approach to improving your organization's security operations.

Skill 2-6: Evaluate a security operations strategy for sharing technical threat intelligence

Threat intelligence (TI) provides additional insights and enrichment for security operations. Larger organizations (like Microsoft) may have their own dedicated TI teams who do their own research and disseminate this information to other security operations teams internally. Smaller organizations may rely on external TI feeds from vendors, governments, and other industry bodies. This section covers the skills necessary to evaluate a security operations strategy for sharing technical threat intelligence according to the Exam SC-100 outline.

Microsoft's threat intelligence strategy

Because the SC-100 exam is a Microsoft exam, let's briefly look at how Microsoft approaches threat intelligence and how it is shared across the organization, Microsoft's customers, and with the wider security community.

 TIP As Microsoft says: To be successful with threat intelligence, you must have a large, diverse set of data, and you must apply it to your processes and tools.

Microsoft is unique because it can gather signals and intelligence from many platforms across the globe. Here are a few of the stats:

- 24 trillion signals are collected daily from Microsoft's platforms (Azure, Windows, Xbox Live, Microsoft 365, and so on).
- There are more than 1.2 billion endpoints. (In other words, any device that can run the Windows OS) running Windows that provide anonymized telemetry.
- Azure has more than 1 billion users of cloud services.
- Xbox Live has more than 65 million active gamers.
- Azure Active Directory processes 630 billion identity transactions per month.
- More than 470 billion emails are scanned every month.

In security operations terms, these collected signals translate to:

- 5 billion threat attempts are blocked every month.
- Microsoft's TI database has more than 300 million entries.
- Microsoft has more than 4 trillion files in their malware sample zoo.
- Microsoft collects more than 8 million indicators of compromise (IOCs) each day.

However, 24 trillion signals per day are not all being looked at by humans. Even a big tech company such as Microsoft wouldn't be able to employ enough people to do this effectively! Microsoft also has research teams that look at the dark web and learning from incident response engagements that add to the bucket of threat intelligence that can be used.

> **NOTE** All telemetry collected by Microsoft is anonymized and only used in ways that their customers have agreed to in writing. If your organization can collect threat intelligence similarly, make sure that you comply with any applicable privacy laws and that your customers have agreed to this use of their telemetry.

All the raw TI goes through a normalization and analytic process using machine learning models, detonation/sandboxing, and so on. When this process is complete, the raw TI will have been distilled down into high-fidelity security insights published via API to the relevant security products and Microsoft security teams. These updates can then be consumed by both external customers of Microsoft and internal teams.

> **NOTE** You can read more about Microsoft's threat intelligence strategy at
>
> - *aka.ms/microsoft-TI*
> - *aka.ms/mcra*
> - *aka.ms/MDDR*

Sharing technical threat intelligence in your organization

While it's very interesting to learn what a large technology company like Microsoft does with its threat intelligence, many organizations do not have the resources to gather their own threat intelligence and are only consumers of TI feeds. This is why vendors and other organizations create TI feeds that can be consumed externally.

Regardless of your organization's size, it is still possible to adhere to the Microsoft-recommended strategy of threat intelligence sharing:

- **Have a large diverse set of data** Consume TI feeds from as many sources as you are realistically able to handle. If there are any specialized TI feeds for your industry, geography, or similar, make sure to include them as the most relevant to your security operations.
- **Apply that data to processes and tools** Make sure that all teams and security tools are consuming the TI feeds your organization has chosen to use consistently across your organization.

Thought experiment

In this thought experiment, demonstrate your skills and knowledge of the topics covered in this chapter. You can find answers to this thought experiment in the next section.

Security operations strategy at Contoso Ltd.

You are the security architect for Contoso Ltd., a large global organization with offices and operations in several jurisdictions. The organization runs a hybrid environment with both on-premises and cloud IT infrastructure that needs to be monitored for security breaches.

You have been tasked with updating the overarching security operations strategy for Contoso Ltd., as their current strategy was created many years ago and only for the on-premises environment. The CISO wants to increase the visibility of the current IT environment and take advantage of new technologies while keeping costs to a minimum.

Current challenges in the security operations environment are as follows:

- The on-premises SIEM is running out of space for new logs.
- No logs are being collected in cloud environments because of the lack of space in the current SIEM.
- There is no automation, and SOC analysts complete almost all tasks manually.
- SOC analysts are too busy and can't investigate approximately 25 percent of the alerts that the SIEM raises.
- There is no budget for additional SOC analysts because of a hiring freeze.
- There is no traceability for the current logs being collected, such as logs being collected by the SIEM, but no one remembers why they are needed.

With this information in mind, answer the following questions:

1. What would you advise the CISO to do regarding the current SIEM strategy?
2. How can you improve the traceability of logs and justify their collection for security operations?
3. How can you decrease the number of alerts the SOC does not investigate?

Thought experiment answers

This section contains the solution to the thought experiment. Each answer explains why the answer choice is correct.

1. An on-premises SIEM has limited storage capacity, and it can be costly to upgrade and increase capacity. You should advise the CISO to move the SIEM strategy toward a cloud-based SIEM, where capacity can scale automatically.

2. For a quick and easy win, if a type of log isn't being used for hunting or detection, questions should be asked about whether it should be collected for security operations. In the longer term, creating use cases for different security operations scenarios and knowing what logs would be required to detect such a scenario is a great way to justify the collection of logs.

3. Humans only have so many hours in the day, so you need to reduce the manual workload of SOC analysts so they can spend more time investigating alerts. Using automation to reduce the repetitive task burden on analysts will free them up for more investigations.

Chapter summary

- Centralizing log collection makes security operations management overhead easier.
- Create use cases to decide which logs have security value to your organization.
- Focus on observability and collect logs from your entire hybrid environment malicious actors look for gaps in monitoring to exploit.
- Consider migrating to/integrating to a cloud-based SIEM and SOAR solution.
- Where possible, use security tools to analyze raw logs and create high-fidelity alerts to ingest into your SIEM rather than large volumes of raw logs.
- Use automation to reduce the repetitive, manual tasks that SOC analysts need to undertake.
- Have clearly defined workflows to respond to and recover from incidents.
- An incident management lifecycle will guide preparation, detection, analysis, containment, eradication, recovery, and post-incident activity.
- Use threat intelligence to enrich security operations and share it throughout your organization.

CHAPTER 3

Design an identity security strategy

Nowadays, many organizations are becoming a mixture of heterogenic infrastructures. It is no longer about everything being hosted within a single common infrastructure and users connecting from one location. Instead, users are more mobile, and they access resources from anywhere. Using identity as the primary security perimeter provides seamless user experiences, unified management, simplified identity governance, lowers the exposure of Privileged accounts, and provides better correlation of information across all the infrastructure.

Microsoft identity solutions provide a common user identity, spanning on-premises and multi-cloud-based workflows. This allows customers to fulfill many business scenarios, integrate signals that provide visibility across the whole environment, and govern environments as if they were using a common infrastructure.

This chapter provides recommendations to strength your identity and access management strategy.

Skills covered in this chapter:

- Skill 3-1: Design a strategy for access to cloud resources
- Skill 3-2: Recommend an identity store (tenants, B2B, B2C, and hybrid)
- Skill 3-3: Recommend an authentication strategy
- Skill 3-4: Recommend an authorization strategy
- Skill 3-5: Design a strategy for conditional access
- Skill 3-6: Design a strategy for role assignment and delegation
- Skill 3-7: Design security strategy for privileged role access to infrastructure, including identity-based firewall rules and Azure PIM
- Skill 3-8: Design security strategy for privileged activities, including PAM, entitlement management, and cloud tenant administration

Skill 3-1: Design a strategy for access to cloud resources

To design a proper strategy for access, you must consider the requirements for enabling a cross-team, organization-wide people, process, and technology approach. The plan should consider the requirements for

- Centrally managing a multi-cloud environment
- Using public and private access to resources anywhere
- Managing and governing identities at scale
- Dealing with emerging threats for all employees, business partners, and consumers

With an assume-breach premise, the focus is to provide the least access by

- Implementing preventative controls to keep attackers away
- Explicitly validating trust for all access requests via Azure AD conditional access
- Enabling automation for rapid response and recovery to reduce the chances of attacks spreading

Although there is often scrutiny about the best way to control access, the most effective access control strategy requires identity and network controls. There will be instances where identity controls will be used more often than network controls (and vice versa) tailored to each environment's opportunities and constraints. By enabling these technologies to work in harmony, you can leverage each control's strengths and minimize its weaknesses by providing a defense-in-depth approach in the environment.

Identity-related access controls

Many people only associate identify with user accounts. However, in modern environments, identity is in every environment resource. There are many identifiable attributes:

- For endpoints, you can identify the operating system, platform (PC, macOS, Linux, iOS, Android, IoT, and so on), and version. Also, you can tell if the device complies with configurations defined for the environment, if it shows indications of compromise, and so on.
- You can identify whether applications are web, database, or regular applications, the name of the application and version, its vulnerabilities, and the like.
- You can identify the data type (file, blob, or database) and the application that created it (Word, Excel, and so on). Also, you can tell if it is encrypted. Certain applications can define the sensitivity of the stored data.
- You can identify the network location, IP address, and ports. You can determine if integrations with third parties ae enabled, such as Cisco ISE, Aruba Clear Pass, and Citrix NetScaler. (More attributes become available for verification, allowing you to control access based on enrollment and device compliance state.
- For infrastructure, you can tell whether it is an SaaS application, the application's name, and whether it is AWS, GCP, Azure, on-premises, and so on.

All resource attributes can be used to identify the resource's state. These attributes can be updated and used to perform verifications before authorizing a resource for access. Automation can be configured to trigger additional protection and workloads if changes are detected in those attributes. And all these verifications can be used whether the resource is on-premises or elsewhere in the world. When thinking about resources this way, many possibilities for verifications are open for enabling Zero Trust.

When architecting a hybrid, multi-cloud environment that follows the Zero Trust principles, it is recommended that you consider how these attributes can be used as part of the authentication and authorization process. For example, Azure Active Directory (AAD) can correlate the information provided by the identity attributes with information such as the type of authentication used when access is requested. Also, it can correlate with where access originates from, whether the tasks performed seem normal or abnormal, and so on. Then, based on calculated risk, different authentication and authorization decisions can be made, such as providing full or partial access while remediation steps run in the background. Careful planning of the steps required after the verification will ensure the user experience and productivity is not affected.

> **MORE INFO** A more in-depth explanation about verifications is found in "Skill 3-5: Design a strategy for conditional access," later in this chapter.

Network-related access controls

Although there is often scrutiny about the best way to control access, an effective access-control strategy requires both identity and network controls. Network controls can view and intercept a broader set of communications, which can help identify threats early on and give network security administrators the best chance of mitigating them. This can be seen by the verifications performed by enterprise firewalls, intrusion prevention systems (IPS), distributed denial of service prevention (DDoS), network analytics services, and so on. Also, network controls help segment resources to isolate resources and make it harder for attackers to move across the environment.

As operational technology (OT) and industrial IoT become more entangled with information technology (IT) systems, network controls must be used to isolate and passively monitor these environments because older OT and IoT systems tend not to focus much on security. In fact, some environments may have machinery that is 50–100 years old that may have been retrofitted with some computer controls to enable IP communication and have no way to implement modern security. Hence, firewalls, Intrusion Detection Systems/Intrusion Protection Systems (IDS/IPS), and other controls will need to be used to protect against unsolicited traffic and defend against atypical access and behavior in the network.

Coordinated identity and network access

When using on-premises and multi-cloud IaaS, cloud-based network services can enable wide visibility across the mixture of infrastructures your organization may have by enabling centrally end-to-end visibility and management of these infrastructures. Then, the centrally collected signals can be made available and shared with other cloud services, which can orchestrate and automate the correlation of information with other signals from other services, including threat intelligence, and come up with better insight into the end-to-end environment state.

Perimeter-based networks assume that all resources within the defined segment are trusted. This means attackers can compromise a single endpoint within a network segment and use that trust to attack the rest of the endpoints. In addition, as datacenter workloads move to the cloud and users access those workloads from anywhere, network controls will be less important. To provide the best defenses for your organization's environment, it is recommended that you coordinate identity access capabilities with your network segmentation capabilities. This will allow you to use your network defenses when available and extend protections by taking advantage of the different identity-related verifications and capabilities that may be available. In other words, when identity and network technologies work together harmoniously, it enables better security for the environment, builds trust, mitigates risks, and protects the organization's resources and data.

Secure Access Service Edge (SASE) uses identity Zero Trust principles, but it extends further by converging deeper network and security services insights into a cloud service model that unifies signals end-to-end for both multi-cloud and on-premises. Currently, no single vendor has the capabilities required to deliver a full SASE solution. This is why the interconnection and collaboration between services and products has become very important. Microsoft has been focusing for years on developing capabilities that enable partners to interconnect their solutions with Microsoft capabilities. Planning for interconnections as part of your architecture ensures that your organization can implement a complete SASE approach.

Interconnection and cross-service collaboration

In 2020, Microsoft published an article explaining how their SOC could handle more than 8 trillion daily threat signals from a diverse set of products, services, and feeds from around the globe (*https://aka.ms/8Trillion*). Microsoft made sure its services—whether first- or third-party—were interconnected and used machine learning, automation, and User Entity and Behavior Analytics (UEBA) to correlate, curate, and auto-analyze signals. This helped them identify threats, sometimes in a fraction of a second. Then, with further automation, they handled many issues automatically, leaving only a few hundred incidents to be handled manually by analysts.

Figure 3-1 shows the Microsoft 365 Defender Incidents queue, which is one of the main services used by Microsoft SOC. For each Incident, there is a Service Sources column, which shows the name of the services that collaborated with data and analysis. By interconnecting the different services and having workloads to query automatically, curate, correlate, and analyze the information, deeper analysis and response are performed in almost real-time. For incidents that cannot be automatically addressed and need additional manual actions, the Incidents queue organizes information to enable analysts to consume it quickly and decide further actions, including triggering scripts to help remediate and recover quickly. Because of all this orchestration and automation, Microsoft could handle 96 percent of the manually handled incidents within an hour of being triggered, ensuring efficiency, flexibility, and speed.

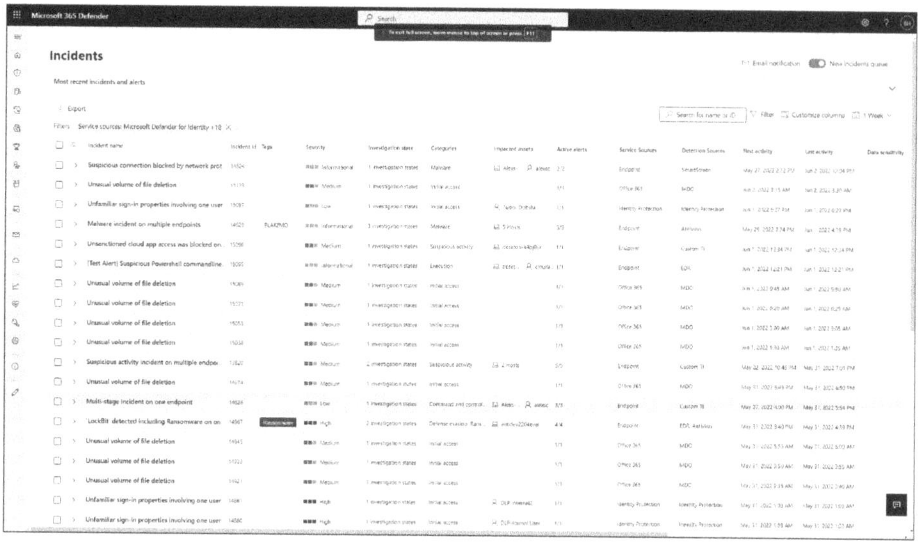

FIGURE 3-1 Microsoft Defender 365 Incidents

Another benefit of this architecture is that it can sustain large-scale change and adapt to volatility. This can be seen in the Microsoft Security Blog "Cyber Signals: Defending against cyber threats with the latest research, insights, and trends" at *https://aka.ms/cybersignals*, where Microsoft reported it had tripled the number of signals received from all its services to 24 trillion in just a few years. Microsoft has sustained that growth because of the integrated services and processes used.

When selecting and architecting your security solutions, make sure that you evaluate the interconnecting and native cross-service collaboration capabilities provided by each of the acquired solutions. Having services with native cross-service orchestration and automation enables deeper insights and frees up your analysts from building and maintaining those automation workflows.

The objective should be to offload the building of cross-service automation and other workloads to the vendors rather than spending cycles and resources building that automation yourself. Doing so minimizes the chances that changes in the platform will affect "custom customer-built" orchestration and automation since the vendors would be responsible for maintaining those workloads and ensuring that they work appropriately when changes in the platform occur, which, as you know, tends to happen often.

By selecting services with many native-built automations, customers do not have to spend cycles building and maintaining their own automations. Not having to build your own automation is very important when your organization does not have dedicated personnel who are continuously aware of changes that might impact those custom-built workflows and update them as necessary.

In the past, customers did not realize platform changes had impacted their custom-built automation and their analysts were unable to detect attacks because of the false positives generated by their custom workloads due to the changes in the platform. In short, ensure that the solutions selected come with as much automation natively integrated with the service or that you have dedicated personnel assigned to continuously maintain the custom-built workloads.

Microsoft Graph

Although identity and access management are the foundation of rapid response and recovery, another very important requirement is the native interconnections between different products and services used in the environment. Many Microsoft services interconnect with each other and with many partners' solutions using Microsoft Graph and other APIs. These APIs serve as an intermediary service (or broker) that provides a single programmatic interface, common schema, and a set of queries that enables services to communicate.

Figure 3-2 shows that third-party services and custom applications can also be interconnected to Microsoft Graph. There are hundreds of Microsoft Intelligent Security Association (MISA) members whose products already interconnect to the Microsoft Graph. In addition, the Microsoft Graph SDK can be used to help interconnect custom applications to other solutions.

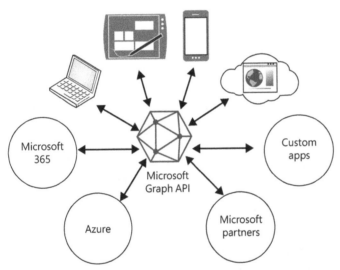

FIGURE 3-2 Many different resources interconnecting to the Microsoft Graph

MORE INFO To learn more about Microsoft Graph, review the following articles:

- Microsoft Graph Beginner's Guide: *https://aka.ms/MSGraphGuide*
- Quick Start – Microsoft Graph: *https://aka.ms/MSGraphQS*
- Microsoft Graph fundamentals: *https://aka.ms/MSGraphFundamentals*

Assume-breach and explicitly verify

By configuring your identity and network-related access controls, you can implement the principle of least-privilege. The configuration used to limit access also means you understand the expected controls, capabilities, and behaviors that should be expected in the environment when enabling these services. That way, you can plan accordingly for the required configuration, processes, and personnel to maintain and govern this configuration.

By architecting the environment with the assumption that everything can be breached, you can use the configuration to drive the verifications that will be performed to reduce the risk of malicious access taking place.

For example, if you have a configuration management solution like Microsoft Endpoint Manager, you can configure and inventory the environment. Then, you can perform compliance checks that the configuration and patches you installed are still in place. Depending on the status of that information, you can define if access should be provided or if certain remediation steps should be taken to reduce the risk. Once the risk is reduced, then you can decide to provide full or partial access.

The health status updates provided by Microsoft Defender for Endpoint (MDE) are another example of the verifications that can be performed. Imagine that shortly after the user logs in, they open a phishing email that executes some malware. MDE detects the threat and performs response and recovery steps for the device. At the same time, it shares status information about the device for other services to use as a possible trigger for orchestration and automation. Because Azure AD monitors that status change, it triggers a re-evaluation of the user session. This re-evaluation may require MFA and other verifications to reauthenticate and reauthorize the requested access. In addition, based on the risk level, the verification process may request recovery steps such as password change to be performed once the user is verified.

> **NOTE** Conditional access Continuous Access Evaluation (CAE) will be discussed later in "Controlling authentication sessions."

People, process, and technology approach

To properly manage identities, network access, people, and processes needed to manage the identity lifecycle for employees, supplier staff, and partners should be modernized. For example, the following are often forgotten by many organizations:

- When enabling new technologies, remember that old processes may tell employees to use older products and services instead of implementing new ones. In addition, the steps required to perform certain tasks may change. Also, certain support areas of the environment are being outsourced; contracts may explicitly specify the applications and tools that the contractors may use.

- Interconnection and automation provide new capabilities that did not exist previously and for which no team or processes existed. Consequently, new teams, roles, responsibilities, and processes will need to be defined. For example, Privileged Identity

Management, conditional access, access reviews, and entitlement management are some capabilities that may not have existed before and for which new personnel may need to be hired and trained to take advantage of these new capabilities.

- Because interconnection and cross-service collaboration are a must-have, acquisition requirements for evaluating products might also need to change.

- Because new capabilities become possible, a single service may replace multiple existing applications. Therefore, an evaluation should be performed to discover which teams are affected, what new processes will need to be defined, and how those teams will interact.

- Implementation of a service is no longer about just implementing the service itself but ensuring that the services are interconnected with many other services.

- People tend to gravitate toward what they know. To ensure employees take advantage of the capabilities provided by the new services, make sure to document some general procedures on how to perform previous tasks and ensure proper training is provided to employees.

- If the organization has outsourcing contracts, these contracts may need to be updated to ensure that they mention the newer services and capabilities.

All these are particularly important for identity and access management. Many new capabilities that did not exist before have been introduced and might need to have additional internal roles and responsibilities defined. In addition, procedures may need to be defined to ensure that the expected outcomes and anticipated goals are achieved for the new services being implemented. Some identity and access management capabilities where people and process modernization may be needed include:

- **Identity and access end-to-end management of on-premises and multi-clouds** While organizations might be accustomed to having a team that manages on-premises identities, the teams might not have the knowledge or personnel to keep up with the new implementation, management, monitoring, governance, and troubleshooting of the added infrastructure, which may include M365, Azure, AWS, GCP, and the like. In other words, personnel will be needed to define, enforce, and monitor that identity and access configuration. This personnel will need to

  - Keep similar security standards across multi-cloud environments

  - Keep track of functionality that may be available in each of the different environments

  - Define the proper steps to reduce the risk of not having certain functionality in place

  - And, most importantly, define events that should be considered anomalous and define the actions that will need to be taken

- **Cloud infrastructure entitlement management (CIEM)** CIEM is another relatively new solution that provides comprehensive visibility into permissions assigned to all identities (users and workloads). Most identities are over-provisioned, which expands the attack surface and increases the risk of misuse. CIEM helps implement Zero Trust security using least-privilege access in Microsoft Azure, Amazon Web Services (AWS), and Google Cloud Platform (GCP). For organizations to take full advantage of this service, the CIEM administrators will need to understand each of the infrastructures, resources, and application permissions required to ensure that the permissions are assigned/reduced properly, continue being enforced, and that all changes are monitored and audited.

■ **Identity governance** Identity governance often needs dedicated personnel for configuring, managing, and auditing the different configurations. Offerings include identity lifecycle for employees' accounts, identity lifecycle for guest accounts, entitlement management, access requests, workflows, policy and role management, access certification, fulfillment, provisioning, reporting and analytics, and auditing. These functionalities drive Microsoft's identity governance approach to provide the right people with the right access to the right resources to secure productivity. However, identity governance is one of the areas in which customers are not fully utilized by many organizations, even though it is one of the Zero Trust principles. Many customers have said they were unaware of the available features and did not understand what they needed, so they failed to include getting the appropriate resources and personnel to perform the work in their plans. Auditing is a perfect example because, to preserve integrity, the configuration auditors should be different than those who create the configuration.

MORE INFO A more in-depth explanation about Privileged access management, entitlement management, and cloud tenant administration can be found in "Skill 3-8: Design security strategy for privileged activities, including PAM, entitlement management, and cloud tenant administration."

■ **Identity lifecycle** The identity lifecyle for employees is something that many organizations are accustomed to, but the interconnection to services like Workday or SuccessFactors might be new for many. In addition, many organizations have not dealt with identity lifecycle management for guests, enabling self-service user provisioning from another Azure AD tenant, direct federation, One Time Passcode (OTP), or Google Accounts. Since all this may be new, developing new processes, defining new roles and responsibilities, and training may be needed to ensure that the organization takes advantage of this functionality.

■ **Continuous updates, interconnection, and cross-service collaboration** This is something many organizations have not had to deal with before. New interconnections with other services and cross-service automation are made available monthly. For example, Azure AD supports interconnection with HR systems, ServiceNow, and others, to continuously keep track of new functionality and ensure that the organization is taking advantage of the investments. Dedicated personnel may be needed to track and plan for the enablement of this functionality.

- **Microsoft Entra Verified ID** is a decentralized identity approach that helps people and organizations interact with each other transparently and securely. Verified ID makes portable and self-owned identity possible. It allows individuals and organizations to decide what information they share, when they share it, with whom they share it, and when they take it back without having to spread identity throughout many providers.

> **MORE INFO** More details will be provided in "Decentralized identities" later in this chapter. For detailed information, see *https://aka.ms/VerifiedID*.

There are many reasons why people, processes, and technology should be tightly integrated. A proper identity and access management architecture will

- Help high-performing organizations energize their people since mundane and tedious tasks will become automated
- Drive trust in being able to execute the strategy since the technology will enable new capabilities
- Drive culture and engagement since the new technology creates opportunities for learning
- Provide room for growth, which, in turn, will motivate them to go beyond the call of duty in pursuit of corporate objectives and innovation

Skill 3-2: Recommend an identity store (tenants, B2B, B2C, and hybrid)

Microsoft recommends using a single tenant when possible. This approach enables consistency in how resources are configured, managed, governed, and supported. However, there are circumstances where a multitenant architecture will be necessary, which introduces many complexities, including the following:

- Defining what you will share with the tenant
- Defining what you will isolate
- Determining what you will monitor and how you will monitor the interactions
- Determining how you will automate Access Reviews and responses to certain events
- Determining how you will govern actions
- Deciding which services you will interconnect to enable all these capabilities

Foundational implementations

As a primary control for least-access, some identity implementations are required to reduce risk and enable end-to-end coverage:

- **Enable single sign-on**   Reduces the number of login credentials that individuals must remember and enables end-to-end visibility of access controls, risks, vulnerabilities, overall configuration and usage, and impact of security events. It also reduces the cost of supporting password-related requests from users.

- **Integrate user provisioning**   Automatically synchronizing or creating user identities in different infrastructures reduces the maintenance and removal of user identities as status or roles change. It also extends the visibility of security services regarding actions taken in the organization's infrastructure. Microsoft Azure AD Provisioning supports System for Cross-Domain Identity Management (SCIM) to connect with applications, automate provisioning and deprovisioning of accounts and groups, govern access, and enable rich customizations. Azure AD supports pre-integrated connectors for many SaaS applications such as DropBox, Salesforce, ServiceNow, and others. In addition, Azure AD user provisioning enables many Human Resources (HR) scenarios by integrating with services like Workday and SuccessFactors. When planning to use HR services as the start-of-authority of newly created digital identities:

  - **Engage the right stakeholders**   Aside from talking to your HR department, other departments may need to be involved when automating provisioning and deprovision of access. For example, an organization may need to talk to the Legal Department and Union organization to reduce friction and ensure that the right parties are aware of procedures that will take place.

  - **Communication plan**   Proactively communicating intent and the status of implementation provides opportunities for users to know what to expect and provide feedback when issues are experienced.

  - **Pilot**   This is another way to proactively get constructive feedback about improving the deployment and perform validation with a group of users before deploying to all users.

  - **Configure the agent**   Configure the Azure AD Connect provisioning agent using a Hybrid Identity Administrator.

  - **Configure the HR app**   Configure the HR app in the Azure portal using an Azure AD application administrator.

  - **Review service integration capabilities**   This includes monitoring and ensuring that these integrations are part of the implementation. Also, update any internal processes and training to ensure that employees take advantage of the new service capabilities.

  - **Review user-provisioning configurations**   Review existing user-provisioning configurations with on-premises and other cloud services to ensure that changes occur as expected.

- **Plan for external collaboration**   Organizations need to collaborate with external users. Microsoft Azure AD Business to Business (B2B) and Microsoft Azure AD Business to Consumer (B2C) enable this collaboration. The next section, "External collaboration," discusses managing these identities and their access.

- **Integrate other software vendors**   Microsoft has partnered with independent vendors to provide API connectors that allow your sign-up user experience to use integrated identity verification and proofing; fraud detection and prevention; MFA and Passwordless authentication; and other capabilities. Consider using these capabilities when creating custom applications requiring security capabilities for the sign-up user experience.

> **MORE INFO**   To learn more about User Provisioning and B2C partner integration, see the following websites:
>
> - **What is user provisioning in Active Azure Directory?**   *https://aka.ms/ AADAppProvisioningVideo*
> - **Application provisioning documentation – Microsoft Entra | Microsoft Docs** *https://aka.ms/AADAppProvisioning*
> - **List of tutorials on how to integrate SaaS apps with Azure AD**   *https:// docs.microsoft.com/en-us/azure/active-directory/saas-apps/tutorial-list*
> - **ISV Partner gallery for Azure AD B2C – Azure AD B2C | Microsoft Docs**   *https:// docs.microsoft.com/en-us/azure/active-directory-b2c/partner-gallery*

External collaboration

Microsoft has several capabilities to enable you to collaborate with external users. The external users can use their own identities, whether corporate or social identity. The following describes in more detail the alternatives:

- **B2B collaboration**   External users can collaborate using their preferred identity— Azure AD, Google, Facebook, or others—to sign in to your enterprise applications. To make this possible, the identity is represented as a guest account and stored in the same directory as your employees. In turn, these guest accounts can be managed as other user objects, including adding them to groups, and using Entitlement Management to define policies allowing users from certain organizations to self-request an access package to certain resources. Also, Access Reviews can be used to schedule reviews to determine whether the guest users have appropriate access or whether some of the access might need to be revoked. There are different ways to invite external users to collaborate in your environment. For example, an administrator can use Azure portal or PowerShell to create user flows to allow external users to sign up for applications themselves or use Entitlement Management to provide access. B2B collaboration is useful when collaborating with these external users using Microsoft Office 365, SaaS, and other applications. Licensing and billing are based on monthly active users (MAU).

- **B2B direct connect**   Enables your organization to establish a mutual, two-way trust with another Azure AD organization. Although B2B direct connect currently supports Microsoft Teams shared channels, connected users aren't represented in your directory, but they're visible and can be monitored in Microsoft Teams admin center reports. A Microsoft Team channel owner can provide access by searching for users from the external organization and adding them to the shared channel. The shared channel's defined policies determine the guest user's access.

- **Azure AD B2C**   AD B2C enables SaaS apps or custom-developed apps to be published for your customers or other consumers to use. Although users can sign in with an identity they have already established, like Gmail or Facebook, you can customize and control the sign-up and sign-in and manage their profiles when using your applications. User objects are created and managed separately from the organization's employee and partner directories.

Table 3-1 provides a summary of the benefits, licensing, and other important information for the different types of external collaborations available:

TABLE 3-1 External collaborations benefits and licensing

Type	B2B Collaboration	B2B Direct Connect	B2C
Intended for	Business partners using their preferred identity provider	Business partners that use Azure AD	Customers using their preferred identity provider
Guest accounts	Represented in the directory as user objects	Not represented in the directory	Represented in the directory as user objects
Management	Entitlement management; access reviews; conditional access	Cross-tenant access settings; Microsoft Teams admin center	Entitlement management; access reviews; limited conditional access
Licensing	Based on monthly active users (MAU)	Based on monthly active users (MAU)	Based on monthly active users (MAU)
Supports	Microsoft Office 365, SaaS, and other applications	Team channels	SaaS apps
Usage	Invitation or self-service sign-up	Invitation or self-service sign-up	Sign-up, user flows
Benefits	Authentication and credential management is handled by the user's home identity provider. The resource tenant controls all access and authorization of guest users. There is no need for federation. Guest users have the same access management as internal users. (There is no need to learn a different interface.)	No need to manage individual user objects	Extend Azure AD capabilities to customer accounts

When implementing any of these external collaboration capabilities, it is recommended that you use a holistic governance approach to reduce possible exposure to sensitive resources and any misalignment to regulatory and compliance requirements that your organization must follow. This includes ensuring proper Access Reviews and making access time-bound where appropriate. In addition, you should implement additional access controls to applications, data, and content, such as Microsoft 365 Purview Information Protection, Data Loss Prevention, Information Barriers, Data Map, and so on.

 TIP Because this data protection is outside the scope of this chapter, we recommend that you review the following article and become familiar with the compliance and data governance technology covered there. The future of compliance and data governance is discussed here: "Introducing Microsoft Purview – Microsoft Security Blog," *https://www.microsoft.com/security/blog/2022/04/19/the-future-of-compliance-and-data-governance-is-here-introducing-microsoft-purview/.*

For B2B, be aware that cross-tenant access settings can be configured to manage whether users can authenticate with external Azure AD tenants. These settings apply to both inbound and outbound collaboration. These settings should not be confused with the external collaboration settings, which can restrict what external users can see, specify who can invite guests, and what domains can be allowed or blocked for invitations.

Controlling external collaboration

Following are some additional recommendations to help you augment the security and governance and help manage the required lifecycle of that external collaboration for B2B Collaboration and B2C. Ultimately, you want a common identity store that enables the same capabilities for securing access, regardless of the application, infrastructure, endpoint, or resource used.

- **Azure AD app gallery** Microsoft has a catalog of thousands of apps that can be easily deployed and integrated to make it easier to configure single sign-on (SSO) and centralized, automated user provisioning. These apps include Workday, ServiceNow, Salesforce, DocuSign, and many others. This reduces the number of identities you have to manage in the environment, and because it provides integration, it helps close blind spots that attackers can use to their advantage. See *https://www.microsoft.com/en-us/security/business/identity-access/azure-active-directory-integrated-apps.*

- **Azure AD Application Proxy** When providing access to internal on-premises applications, Azure AD Application Proxy helps bring SSO, conditional access, and other benefits across the internal on-premises access. This is a better solution than VPN access because access is controlled via user-to-application rather than user-to-network. Using a user-to-application access segmentation approach prevents an attacker from using lateral movement and privilege escalation as a tactic to access the environment.

- **Integrate user provisioning** Use SCIM to automatically provision users and groups between your applications and Azure AD. This helps keep user access consistent and enables more integrated monitoring.

- **Azure AD entitlement management** Entitlement management defines policies for users from specified organizations to self-request an access package, automatically providing defined permissions to certain resources. This helps document and control access to resources from a centralized location. In addition, it helps manage access to resources from a centralized location.

- **Azure AD Access Reviews** Schedules Access Reviews to be performed in a scheduled manner to verify whether users have appropriate access or if some access needs to be revoked. This helps reduce excessive permissions provided in the environment.

- **Azure AD Dynamic Groups** You can use attribute-based rules to control the membership for a group in Azure AD dynamically. For example, you can use a department, user title, or another custom attribute to enable membership. Then, if that information changes, the user is auto-removed from the group. This is another tactic to reduce excessive permissions over resources.

- **Microsoft Entra permissions management** Entra is a cloud infrastructure entitlement management (CIEM) service that lets you discover, remediate, and monitor permissions on multi-cloud environments, including Microsoft Azure, AWS, and Google. Entra allows you to have granular visibility, enforce least-privilege, and detect anomalies.

By incorporating these capabilities, you can bring uniform capabilities across and centralize the management and monitoring of the different infrastructures. In addition, it will reduce the amount of different infrastructure-focused services your team needs to manage.

Skill 3-3: Recommend an authentication strategy

Authentication (AuthN) is the process of proving that you are who you say you are. Since determining whether the requestor is known is the first decision you must make, AuthN is crucial for the security of the whole environment. When planning your authentication strategy, you should start by planning with privileged, specialized, enterprise, and consumer accounts. This skill provides general guidance for enterprise and specialized accounts. Consumer accounts were discussed in "Skill 3-2: Recommend an identity store (tenants, B2B, B2C, hybrid)," earlier in this chapter, and privileged accounts will be discussed in "Skill 3-7: Design security strategy for privileged-role access to infrastructure, including identity-based firewall rules, and Azure PIM," later in this chapter.

Enterprise accounts

To meet your organization's security and compliance requirements, your authentication strategy needs to consider existing infrastructure, the silos that will be required, the interconnections available, and the supported authentication methods. Azure AD supports the following authentication methods for hybrid identity solutions:

Cloud authentication

Azure AD handles the authentication. The following sections explain the options available in cloud authentication.

AZURE AD PASSWORD HASH SYNCHRONIZATION

When using on-premises to synchronize directory objects into Azure AD, a hash representation of on-premises AD stored passwords is synchronized using AD Connect Sync. This value results from a one-way mathematical function that cannot be reverted to the plain-text version of a password.

When you first enable password hash synchronization, all in-scope users' passwords are synchronized. You cannot explicitly define a subset of user passwords to be synchronized, but if multiple connectors are configured, you can disable password hash sync for some connectors using the Set-ADSyncAADPasswordSyncConfiguration cmdlet. Synchronization is only supported for the Azure AD object user type. There is no support for iNetOrgPerson.

iNetOrgPerson, defined in RFC2798, is a class used by Active Directory Domain Services as a security principal to help migrate user accounts from third-party directories. However, it can introduce issues with certain third-party applications.

Be aware that some premium features of Azure AD, such as identity protection and Azure AD Domain Services, require password hash synchronization. When possible, we recommend that you use this type of synchronization in conjunction with AD Identity Protection because it helps identify many risks, such as impossible travel, abnormal sign-in locations, password spray, leaked credentials, and so on.

The leaked credentials feature uses Microsoft threat intelligence; Microsoft has accumulated this intelligence by analyzing trillions of signals and gathering information from using Bing searches to uncover passwords that may be sold on the dark web. By converting those passwords to hash and comparing them with what is used to authenticate in Azure AD, Azure AD can identify potential risks to the authentication and trigger remediation steps, such as a password change.

AZURE AD PASS-THROUGH AUTHENTICATION

Certain organizations might require authentication to happen using on-premises AD. When the Azure AD pass-through authentication method is configured, password validation doesn't happen in the cloud. Instead, the authentication request is passed to on-premises AD Servers using a software agent that runs on those on-premises servers. This method might be necessary for companies that require on-premises user account states, password policies, and sign-in hours to be immediately enforced.

Azure AD Identity Protection provides many benefits, including not storing on-premises passwords (in any form) in the cloud, working seamlessly with Azure AD conditional access policies (including multifactor authentication), blocking legacy authentication, and filtering out brute-force password attacks.

However, you will never be able to use Azure AD Identity Protection with Azure AD pass-through authentication. Also, if there are ever issues with on-premises AD, AD federation services, or network connectivity to on-premises, users will be unable to authenticate to cloud services.

FEDERATED AUTHENTICATION

This authentication method handles the authentication process by a trusted system that validates the user's password. Usually, organizations want to use authentication methods offered by Active Directory Federation Services (AD FS) if there is a sign-in requirement that is not natively supported by Azure AD. For example, the use of smart cards was one of the reasons many organizations started using AD FS. Recently, Azure AD added support for X.509 certificates on smart cards. One of the reasons to avoid using AD FS is that it extends the attack surface that can be used to gain control of both on-premises and cloud infrastructure. When using AD FS, we recommend that you run an identity threat protection solution, such as Defender for Identity. The sensor should be installed on all domain controllers (DCs) and AD FS Servers for full coverage.

Figure 3-3 shows a summary decision-making chart to help you define the type of authentication that should be used. If you have an on-premises environment, need authentication to happen on-premises, and do not need federation (AD FS), then you will use pass-through authentication. If you need federation, require sign-in using on-premises MFA Server or a third-party authentication, or need multi-sided on-premises authentication, then you will use AD FS. If you do not need authentication to happen on-premises or want to implement Azure AD Identity Protection or Azure AD Domain Services, you need password hash authentication.

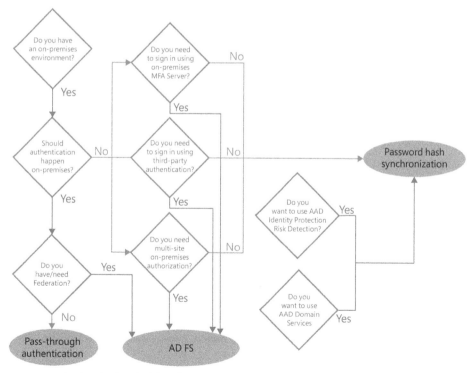

FIGURE 3-3 Authentication decision chart

Other things that may affect your architecture decision include the following:

- Suppose you need to apply user-level AD security policies such as account expired, disabled account, password expired, account locked out, sign-in hours, and so on. In that case, you will be required to use on-premises authentication.

- When using federation, you can do a password hash sync to enable other Azure AD capabilities, such as Azure AD Identity Protection and Azure AD Domain Services.

- Password hash synchronization is the easiest to deploy and maintain since it does not require an infrastructure.

- Password hash synchronization is highly available as a cloud service that scales to all Microsoft datacenters.

- With all authentication methods, it is recommended that you deploy single sign-on (SSO) to provide a better user experience.

- If you have Azure AD Premium P2, it is recommended that you enable Azure AD Identity Protection. As mentioned, password hash synchronization will be required.

- Pairing AAD Identity Protection with conditional access allows you to control access by checking to see if the sign-in risk is set to Low, Medium, or High. In addition, you can trigger the remediation steps to be taken. For specific applications, you can address risks by configuring adaptive authentication. With this, you can configure a specific set of users to provide a second authentication factor or block access based on the level of risk detected.

- When an on-premises user account state changes (for example, disabling accounts), password hash synchronization doesn't immediately enforce changes. This means that a user will have access to cloud applications until the user account state is synchronized to Azure AD. Organizations might want to run a new synchronization cycle after bulk updates to overcome this situation.

- Pass-through authentication needs lightweight agents installed on existing servers (three servers are recommended). These agents need unconstrained network access to all domain controllers and outbound access to the Internet. Deploying the agents in a perimeter network is not supported.

- Although this change does not happen automatically, when using pass-through authentication, you can configure password hash synchronization as a backup authentication method in case of a significant on-premises failure. Azure AD Connect will have to be used to switch the sign-on method manually.

The following scenarios will need federation services to be implemented:

- On-premises MFA servers or third-party multifactor providers requiring a federated identity provider

- Authentication by using third-party authentication solutions

- Sign in that requires a `SamAccountName` (for example, `Contoso\username`) instead of a User Principal Name (UPN) (for example, `Orguser@contoso.com`)

Federation services usually require more significant investment in on-premises infrastructure to provide the required services and high availability. This requires a lot of maintenance and security to be put in place to prevent attacks, as seen in the Solarwinds incident (Solorigate). We recommend you deploy endpoint threat protection and identity protection services such as Defender for Identity and Defender for Endpoint to reduce these risks and protect this infrastructure. Also, Defender for Cloud can help with configuration recommendations, server focus, and malicious behaviors, such as suspicious processes, dubious sign-in attempts, and kernel module loading.

Road to passwordless sign-in

Sign-in authentication is when a user, application, or device presents their credentials (account with password/PIN, certificate, and so on) to attest they are the resource they are claiming to be.

Although in the past, passwords were the only recommended methods for authentication, there are a number of reasons using passwordless sign-in presents a variety of risks, including:

- Passwords tend to be easy to guess.
- Users often reuse the same password for different services.
- Passwords are sometimes shared between users.
- Passwords are easily stolen through social engineering or unsecured network transmissions.
- Users write down passwords in documents.
- Key loggers can capture typed passwords.
- Organizations' password databases get stolen and sold on the dark web.

Try to eliminate the use of passwords in the environment to eliminate these risks. Some newer authentication methods can be used for sign-in, including the Microsoft Authenticator App, FIDO2 security Keys, Windows Hello for Business, and SMS. Table 3-2 summarizes these authentication methods.

TABLE 3-2 Authentication methods

Method	Quality	Usability	Availability	Primary Auth
Authenticator App	Better (push notifications) Best (phone sign-in)	High	High	Yes
FIDO2	Best	High	High	Yes
Oath Hardware tokens	Better	Medium	High	No
Oath Software tokens	Better	Medium	High	No
Windows Hello for Business	Best	High	High	Yes

Method	Quality	Usability	Availability	Primary Auth
SMS	Good	High	Medium	Yes
Voice	Good	Medium	Medium	No
Password	Bad	High	High	Yes

MICROSOFT AUTHENTICATOR APP

The Microsoft Authenticator app can be used to turn any iOS or Android phone into a strong, passwordless credential. See Figure 3-4.

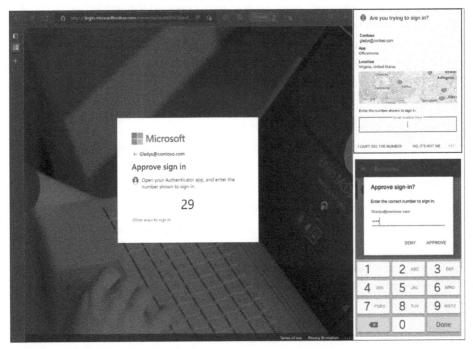

FIGURE 3-4 Passwordless authentication

On the left side of Figure 3-4, a passwordless authentication is shown, where upon entering the username, the application asks to open the Authenticator App and enter the number shown. In the top-right corner, the Authenticator App sign-in interface requests the code provided at the left. Additional context about where the authentication originated from is also shown.

If the user shown isn't accurate, the user can click No, It's Not Me. The Authenticator App also provides an option in case there is a problem with the number displayed. The bottom-right corner of Figure 3-4 shows the prompt triggered by having an Authenticator Phone Sign-in as your verification method. The prompt asks the user to enter their PIN to approve the sign-in.

Because security keys require something you have (physical device) and something that you know (PIN), it is a stronger verification method than other authentication methods, such as username and password. Besides using it as a primary authentication method, it can also be used as a secondary authentication and for Self-Service Password Recovery (SSPR).

FIDO2 SECURITY KEYS

One of the benefits provided by FIDO2 keys is that they are un-phishable. This is done by allowing users to sign-in without a username or password by using a security key stored in an external device. Because there is no username or password, they cannot be exposed or guessed. FIDO2 can be used to sign in to supported browsers, Azure AD, or hybrid AD–joined Windows-supported devices. For more information about the supported Windows client OS, see *https://aka.ms/SupportedWinOS*. Besides using it as a primary authentication method, it can also be used as a secondary authentication.

WINDOWS HELLO FOR BUSINESS

As shown in Table 3-2, Microsoft understands that not all applications support this type of authentication. Organizations might require other types of sign-ins or that different authentication areas be secured. To secure the login of Windows endpoints and remove the possible risk of replay attacks, Microsoft provides Windows Hello for Business, which supports facial and Fingerprint recognition. The biometric data is stored only on the local device.

Windows Hello for Business is based on a cryptographic key pair bound to the Trusted Platform Module (TPM). When a PIN or gesture is entered, it is used to unlock the cryptographic, and then the identity provider can tell the user identity has been authenticated. That trusted relationship between the identity provider and the user is established when Windows Hello for Business and the PIN are configured.

Windows Hello for Business can use key-based and certificate-based authentication. For organizations that do not have a public key infrastructure (PKI), we recommend that you use key-based credentials because it reduces the necessary effort to manage that infrastructure.

> **CAUTION**   Be aware that RDP doesn't support key-based authentication. It only supports Windows Hello with certificates.

OATH HARDWARE TOKENS

Azure AD supports OATH TOTP SHA-1 tokens. A secret key is preprogrammed in the token and must be input into Azure AD using a comma-separated values (CSV) file. A header must be in the first line, and the values of each OATH token for UPN, serial number, secret key, time interval, manufacturer, and model must be in subsequent lines. Up to 200 OATH tokens can be activated every 5 minutes. Users may have up to five OATH hardware tokens or authenticator applications for use at any time. OATH tokens can also be used for secondary authentication and self-service password recovery (SSPR).

OATH SOFTWARE TOKENS

Software OATH tokens are authenticator applications, such as third-party apps or the Microsoft Authenticator App. Software OATH tokens can also be used for secondary authentication and self-service password recovery (SSPR).

SMS-BASED AUTHENTICATION

With SMS-based authentication, users can sign-in without providing their username and password. It can also be used for secondary authentication and self-service password reset (SSPR). SMS-based authentication isn't recommended for B2B accounts and isn't compatible with native Office applications.

VOICE-CALL AUTHENTICATION

An automated voice call is made to the phone number registered for the user to complete the sign-in process by pressing # or entering a PIN registered on their keypad.

NUMBER MATCHING AUTHENTICATION

When users attempt to authenticate, they are presented with a number that must be entered into the Authenticator App to complete the authentication. AD FS supports number-matching after installing an update for Windows Server 2016 or later.

Authoritative sources

When considering authentication strategy, you should also plan for the authoritative sources for account or access creation. Organizations can have many sources, including on-premises Active Directory, cloud infrastructures, and HR management systems. Microsoft on-premises HR provisioning uses Microsoft Identity Manager to trigger the provisioning. Cloud HR applications like Workday or SuccessFactors can integrate with the Azure AD user provisioning service to provision users to on-premises AD and cloud-only and writeback information such as email addresses and usernames to the HR app.

By integrating Cloud HR services, automation can be enabled for creating user accounts automatically, updating employees' attributes (such as name, title, and name), automatically disabling accounts upon termination of employment, and reactivating old accounts upon rehiring. Besides automatically running these workloads, the organization will see increased productivity because the employees do not have to wait for accounts to be manually created, therefore reducing the risk created by termination. Also, changes in title or other attributes may trigger further automation from access reviews or AD dynamic group membership, which might automatically provide and/or remove access. Finally, because Azure AD supports native audit logs for user provisioning requests, you can track provisioning and access, enabling organizations to address compliance and governance requirements.

Specialized accounts

Many attacks use broken authentication and session management to bypass the authentication methods used by applications. Recently, attackers have even hidden their code to run under organization-sanctioned applications, hoping the malicious actions go unnoticed. This section explains the different functionality Microsoft has developed to reduce application authentication and access-related risk and will provide guidance for planning your architecture.

Service principals

Similarly to a service account in ADDS, you must register the app in Azure AD to set up the trust between an application and the Microsoft Identity Platform. When you register the app, the platform provides some attribute values, while others are manually set up by the person registering the app. The Application (client) ID and the Redirect URI values are very important. The Application ID is assigned by Azure AD to uniquely identify your app. The authorization server uses the Redirect URI to direct the web browser or mobile app to the destination where the application code is located if required. Upon registering the application, the service principal is created.

A service principal functions as the application's identity in the tenant where the application is used. It defines which resources the application can access and who can access the application. A service principal is created upon the user's consent to use the application or API. A service principal must be created on each tenant if the application is used in multiple tenants.

Service principals use two authentication methods: client certificates and client secrets. When possible, use client certificates because they cannot be accidentally embedded in code and can be protected using Azure Key Vault.

You will face several security challenges when using service principals, such as reviewing the service principals' assigned privileged roles, access, credentials, and the provided authentication methods. In addition, many applications tend to be over-permissioned. Although Microsoft is working to improve the experience with many of these challenges, such as developing access reviews for service principals assigned to privileged roles, you should consider using managed identities instead of service principals.

Managed identities

Managed identities allow any service supporting Azure AD authentication, including Key Vault, to authenticate to each other without presenting explicit credentials via code. This approach is secure because the managed identities eliminate the need to store credentials that might be leaked inadvertently (such as passwords or cryptographic keys). There are two types of managed identities: system-assigned managed identities and user-assigned managed identities.

System-assigned managed identity   A system-assigned managed identity is created when the resource gets created in Azure. When the resource is deleted, Azure automatically deletes the identity. This means that they have a 1:1 relationship with the resource created. For example, each VM has its own managed identity.

User-assigned managed identity A User-assigned Managed Identity is managed separately from the lifecycle of the Azure resource. After the resource gets created, you must manually create the identity. If the resource gets deleted, the identity remains. The identity object can be assigned to multiple resources.

By eliminating explicit credentials, risks such as user authentication credentials not being protected when stored and predictable login credentials are eliminated. In addition, broken authentication-related issues such as password length, password complexity, username, password enumeration, and brute-force login for application accounts will not be an issue because credentials are fully managed, rotated, and protected by Azure.

Controlling authentication sessions

The Azure AD default configuration for user sign-in frequency is 90 days. This sounds like a lot of time, but any violation of policies such as change of password, device health, account disabled, and others will revoke the session. Also, remember that whenever a user locks their computer, they reauthenticate to unlock it.

Conditional access sign-in frequency

There might be some special circumstances that could require restricting the sessions to less-than-default values. Some use cases include having sessions that provide access to sensitive information from external networks, sessions from unmanaged or shared devices, sessions made by high-impact users, and sessions that use critical business applications.

For those scenarios, Microsoft provides options to define the number of days or hours a reauthentication will be required. The session frequency can be changed by enabling user risk or sign-in risk, configuring the conditional access sign-in frequency, and defining the number of days or hours. You can also select **Every Time** instead of defining hours or days or even require reauthentication during the Intune device enrollment. We recommend that you do not require a very low reauthentication interval because it can affect the user experience.

> **CAUTION** Be aware that Microsoft will not prompt users for additional MFA if they have done MFA in the last 5 minutes.

This sign-in frequency works with most Microsoft native apps for Windows, Mac, and mobile, as well as third-party Security Assertion Markup Language (SAML) applications and apps that have implemented OATH2 or OIDC (OpenID Connect) protocols. Besides requiring OATH2 or OIDC, the applications must also not drop their cookies or get redirected to Azure AD for authentication.

Conditional access evaluation

As mentioned above, a violation of policies, such as a change of device health, can cause the revocation of the user authentication token, causing the user to have to reauthenticate. This resiliency is built by using conditional access policies that rely on Continuous Access Evaluation (CAE). CAE-aware applications can be notified when critical events occur, such as the user endpoint showing an indication of compromise (IOC), triggering a rejection of unexpired tokens, and forcing reauthentication. Microsoft services such as SharePoint Online, Teams, and Exchange support CAE. In addition, Outlook Web App (OWA) and some Office 365 clients support CAE.

Microsoft is working with the industry for CAE to become a standard supported by more third parties. To help third-party vendors to take advantage of CAE capabilities, Microsoft has released a CAE API (*https://aka.ms/CAEAPI*). In addition, Microsoft is extending CAE for workload identities, and the preview currently targets service principals. Based on the risk detected, service principals may be disabled or deleted. This prevents malicious changes to applications that might otherwise go undetected.

To better understand how this technology works, see Figure 3-5, which shows the following flow of events:

1. A CAE user signs in and requests an access token.

2. The identity provider provides a token.

3. The user sends the token to the resource provider to access the resource.

4. Shortly, policies running in the environment notice changes in the account's health, the device's health, or even changes made by an administrator affecting the involved resources. This causes an event to be generated and made available for other CAE services to consume. In Figure 3-5, Azure AD shares a revocation event.

5. The CAE-aware resource provider notices the raised revocation event, rejects the token by sending a 401 (unauthorized HTTP status code), and sends a claim challenge back to the client.

6. The CAE client understands the challenge and restarts the reauthentication process described in step 1, and the cycle continues.

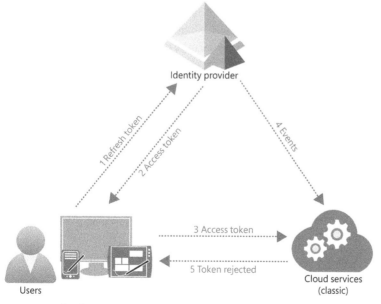

FIGURE 3-5 Continuous Access Evaluation token cycle

MORE INFO   To learn more about CAE, see "Skill 3-5: Design a strategy for conditional access."

Persistent browser sessions

Persistent browser sessions allow the user to remain signed-in even if they close the browser session until the session timeout is reached. This includes users signing in from personal devices. By default, Azure AD allows browser session persistence to be determined by the user by prompting them to remain signed-in after a successful authentication. With conditional access, you can choose to make the session non-persistent. If a user receives a prompt triggered by their company's conditional access settings to remain signed in, the configuration defined in the persistent browser session will overwrite that setting.

Block legacy authentication

To reduce risk from password spray and credential-stuffing attacks, ensure that all users are MFA-enabled and conditional access policies are used to block legacy authentication. Protocols like POP, SMTP, IMAP, and MAPI do not enforce MFA. Customers using the security defaults automatically block legacy authentication.

Key recommendations

Following are some recommendations:

- Evaluate the organization's identity solutions, HR provisioning, and user requirements to identify how users will be created and maintained.
- Interconnect and synchronize all identity systems, including HR-provisioning services and cloud and on-premises directories (except for high-privilege accounts). This ensures consistency, reduces errors, and helps improve security efficiency because security tools can analyze the impact users/resources might have in the whole environment after a malicious event. It also enables the orchestration and automation to speed up the response and recovery.
- Enable SSO.
- Use passwordless methods that require MFA and plan the implementation in a way that does not significantly affect operations. This includes Microsoft Authenticator, smart card authentication, or any other client certificate-based authentication.
- Use managed identities when possible.
- Consider moving away from service principals to managed identities because it eliminates the need to protect, rotate, and manage credentials.
- If you must use service principals, use a client certificate for authentication because it cannot accidentally be embedded in code as client secrets can.

- Use Azure Key Vault for certificate and secrets management. Also, you can encrypt .pfx files, passwords, authentication keys, storage account keys, and data encryption keys by using keys protected by hardware security modules.

- Use the Sensitive Operations Report workbook to identify modifications to applications' service principals' credentials or authentication methods.

- Look for opportunities to convert explicit credentials (such as connection strings and API keys) to use managed identities.

- Standardize on using managed identities where possible.

- Review and document the service interconnections and the permissions setup across them and use this information when performing audits or configuration reviews.

- Review organization processes and policies that may describe how identities should be used and the systems they should interconnect to reduce employee friction and confusion on how the service should be configured.

- Ensure that the monitoring systems and alerts are interconnected and that the required organization teams, including the SOC, have access to the required insights.

- If you are considering enabling sign-in frequency, make sure there is no other conditional access policy enabling the configurable token lifetime feature for any of the users for which you are enabling sign-in frequency. Microsoft does not support this configuration because the configurable token lifetime feature was retired in January 2021.

- Do not overuse the sign-in frequency >every time setting. Only use it for specific business needs because it can affect productivity and increase the risk of users approving authentications they might not have initiated because they have grown numb to the prompts.

- Disable legacy authentication using a phased approach. First, you might want to disable basic authentication on a per-protocol basis using Exchange Online authentication policies. Then you might want to extend the protection using conditional access.

- Use a single identity provider that supports all platforms, including operating systems, cloud providers, and third-party services.

- For older tenants that explicitly disabled the CAE preview or only explicitly enabled some users using the old experience, CAE is not enabled by default. Consider enabling it. You do this by selecting **Azure Active Directory > Security > Continuous Access Evaluation** and selecting **Migrate**. This process will create a new conditional access policy named **CA Policy Created From CAE Settings**. For newer tenants or customers that explicitly enabled CAE for all users using the old experience, CAE is automatically enabled, and no migration is needed.

- Be aware that not all services support CAE, though Microsoft is working on extending that support for both Microsoft cloud and third-party services.

- Update your organization code to use CAE.

Skill 3-4: Recommend an authorization strategy

The previous skill focused on describing authentication approaches to ensure the identity is known and trusted. For this skill, the focus will be extending the validation to check the trust factors of that identity and ensuring that the right authorizations are provided. However, we must first start with provisioning the required access for the right authorizations to take place. After all, authentication is the act of granting permissions to perform certain required tasks.

Configuring access to support authorization

Different authorization methods can ensure the resource has the required access. People often plan for authorization to be driven mostly by user accounts. However, as mentioned earlier, in order to get the best security and Zero Trust strategy, all identities and network capabilities should work in harmony to properly authorize the required access. Because of this, the type of access controls and verifications needed to properly authorize a session will be very diverse and will include checking

- **What devices are authorized to communicate with another device** An SQL server may only need to communicate with the identity provider and supporting websites. In addition, most on-premises user workstations do not need to communicate with other workstations. They only need to communicate with servers/applications. This means you can use micro-segmentation capabilities to only allow the required traffic requirements. Some capabilities that can be used include implementing host firewall policies through Microsoft Endpoint Manager, using Azure Network Security Group (NSG), and using Azure Firewall to limit open ports and traffic paths. Be aware that this strategy might not work for mobile workloads, but it can reduce risk on server workloads and specialized endpoints that do not move across environments. For example, on-premises Privileged Access Workstations (PAW) can be used to administer IaaS and on-premises server workloads. (See "Skill 3-7: Design security strategy for privileged-role access to infrastructure, including identity-based firewall rules and Azure PIM," later in this chapter.)

- **What roles and group membership should a user belong to, and whether the access should be time-bound** Group membership helps provide common permissions to a group of users. Some memberships might be permanent, while others, like privileged groups, might not need to be if a just-in-time (JIT) service is used to grant time-bounded granular elevated privileged access in real-time. In addition, membership of a group may be controlled dynamically based on the value of an attribute defined within the identity object—for example, the user's title or department or portions of the device's name.

- **What data may need to be accessed and when** Permissions can be assigned to control data access. However, other capabilities, such as Microsoft Data Loss Prevention (DLP) and Microsoft Sensitive Labels, use attributes defined within the data to drive access control. In addition, retention labels and policies can control the time a file or data may be available.

- **What explicit permissions are applied, and which service controls it** Microsoft Office 365 applications like SharePoint and Teams can be controlled using their own permissioning system or Azure AD specialized groups (Microsoft 365 group). In addition, Azure AD entitlement management can automate the provisioning and revocation of access based on group membership or attributes defined within the user object. To ensure that proper authorizations are in place, there must be an understanding of the different provisioning services available and how they overwrite each other to reduce the friction that these services may otherwise create. This means that processes must be defined and made available for administrators to follow to reduce conflicts that may be created. In addition, audits should be planned to review the different access provided by these services and ensure that excessive permissions are not being granted.

- **Who should you share data with** DLP can be used to control what data should be shared based on the content of that data. For example, the organization may define that no file containing a Social Security Number will be shared externally. Microsoft Defender for Cloud Apps can use policies defined by DLP and Information Protection to search for sensitive data that may be shared externally through the different Software as a Service (SaaS) applications used by the organization. Then, Defender for Cloud Apps can take the proper steps to either remove the data or set the proper permissions so the data is not exposed externally. Microsoft Purview Information Barriers is another example of how you can control shared data; this compliance solution prevents two-way communication and collaboration between groups and users meeting certain criteria. For example, finance personnel might be unable to communicate and share information with certain groups within their organization, such as marketing.

All these capabilities enforce least-access/privileged access, which, in turn, ensures that the proper authorization to resources is provided. By incorporating all access controls from network, privileged, identity, external, endpoint, and adaptive access, you can implement a defense-in-depth approach, where each layer supports the others and helps contain threats. More detailed recommendations will be discussed in subsequent sections.

Network access

Nowadays, many organizations are migrating to the cloud. However, many still have network management infrastructure (such as IaaS and on-premises). To protect anywhere, security must have a cloud-delivered capability and be interconnected, so insights can be shared across services. This is because isolated signals can create blind spots that will prevent analysts from determining if malicious events have occurred and cannot verify if the attackers have used those blind spots to jump to other environments in the organization.

Secure Access Service Edge (SASE) is a framework that tries to interconnect signals from cloud-native security technologies such as Secure Web Gateway, Cloud Access Security Broker (CASB), Firewall as a Service (FWaaS), Remote Brower Isolation, encryption, and software-defined WAN (SDWAN). This interconnection of signals helps you gain end-to-end visibility of the environment, consistent policy enforcement, control of sensitive data, and so on.

Besides the capabilities mentioned, there are other functionalities you should consider using a threat protection solution to uncover network misconfiguration and improve the environment's security posture. For example, Defender for Cloud provides capabilities to control network access, such as:

- Adaptive network hardening helps filter traffic to and from resources by using network security groups (NSGs). It also provides hardening alerts and recommended policy rules.
- Network map provides a graphical view of the connections between your virtual endpoints and subnets to provide insights that help harden the environment. Figure 3-6 shows how Microsoft Defender for Cloud reports the network-related recommendations.

> **MORE INFO** A list of Defender for Cloud network alerts can be seen at *https://aka.ms/ NetworkAlerts*. Also, the network map helps uncover unwanted connections, enabling you to better isolate workloads and subnets.

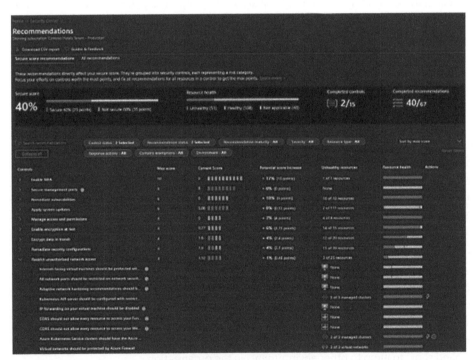

FIGURE 3-6 Defender for Cloud Recommendations

Defender for IoT provides insights through the Device Map, such as the capabilities of Defender for Cloud Network Map, which can help define segmentation rules to isolate devices. In addition, the user interface provides capabilities to search by IP, MAC, protocols, known applications, and so on, which can help uncover unexpected connections and enable continuous configuration improvements in the environment. Defender for IoT interconnects with

Defender for Cloud, Defender for Endpoint, Sentinel, and others to help provide an end-to-end view of the environment. Figure 3-7 shows the Defender for IoT Device Map.

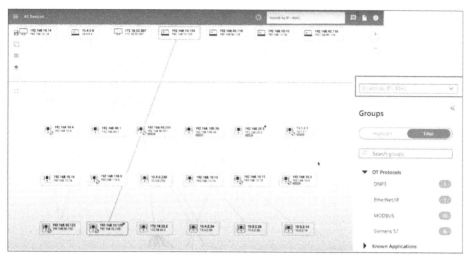

FIGURE 3-7 Defender for IoT Device Map and network-related filtering capabilities

There are many other network-related capabilities from Microsoft. However, this section focuses on network capabilities that help enforce least-access to ensure proper authorizations occur. You can create a comprehensive authorization strategy by incorporating these approaches with other access controls described in the following sections. In addition, the configuration baseline created by these approaches helps provide information supporting audits and/or investigations of unexpected configurations in the environment.

Privileged access

When starting an attack, cybercriminals target privileged accounts to quickly spread and attain wide access across the environment. Therefore, it's important to make it difficult for attackers to find sources that can provide privileged access and carry the attack further: Make sure attackers cannot see who the members of the privileged groups are. Make sure attackers cannot use well-known and easy-to-use attack vectors to compromise users (email and Internet browsing). And make sure those identities never have excessive permissions.

> **MORE INFO** Because of the extensive number of privileged access solutions provided by Microsoft, "Skill 3-7: Design security strategy for privileged-role access to infrastructure including identity-based firewall rules and Azure PIM," describes these capabilities.

Identity access

Security group membership, role-based access control, security namespaces and permissions, feature flags, and access levels are some of the capabilities that can help the proper authorizations take place. To ensure proper authentication takes place and the least-access principle is applied, some configurations that you should consider when architecting your authentication strategy include the following:

- Security namespaces in Azure DevOps is a functionality that stores access control lists (ACL) in tokens to determine the level of access that different entities must perform over a resource.
- Feature Flags in Azure DevOps deployments is a technique that uses conditional logic to control the visibility of certain application functionality for users, for example, deploying functionality only to a limited audience for testing or paying higher subscription fees or others.
- Access Levels grants or restricts access to select web portal features.
- Microsoft Office utilizes its own Microsoft 365 roles and Azure AD Microsoft 365 groups to control access to Microsoft Office resources.
- SaaS applications such as ServiceNow, WorkDay, and SuccessFactors use their own access management systems in conjunction with Azure AD or other identity providers to control access to their services.

As seen, user access is controlled in many areas of the environment. To control all the access levels, organizations should dedicate personnel for auditing all these different accesses and develop guidance for employees to follow when granting and revoking access. To help with the organization's governance needs, Microsoft has released many different governance solutions, such as Azure AD Entitlement Management, which controls permission granting and revoking.

When planning, it is also important to try to automate and simplify the environment's permissioning for the environment. Consider these questions:

- Should you use dynamic groups that populate membership based on some value within the user object (such as department) and then use those groups to provide access within the applications?
- Do the applications support using dynamic groups to assign permissions?
- Should you use services like Entitlement Management for granting and revoking access?

Some organizations work on projects that have citizenship, education, certification, or other employee requirements. They might need employees to sign yearly agreements and take yearly training for them to be able to work on those organization projects. This means that you should consider whether information should be populated from an HR or personnel system to drive automated workloads around employee screening, clearance, training, and other requirements. And you should consider the type of access needed once that information is verified.

External access

External access is more than the access from your organization users to your internal or DMZ resources. Now you must deal with:

- External collaborations (B2B and B2C) as described as part of "Skill 3-2: Recommend an identity store (tenants, B2B, B2C, and hybrid)"

- Federations you may have configured with other organizations
- Access provided by services such as Azure Bastion, which allow you to RDP to devices using the Azure portal
- Access provided by cloud web gateways such as Azure AD Application Proxy, which enables access to internal on-premises applications
- External capabilities provided by SaaS applications, such as OneDrive, Box, DropBox, GitHub, and AWS, the sensitivity of the data being shared, and the services that can help manage the risk, such as Defender for Cloud Apps, Data Loss Prevention, Sensitive Labels, and so on

When architecting controls for this type of access, ensure a continuous posture assessment is performed. Services such as the Microsoft Defender for Cloud Secure Score, recommendations, and alerts can provide guidance on improving external access securely. Also, the Microsoft Purview Compliance portal can provide guidance on how current access configuration changes the organization's compliance posture and access to different areas of the environment.

Remember that these new governance components provide organizations with capabilities that most organizations did not have before. This means that the organization may need to create new roles and responsibilities to ensure that the proper checks and required remediation actions are scheduled and comprehensive.

Endpoint access

Besides implementing regular file and group permissions, Windows endpoints have a diverse functionality that helps control access within the endpoint itself. For example, Windows Defender Application Control can define what can run on devices you manage. This is an allow list/block list functionality. Windows Defender SmartScreen protects against phishing, malware sites, and applications by blocking access to potentially malicious content.

Windows Defender System Guard protects and maintains the system's integrity as it starts up and validates the system's integrity has truly been maintained through local and remote attestation. Windows Defender Exploit Guard provides attack surface reduction, controlled folder access, and exploit and network protection. Windows Defender Firewall can be used to control communications in and out of the endpoint. Using a firewall capability may not be a suitable solution for certain endpoints.

Adaptive access

Azure AD provides several capabilities that help provide adaptive access, including Dynamic Group Membership and Azure AD Entitlement Management.

However, the adaptive access capabilities provided by conditional access are even more powerful. Not only does conditional access verify the first time the user is authenticated, but it also keeps monitoring the health status of the user identity and the device, connection, data, and application. If something risky is found, Azure AD revokes the session token, and the user will be issued a challenge for re-authentication and re-authorization.

Because these policies can be enforced tenant-wide, a consistent policy-driven access control architecture for all technologies and scenarios can be implemented.

Decentralized identities

Although centralized identities allow consistency in how resources are configured, managed, governed, and supported, regulations such as the General Data Protection Regulation (GDPR) require organizations to provide better data protection, privacy, and control of shared personal data for individual users. But at the same time, improved verifications are required. To help meet these requirements, Microsoft has released the Microsoft Entra Verified ID, which provides capabilities for Decentralized Identifiers (DIDs).

DIDs are global, unique self-owned identities that are easy to use and provide complete control over how identity data is accessed and used. They also assure immutability, censorship resistance, and tamper evasiveness characteristics. Microsoft has been collaborating with the Decentralized Identity Foundation (DIF), the W3C Credentials Community Group (*https://www.w3.org/TR/did-core/*), and other groups to develop the standard that is being implemented in Microsoft services.

Microsoft's Verifiable ID solution uses DID to cryptographically sign and attest the ownership of the Verifiable ID. For example, see Figure 3-8, which shows a use case where Mary wants to buy something from ProseWare using the discounts that ProseWare provides to employees of Contoso.

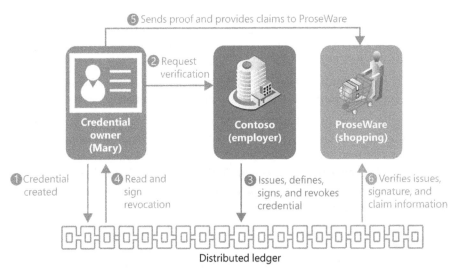

FIGURE 3-8 How DIDs are used for authentication

Figure 3-8 is explained in more detail here:

1. To prove to ProseWare that she is a Contoso employee, Mary requests proof of employment from Contoso by signing into the Authenticator App.

2. With the request, the app passes an ID token to Contoso.

3. Upon validating the ID token, Contoso issues a signed verifiable credential that includes claims about Mary and signs it with Contoso DID.

4. Now, when ProseWare requests proof of employment from Mary, she uses the Authenticator App to scan the QR code provided by ProseWare to start the verification.

5. The request is approved and sent to ProseWare.

6. A signed verifiable presentation (VP) with her DID is provided to ProseWare using their public key.

> **NOTE** When this book was written in late 2022, the capabilities of Verified IDs were just getting started, but you should start planning how you can use proof of employment, certification, college diploma, residency, training taken, and so on to perform an adaptive access decision. Although many applications could not take advantage of these capabilities yet, Microsoft APIs allow developers to discover credential types and issue and verify credentials. In addition, any version of Azure AD, including the free version, can request and verify credentials without requiring any custom integration with issuers.

Key recommendations

Following are some key recommendations:

- VPN access tends to provide wider access to users than necessary. To segment sessions further, we recommend that you use a user-to-application segmentation solution, such as the one provided by the Secure Web Gateway service. This type of service enables organizations to proxy access to individual, user-selected, on-premises applications without needing VPNs. Therefore, we recommend that you replace legacy VPNs with Secure Web Gateway solutions, such as Azure AD Application Proxy.

- Implement least-access/privileged access at all access levels and use policies that allow this configuration to work harmoniously.

- Implement Zero Trust for all users, regardless of location, including on-premises users.

- Consider monitoring your application permission changes. After attackers compromise an infrastructure, they tend to modify application permissions and run their payloads behind the organization's applications. This is because they know that organizations tend to trust their own applications and not scrutinize changes as often.

- Use Secure Access Workstation to protect your privileged users. Reduce Internet browsing usage to only approved sites and eliminate or reduce access to email, if possible.

- Use just-in-time capabilities to assign time-bound group membership.

- Assign time-bound access to resources.

- Conduct Access Reviews to ensure users require roles assigned to them.

- Perform audits of privileged access requests and configuration changes.

- Implement endpoint access controls to minimize risk and the chances of a compromise spreading into the endpoint.
- Allocate a considerable amount of time for managing external access.
- Use adaptive access controls to automate the granting and revoking of access.
- Create new roles and responsibilities to deal with the new governance capabilities.
- Update internal processes to align with new capabilities.
- Plan for how verifiable IDs can be used in your environments.

Skill 3-5: Design a strategy for conditional access

Conditional access is the heart of the Microsoft Zero Trust approach. It analyzes and verifies signals from different sources to make adaptive access decisions that reduce risk when authenticating and authorizing access. The following verifications can be performed to support the Explicit Verify Zero Trust principle (some of which also can be seen in Figure 3-9):

- MFA Usage.
- Real-time detection checks to see if the leaked credentials are being sold on the web; and if there has been any password spray against the account. It also evaluates many things, including
  - Whether the sign-in is using an anonymous IP address
  - Whether the sign-in is deemed from a location (impossible travel)
  - Malware delivery has been linked to a location the user has never signed in from before
- Group Membership.
- Legacy Authentication used.
- To support device verifications, the following checks are performed:
  - Joined to AAD.
  - Configuration is compliant.
  - Microsoft Defender for Endpoint can alert you if indications of compromise (IOCs) have been detected.
  - Filter by platform or value assigned to an identity object attribute. For example, `extendedAttribute1` = PAW. This can be used to restrict access to privileged resources.
  - No persistent browser session.

- To support application verifications, the following checks are performed (see *https://aka.ms/caapps*):

  - Users attempting to access specific applications.

  - Modern authentication client users, including browsers, mobile apps, and mobile desktop clients.

  - Legacy authentication clients.

- To support network verifications using IP location information:

  - Administrators can create trusted IP address ranges to be used when making policy decisions.

  - Entire countries/regions IP ranges from which to block or allow traffic.

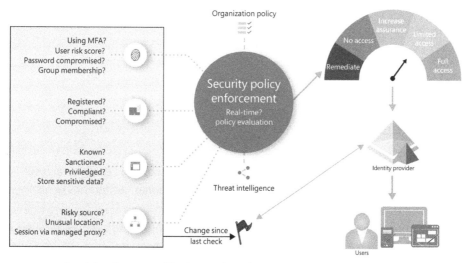

FIGURE 3-9 Conditional access verifications and continuous access evaluation

To use conditional access, you must have an Azure AD Premium P1 license or Microsoft 365 Business Premium. Risk-based policies require Identity Protection, which is an Azure AD P2 feature.

Microsoft is working on making the Azure AD administrative console more user-friendly. As part of the rebranding of Microsoft Entra Azure AD, you can see that Microsoft has created templates for the most used conditional access scenarios. Figure 3-10 shows some of the conditional access templates being provided.

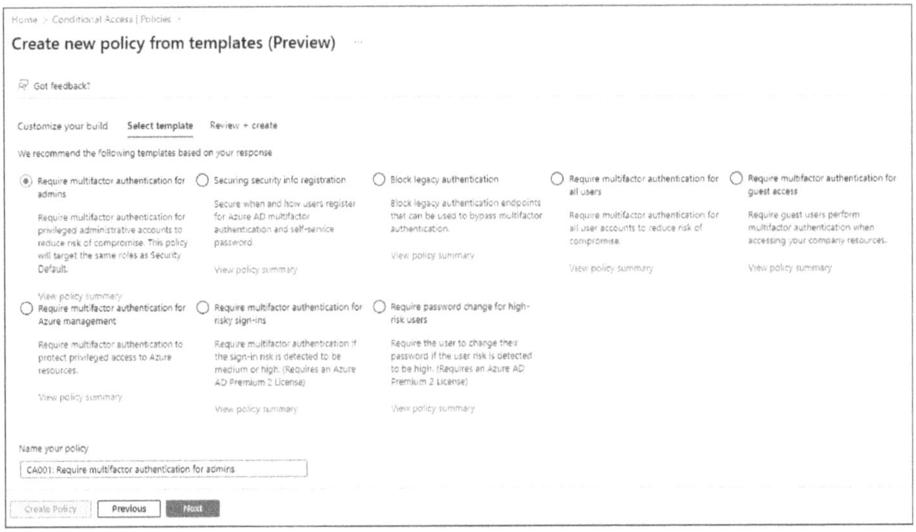

FIGURE 3-10 Create policy from templates

Key recommendations

Following are some key recommendations:

- It is recommended to structure conditional access policies based on common access needs by different groups of users. For recommended personas, see *https://aka.ms/ CAAccessPersonas.*

- Set naming standards for your policies. Possible naming structure to use may be found in the following URL: See *https://aka.ms/CANamingConvention.*

- Enable Conditional Access Evaluation (CAE) in your environment. If CAE is already enabled, there are some migration steps that may need to be taken.

- Exchange Online, SharePoint Online, and Teams should be subscribed to critical Azure AD events for them to use CAE. These three services support CAE using Windows, iOS, Android, and macOS. Microsoft is working on adding support for CAE on all Microsoft and partners services.

- Consider preparing your custom applications to use CAE with the CAE API.

- When using location awareness as a verification, be aware that location can be spoofed.

- Conditional access can also be enforced for B2B collaboration.

- Be aware that the conditional access policy can apply to service accounts which may create issues with some of your applications.

- Consider implementing conditional access to control every application. Azure AD integrated applications, including gallery, non-gallery, and applications published through Azure AD Application Proxy are supported.

- Use **Report-Only** mode and the **What If** tool to understand the behavior of the policy before implementing it. **Report-Only** mode allows you to see the impact on real-time sign-ins on the **Sign-In Logs** > **Event** > **Report-Only** tab. The **What If** tool provides an analysis under hypothetical circumstances.

- Use the Conditional Access Insights And Reporting workbook under **Azure Monitor** to view the aggregate impact of your conditional access policies.

- Minimize the number of conditional access policies to ease management.

- When planning for disruption while implementing conditional access policies, develop a communication plan to let users know what is being done, what to expect, and what to do if they encounter any issues. This includes who to contact and what information to include as part of the communication.

- Consider using `extensionAttribute` to apply conditional access policies to groups of devices. For more information, visit *https://aka.ms/extensionAttribute*.

- Have a contingency plan in case something does not work as expected. Review the tutorial at: *https://aka.ms/CAContingency*.

- Create policies that will be used only in an emergency and leave them in a disabled state. This will enable the opportunity to roll back changes in the event of a previous policy implementation lockout.

- To roll back a policy, you can disable it or exclude a user or group from the policy.

- Back up all conditional access policies using Microsoft Graph API. See the Github repository for help with this task.

- Be aware that selecting All Cloud Apps under **Conditional Access > Cloud Apps** can inadvertently block user access because the policy will be enforced for all tokens issued to websites and services. So, although there are many advantages to using this option, familiarize yourself with the list of applications that have gone through onboarding and validation from Microsoft and test all other applications in your environment before implementing the All Cloud Apps setting. Otherwise, consider using a targeted approach for protecting applications.

- Familiarize yourself with the conditional access dependencies and relations with other technologies and services. Some conditional access functionality may not be available unless the proper requirements are met. For example

  - For device compliance to work, you will need Microsoft Endpoint Manager.

  - For device risk, you will need Microsoft Endpoint Manager.

  - For user risk, you will need Azure AD Identity Protection.

  - Consider putting processes in place to monitor conditional access admins as they can bypass Zero Trust controls.

Skill 3-6: Design a strategy for role assignment and delegation

Your organization's security depends heavily on how well you control privileged access. Cyber-attackers target privileged users to expand their reach across the environment, so thorough planning needs to be performed to reduce overpermissioning. Some of the best practices to adhere to when planning include:

- Provide least privileged access to perform the tasks at hand. When possible, use built-in roles rather than creating your own.

- Role assignments should be provided by Privileged Identity Management (PIM) functionality instead of assigning groups directly to roles. Assigning a group to be eligible for role assignment in PIM makes each group member eligible to activate the roles for a limited period, and the access is revoked afterward. In turn, this reduces the risk of exposure since privileged accounts will not have long-term access making it more difficult for attackers to find an account to target.

- When using PIM to protect Azure resources, a service principal is created for PIM and assigned as a User Access Administrator for the resource.

- When role assignment cannot be done through PIM, assign roles to groups rather than users. This simplifies assigning roles to many users.

- If multiple roles are required to perform tasks, use privileged access groups to grant permanent access to multiple roles and then make the users eligible for that privileged access group membership.

- Limit the number of Global Administrators to less than five users.

- Define at least two emergency access accounts to the Global Administrator role to be used in a "break glass in emergency" way. Ensure that they have different MFA mechanisms from other global administrators in your organization and that you control and monitor account usage.

- Do not sync administrative accounts from on-premises. If on-premises is compromised, the attacker can automatically obtain privileged access to the cloud. Instead, all administrative accounts should be cloud-native accounts.

- Conduct periodic inventories of services, owners, and administrators. Use Privileged Identity Management Discovery and Insights to help with this inventory.

- Global Administrators in Azure can assign themselves to access all Azure subscriptions and management groups in your directory. When that access is elevated, the account is assigned to the User Access Administrator role in Azure root scope (/). This provides access to view all resources and assign access to any subscription or management group in the directory. Configure Access Management For Azure Resources under the Directory Properties to get that access. We recommend that you audit this request on a recurrent basis. You can get a list of role assignments at the root scope by using the

`Get-AzRoleAssignment` PowerShell command. To list the User Access Administrator role assignments, use the `az role assignment list` command.

- Review the Elevate Access Logs regularly by choosing **Monitor > Activity Log > Activity > Directory Activity**. You will see a list of access elevations that have been performed in the environment and who performed them. To delegate access to view the Elevate Access logs, follow the instructions outlined at *https://aka.ms/ElevateAccess*.

- To ensure that the role assignments have the right membership, configure recurring Access Reviews to revoke unneeded privileged assignments.

- Identify Microsoft accounts that are members of any administrative roles and switch them to work or school accounts. (For example, Microsoft accounts may have been used when Azure AD was first enabled.)

- Administrative Users should have two accounts—one dedicated for performing administrative tasks and one used for day-to-day work. The administrative accounts should have reduced email and Internet browsing.

- Inventory your configured privileged accounts on VMs.

- Review the membership for built-in Microsoft 365 admin roles.

- Most Azure logs, such as Azure Activity and Azure Resources logs, are retained for only 90 days if not stored in external storage, such as Azure Log Analytics or Microsoft Sentinel.

- Azure Lighthouse enables service providers to deliver managed services using comprehensive tooling built into Azure. This means customer subscriptions and resource groups can be delegated to specific users and roles so they can manage the tenant. The activity log shows the changes performed and who made them.

- Review and modernize internal organization processes for role assignments and delegation.

- Assign Audit Global Administrator or Privileged Role Administrator membership because they can modify Azure AD role assignments.

Delegating to non-administrators

There are instances in which access needs to be delegated to non-IT users. For example, auditors might need to assess the environment and access to the capabilities provided by Microsoft Purview services, such as eDiscovery, Data Loss Prevention, Information Protection, Insider Risk Manager, Communication Compliance, and Compliance Manager.

Figure 3-11 shows the Microsoft 365 Compliance portal with blades for each of the different governance services available. First, navigate to the Microsoft Compliance portal and select the **Permissions** blade. There, you will see that you can delegate access by using the Azure AD Roles, or if you want to provide solution-specific roles, you can use Microsoft Purview.

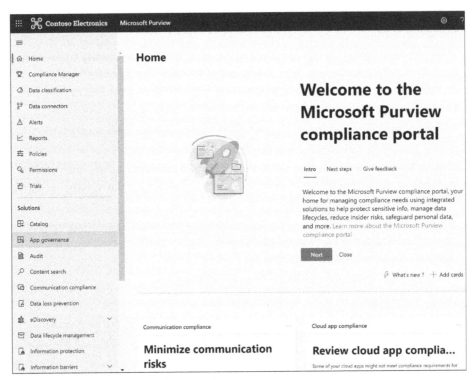

FIGURE 3-11 Microsoft 365 Compliance portal

Before deciding which solution to select, let's talk about how access has been given in the past. In on-premises environments, customers were accustomed to purchasing a single application to provide a capability to a group of users. Administrators provided most employees with permissions in only one application. Nowadays, services integrate and cross-collaborate, easing the workload and enabling many new analytics and reporting that were not possible before. To provide access to all those enhanced capabilities, you must look at the work that users do, the functionality they need, and how different services interact with other services to provide those extra capabilities to the user.

Once you understand those interactions, you need to analyze the data provided by those interactions and decide what type of access you want the user to have. This information will guide you in choosing the role you will need to provide within the solution. In other words, interconnection and cross-service collaboration change how access management is performed because the strategy is no longer about providing access in a single application. Instead, the strategy is to provide roles that allow cross-service usage.

However, most administrators still believe that you provide access at the application level and might be tempted to provide access for each required service. So, when they start planning, they tend to provide permissions focusing on individual services. After several months of using the solution and getting user feedback, they begin to realize that for the users to perform end-to-end analysis, a different method for delegating permissions is required. Slowly, they begin being added to the built-in roles provided by Azure AD.

For example, let's walk through what a possible auditor would need to investigate data exfiltration:

1. They might start checking Microsoft Purview Insider Risk Manager and Communication Compliance to see if there are indications and motives for a user to exfiltrate data.

2. Then, they might use Microsoft Purview eDiscovery to uncover communication or review emails that may exfiltrate data.

3. Next, they might want to review the sensitivity of that data using Data Loss Prevention and Information Protection.

4. They also may want to review logs of actual data being exfiltrated to different external SaaS solutions, which might require access to Microsoft Defender for Cloud Apps.

5. The auditor might need access to Log Analytics and/or Microsoft Sentinel if the analyzed timeframe is longer than what the service stores (usually 90 days).

6. Because of the wide number of services that the auditor needs, the roles of Security Reader and Compliance Administrator may be a better fit for this Auditor role.

In summary, role assignment requires analysis of the user-required activities before even looking at the necessary services.

> **MORE INFO** To help with that analysis, Microsoft provides guidance on defining and using personas and making role assignment decisions at *https://aka.ms/CAAccessPersonas*.

Once you understand the user activities, you must look at the initial services needed and the interconnections enabled with those services to allow extra capabilities needed by a user. This type of approach should be used for all access decisions. Doing so will help you reduce unnecessary role creation, simplify role assignment, and access delegation for your organization.

Delegating access to service providers

With the increasing set of capabilities being made available and the increasingly complex security landscape, organizations often partner with service providers to obtain the help and expertise needed to manage the infrastructure.

To view and manage your service partners in a centralized user interface, you can use Azure Lighthouse Service Providers in the Azure portal. Figure 3-12 shows the **Service Providers** blade, where you can view details about your service partners and their offers and delegations made to specific resources.

FIGURE 3-12 Service providers

When you select Add Offer from the Delegations blade, you see a list of offers from different companies. When you select an offer, you can configure the delegations you want to provide to the Service Provider. Be aware that Microsoft has released a new granular delegated administrative privilege (GDAP), which provides partners with least-privilege access by allowing them to configure granular and time-bound access to their customers' workloads. You can assign approved Azure AD roles to the specific security groups created by the partner in the Partner Center dashboard, which will grant granular delegated admin privileges (GDAP) to those security groups.

Once the delegations are enabled, you should use the built-in Azure policy definition to audit delegation of scopes to a managing tenant. You can also restrict delegation to specific managing tenants, so any attempts to delegate those subscriptions outside the ones you have approved are denied. Then you can view Azure Activity Log to see all actions performed. Remember to store Logs in Log Analytics or Microsoft Sentinel if you want to retain them for over 90 days.

In Microsoft 365, you can delegate administration to a Microsoft partner by selecting the subscription you want to delegate at **Microsoft 365 Admin Center > Settings > Partner Relationships**. If you're not currently working with a partner, you can also find one on the Microsoft Pinpoint website at *https://pinpoint.microsoft.com*.

Once the partner is selected and you accept the invitation, give them Global Administrator and Helpdesk Administrator roles. With the new GDAP, you can configure more granular access. The access is explicitly granted by customers to partners after the partner configures a request for a granular administrator relationship with the customer from the Partner Center.

Your organization can approve the request by selecting **Microsoft 365 Admin Center > Settings > Partner Relationships**.

For Microsoft Dynamics 365, delegated administrators are not visible in your Azure AD user list until the delegated administrators log in to Dynamics 365. All actions performed by the delegated admin are logged in Dynamics 365 and associated with their ID in the partner's Azure AD. You will be able to see the changes made and which partner made them, but you will not be able to see usernames.

Because of these delegations, we recommend that you regularly review the following things:

- The Partner Relationships set
- Your organization's Global Administrator and Helpdesk Administrator roles

Skill 3-7: Design security strategy for privileged-role access to infrastructure, including identity-based firewall rules and Azure PIM

Throughout this chapter and book, we have emphasized how capabilities should work together to provide a defense-in-depth that effectively adapts to the complexity of the modern environment.

This is even more important for a privileged access role access to infrastructure. As mentioned, attackers target privileged role users to get wider access to the environment. In the past, it was harder to centrally manage individual resource roles. However, as you will see in this skill, Microsoft provides ways to centrally manage all those roles. In this section, we focus on the approaches that can be used to secure privileged access to infrastructure.

Privileged Access Workstation (PAW)

You can make it difficult to attack privileged users by removing email and Internet browsing risks. Some organizations might still need to provide administrators with these services, but you can reduce much of the risk by reducing the sources from which the administrators get emails and the external sites that administrators browse.

Also, you can reduce the attack surface by not installing many everyday applications on these workstations (such as Outlook and other productivity applications). Make sure security features like Credential Guard, Exploit Guard, System Guard, Application Guard, and Firewall are turned on to protect against and isolate threats.

Create conditional access policies to enforce modern authentication and require installing threat protection services like Microsoft Defender for Endpoint. Tight access rules must be configured to reduce these workstations' incoming and outgoing connections. These workstations should only be able to communicate with the resources it needs to manage. For example, there is no need to use a day-to-day productivity user workstation to communicate with these

SAW devices. Configuring policies to prevent unexpected communications from unexpected sources should help prevent attackers from getting privileged access.

Privileged Identity Management (PIM)

PIM simplifies and helps improve the protection and manage privileged access for your Azure resources. PIM allows organizations to limit when privileged access is active and provides an auditable log of privileged access. Figure 3-13 shows the Azure resources that PIM has discovered. When you first set up PIM, it asks if you need to discover Azure resources.

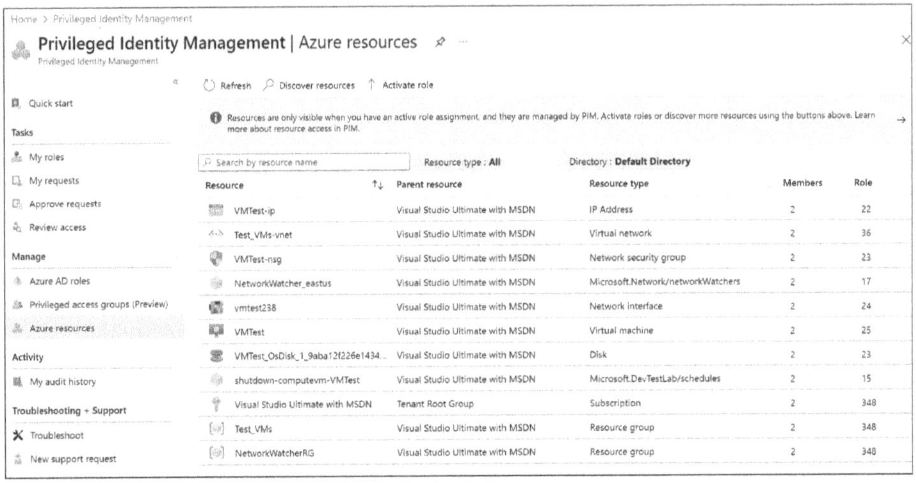

FIGURE 3-13 Privileged Identity Management

Discovering resources causes PIM to create a service principal that gets assigned to the User Access Administrator role for each of the Azure resources discovered. The User Access Administrator role for the resource provides PIM with the `Microsoft.Authorization/roleAssignments/write` permission, which enables PIM to manage each of the resources.

Figure 3-14 shows the PIM service principal account as part of the User Access Administrator. As you can see from the image, the assignment Membership is set to Direct, the State is set to Assigned, and the End Time is set to Permanent. Be aware that the user who created the resource is also configured with the same assignment. You might want to audit resources for this behavior and remove any nonrequired direct assignments.

> **CAUTION** Do not delete the MS-PIM assignment because that will disable PIM from managing the different resources.

FIGURE 3-14 User Access Administrator membership defined under a PIM Resource

Assignment duration

PIM allows you to select two types of assignment duration options (**Eligible** and **Active**), and within those two assignments, there are configurations you can set:

- **Eligible**   For most accounts, we recommend that the assignment be configured as **Eligible** because they must use PIM to activate the role to use it.

- **Active**   Configure the assignment to **Active**, which means the role will be activated when the user logs in to the environment. This might be necessary in larger organizations where administrators perform tasks from the moment they log in until they are done for the day. If they are not configured as **Active**, the user will have to go to PIM, request activation, log out, and log in for a refresh token to be issued before they can do their work.

- **Permanently Eligible**   We recommend that you set the assignment to **Permanently Eligible** because you want to evaluate their ability to elevate every so often, such as when a user has changed positions and no longer needs access. Perhaps the user has asked for access to complete an audit, so the access is needed for a short time. This setting ensures a reevaluation if the access occurs, and if it does not happen, their capability to activate is removed. In larger organizations, it may be difficult to manage all administrative accounts using this method because the timeframe is managed for each user assignment by assigning individual start and end dates. Instead, you may rely on Access Reviews, which enable a group of users to be verified at once.

> **MORE INFO**   Access Reviews are discussed later in this chapter in "Access Reviews."

The two break-glass accounts should be configured with allowed permanent active assignments. Also, these accounts should not be configured to require MFA on active assignment either. You will be dealing with an emergency when you use either of these accounts, so you want to minimize disruption when using them. Of course, because of how these accounts are configured, heavy monitoring should be enabled, including releasing alerts when anyone signs in using them.

EXAM TIP   Be aware that when you disable the **Permanently Eligible** assignment and assign a **Start Date** and **End Date**, if the assignment expires, the user can request that the assignment be changed to **Extended**. When they request the extension, the administrator receives an email notification to review the extension request.

Delegation

When adding an assignment, select the resource and click **Roles**. This will allow you to see all roles available for that resource and add the proper assignments. When possible, it is recommended that assignments be enabled at a higher administrative level than an individual resource (such as a Resources group). This will help to simplify the management of those resources.

Review access

We recommend that your organization review assignments regularly to reduce the risk associated with stale role assignments. When you perform a review, you can define how frequently you want the review to be triggered (weekly, monthly, quarterly, semi-annually, or annually).

You can also define the scope of the review (**All Users And Groups** or **Service Principals**), what assignment type you want to review (**All**, **Active**, or **Eligible**), and who will be the reviewers (**Selected User Or Group**, **Manager**, or **Self**). The **Manager** option refers to the manager of the user or group being reviewed.

Lastly, you can decide what should happen if there is no response (**No Change**, **Remove Access**, **Approve Access**, or **Take Recommendations**) and send a notification to additional users or groups to receive completion updates.

Alerts and audits

You can configure PIM to alert when suspicious behavior is detected. You can do this for Azure AD roles, privileged access groups, or Azure resources by clicking **Alerts** and then activating the checks. For example, Figure 3-15 shows the Alert Settings, which shows the types of alerts that can be detected in an environment.

FIGURE 3-15 Alert Settings

As seen in Figure 3-15, each alert shows a **Risk Level** and whether the alert is **Active** (**Yes** or **No**) or **Disabled** (**Yes** or **No**). Click an alert for more information about it.

Microsoft Entra Permissions Management

Permissions Management is a cloud infrastructure entitlement management (CIEM) solution that provides visibility into permissions assigned to all identities across Azure, Amazon Web Services (AWS), and Google Cloud Platform (GCP). It monitors for unused and excessive permissions to help you implement least-privileged access. It inventories and provides a risk classification of privileged entitlements across all resources.

To enable Permissions Management, go to *https://entra.microsoft.com/* and select **Permissions Management**. If you have not previously used permissions management, you will be asked to try or purchase it. After the license is enabled, the Microsoft Entra Permissions Management dashboard, as shown in Figure 3-16, will show where you can create a configuration for your AWS, Azure, or GCP environments.

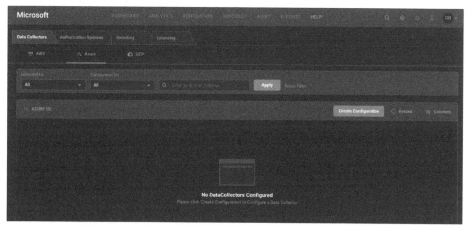

FIGURE 3-16 Microsoft Entra Permissions Management dashboard

To get started, you can select the infrastructure that you want to configure (**Azure**, **GCP**, or **AWS**) and click **Create Configuration**. Steps to onboard can be found at *https://aka.ms/EntraPM*.

After onboarding and discovery and analysis of your environment are completed, you see a summary of key statistics and information about your identity environment, including

- **Permission Creep Index (PCI)**   The PCI provides information about the users who have been granted high-risk permissions but have not used them.
- **Analytics dashboard**   The Analytics dashboard provides a snapshot of permission metrics in the last 90 days.

By selecting **Permission Creep Index** and clicking the statistics, you can see either a list of **Users**, **Applications**, and **Managed Identities** or other findings with detailed information found for those resources, including

- The PCI index calculated
- Number of permissions granted

- Number of permissions that have been used
- The last time the permissions were used

For remediation, you can create a custom role and provide the permissions required to make the user eligible for the role in PIM.

Key recommendations

Following are some key recommendations:

- Azure AD Resource administrator permissions are needed to manage resources under PIM. The Owner or User Access Administrator subscription roles and Azure AD Global Administrators have this permission by default.

- Once a management group or a subscription is selected to be managed under PIM, it cannot be unmanaged.

- You might want to audit resources that have users with **Permanently Assigned** roles other than your break-glass roles and other exceptions. You might want to configure automation to remove those users from the **Permanently Assigned** role.

- Do not delete the MS-PIM assignment since that will disable PIM from managing the different resources.

- You might need to elevate your access to gain access to all subscriptions and management groups in your directory. This applies to Global Administrators since Azure resources are secured independently from Azure AD. Azure AD role assignments do not automatically grant access over the Azure resources. When you elevate your access, your account is assigned to the User Access Administrator role in Azure root scope (/). This provides access to view all resources and assign access to any subscription or management group in the directory. To get that access, configure **Access Management For Azure Resources** under the **Directory Properties.** We recommend that you audit this request on a recurrent basis. You can get a list of role assignments at the root scope by using the `Get-AzRoleAssignment` PowerShell cmdlet. To list the User Access Administrator role assignment, use the `az role assignment list` cmdlet.

Skill 3-8: Design security strategy for privileged activities, including PAM, entitlement management, and cloud tenant administration

All the recommendations discussed as part of Skill 3-7 apply to privileged activities. The administration of PIM is a bit different because rather than selecting Azure Resources, you will be selecting Azure AD roles, which are a bit different. This skill focuses on defining the PIM-related differences for managing Azure AD Roles and providing the many other capabilities that can be used as part of the security strategy for privileged activities.

Privileged Access Workstation (PAW)

Privileged users should use PAWs to make it difficult for attackers to access privileged credentials. As discussed in other sections, eliminating or reducing email and Internet browsing access can lower the risk of phishing.

In addition, because this type of workstation will be used only for privileged activities, many of the organization's required applications will not be needed on them, which reduces the attack surface. In addition, more Windows and threat protection capabilities can be added to monitor these critical assets without impacting productivity. We recommend that these workstations be implemented to protect privileged activities.

Privileged Identity Management (PIM)

In the previous section, we focused on showing how PIM simplifies and helps improve protection on how you manage privileged access for your Azure resources.

This section focuses on how PIM helps with Azure AD Roles and other Microsoft services, such as Microsoft 365 and Intune. It enables organizations to limit when privileged access is active and provides an auditable log of privileged access.

You can view activity, activations, and audit history for all the roles within your organization. Figure 3-17 shows the functionality provided by Privileged Identity Management for managing Azure AD roles.

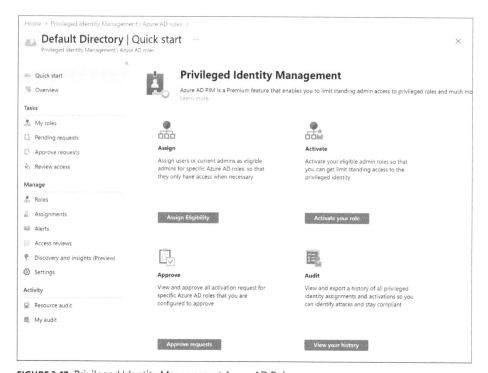

FIGURE 3-17 Privileged Identity Management Azure AD Roles

Most of the functionality for Azure AD roles is the same as managing Azure resources. You can manage roles, assignments, and alerts. You can create Access Reviews and configure settings. However, there is a Discovery and Insights (Preview) blade that shows you the findings, such as

- The number of accounts with permanent membership
- The number of accounts with assignments to privileged roles
- The number of service principals with privileged roles assignment
- Ways to remediate issues presented in the report

We recommend that you review the findings in this report and try to remediate them.

Microsoft Entra Permissions Management

Similar to PIM, most of the capabilities provided for Microsoft Entra Permissions Management (described in the previous section) to protect the infrastructure can also be used to protect general privileged activities.

One difference between Entra Permissions Management for AWS and Google and the Azure AD capabilities is that Entra Permissions Management for Azure AD can interconnect with PIM. This interconnection allows information to be displayed, such as

- Whether identities are assigned as permanent or time-bound
- Whether the assignment is active

Because PIM shares this information with Microsoft Entra Permissions Management, the service can consider that information when providing guidance about reducing the access risk.

Thought experiment

In this thought experiment, demonstrate your skills and knowledge of the topics covered in this chapter. You can find answers to this thought experiment in the next section.

You are one of the Azure administrators for Tailwind Traders, an online general store specializing in various products around the home and office. You are provided with the following background:

- Tailwind Traders have been migrating many of its resources to the cloud, but it still has many resources on-premises.
- Tailwind Traders is using a multi-cloud environment to ensure redundancy and availability.
- The company uses ADFS to provide smart card capabilities for its users.
- Tailwind Traders has purchased Defender for Endpoint, Defender for Identity, and Microsoft Endpoint Management to secure their workloads.

- Azure AD is the company's primary identity access management system and Azure AD P2.

- Also, the company wants to meet the Zero Trust requirements.

You have been contracted to architect an identity security strategy that takes advantage of these newly purchased capabilities. What are the possible implementations that Tailwind Traders should consider doing to take advantage of their investments?

Thought experiment answers

This section contains the solution to the thought experiment. Each answer explains why the answer choice is correct.

1. Based on this scenario, you will need to enable Defender for Endpoint, Defender for Identity, and Microsoft Endpoint Management.

2. Under Microsoft 365 Defender, click Identities to prepare the sensor agent that needs to be installed on all on-premises domain controllers, ADFS Servers, and Azure and AWS domain controller VMs. Once you download the agent, install it in all DCs and ADFS servers.

3. Once Defender for Endpoint and Microsoft Endpoint Management are configured for all endpoints, navigate to **Conditional Access > Access Controls > Grant** and select **Require Device To Be Marked As Compliant** and **Require Hybrid Azure AD Joined Device**.

4. Navigate to **Conditional Access > Conditions > Sign-In Risk** and set **Configure** to **Yes**. This is available for customers with Identity Protection, which is provided as part of Azure AD Premium P2 licenses. This enables different risk detections to be performed, such as anonymous IP, atypical travel, malware-linked IP, leaked credentials, and more.

5. Choose **Conditional Access > Access Controls > Grant > Require Multi-Factor Authentication**.

6. Configure two break-glass accounts and exclude them from implementing any of the conditional access options except MFA.

7. Enable PIM and onboard all accounts. Remove all the **Permanently Active** assignments, except both break-glass accounts, which should appear as **Allowed**. This will ensure that privileged accounts are only available when needed. Also, if there is a problem with PIM, you can use your break-glass accounts.

8. Ensure that service principals are not impacted by conditional access because this will affect applications being run on the environment.

9. Browse to **Azure Active Directory > Security > Continuous Access Evaluation**. Click **Enable** and click **Save**. This enables token revocation to take place when an indication of compromise (IoC) is detected on the device.

Chapter summary

This chapter provides recommendations to strengthen your identity and access management strategy. For the most part, we assumed you understand the basics of Microsoft Identity.

> **NOTE** For more information, review the material about the Exam SC-300: Microsoft Identity and Access Administrator exam at *https://docs.microsoft.com/en-us/learn/certifications/exams/sc-300*.

Because of the number of recommendations we provided to help with your identity security strategies, summarized recommendations were provided with each skill. However, below is a list of key recommendations to help guide your wholistic strategy:

- Remember, every resource—whether a user, application, data, device, or network—is an Identity. All these need to be updated, hashed, and healthy. By treating all resources as identities with attributes that can be verified, you extend your Zero Trust capabilities.

- The Interconnection and cross-service collaboration enable almost real-time automation and analysis that was not possible before cloud capabilities were available. However, this also brings complexity to the environment because you aren't providing permissions at the service or application level. Instead, you must understand the user roles and responsibilities, the initial services that the user needs, and the interconnections to other applications that will further expand the user experience to decide what type of role the user needs for them to obtain the right access. In addition, when replacing or changing services for other vendor solutions, you must understand all the functionality that will be affected.

- Establish a least-privilege configuration and explicit validation of sessions and authorized elevation paths.

- Mitigate movement across the environment.

- Use Rapid Threat Detection and Response to limit adversary access and time in the environment.

CHAPTER 4

Design a regulatory compliance strategy

Regulatory compliance for security is a key part of a security governance strategy. Security governance ensures that security meets all requirements and that security controls are implemented consistently across the organization. The regulatory compliance function of security governance ensures that security controls and processes comply with external regulatory bodies' requirements.

Regulatory standards capture security best practices and define a minimum due diligence for security controls to help you avoid being negligent of well-known security best practices. While many of these standards are outdated and were written before cloud services, it's critically important for an organization to meet them and report compliance to avoid fines, loss of authority to operate the business, and other negative consequences.

The regulatory compliance function ensures that the organization follows these standards and can report on that to regulatory bodies.

Skills covered in this chapter:

- Skill 4-1: Interpret compliance requirements and translate them into specific technical capabilities (new or existing)
- Skill 4-2: Evaluate infrastructure compliance by using Microsoft Defender for Cloud
- Skill 4-3: Interpret compliance scores and recommend actions to resolve issues or improve security
- Skill 4-4: Design implementation of Azure Policy
- Skill 4-5: Design for data residency requirements
- Skill 4-6: Translate privacy requirements into requirements for security solutions

Overview of security governance

Cybersecurity architects need basic literacy about security governance functions to effectively support regulatory compliance. Security architects should be aware of the major functions of security governance, how architects support these functions, and the key relationships between them.

Security governance is composed of multiple functions that collectively ensure that the organization consistently meets the various security and compliance requirements. Security governance functions help drive consistency across the technical estate and processes of the security program. They also ensure that everything is on track to meet internal and external obligations. Governance functions also maintain key relationships with other teams and external organizations that affect the whole security program.

Security governance is a unifying force within the security team and is becoming a dynamic, agile discipline as organizations adopt Zero Trust. This is because the technical estate, security requirements, compliance requirements, and attackers are constantly in motion, requiring security teams to constantly adjust to meet these challenges.

During a Zero Trust transformation, security governance functions ensure technical teams shift to a continuous improvement approach (if they are not already in that mode). The governance functions provide architectural guidance, policy, and oversight to ensure that teams adapt technology, process, and skill sets for these changes.

The security governance functions are shown in Figure 4-1, including key external relationships for these functions:

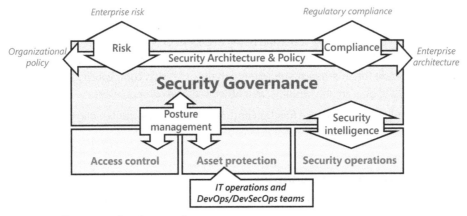

FIGURE 4-1 Governance function overview

The functions described in Figure 4-1 are explained below:

- **Risk** The risk function in security translates security risk into organizational risk and vice versa, ensuring security risk is managed within the organization's risk framework. Without this, the organization may not be considering risk in security decisions, and the security team may be focusing on areas with little impact on business risks.

- **Security architecture and policy** These provide a unified, clear vision that serves as the authoritative technical vision and rulebook that makes the strategy real and actionable.

- **Security architecture** Security architecture is similar to building architecture, providing a clear end-state vision of all the components and how they fit together. Security architects create diagrams and documents that identify, document, and rationalize all the components to ensure they all fit together and meet the requirements.

- **Security policy** Security policy authoring and approval functions provide clear security rules of what must and must not happen (and what should and should not happen).

This provides teams across the organization with guardrails that help ensure they stay on track. Without this, the organization's teams will have difficulty consistently executing security controls and reducing risk. The security policy also works closely with other policy teams to ensure security policy elements are integrated into the organization's other policy frameworks, like employee policy.

- **Security intelligence**   Security intelligence provides accurate and useful insights into the threats the organization has and will face and other external events of interest. Strategic threat intelligence is the portion of this discipline that acts as a governance function, providing insights to leaders and teams across the organization. This helps architects better plan and prioritize activities and reduce organizational risk from known threats, attacks, and common mistakes. Strategic threat intelligence complements (and works closely with) other technical and tactical functions of threat intelligence that provide technical tools and processes with more specific signals.

- **Posture management**   Posture management is an operational function of the governance team, ensuring the organization has a clear understanding of the actual security risk they are carrying at any moment and working across teams to continuously reduce that risk. Without this, the organization is constantly surprised as attackers find new ways to attack the organization, and the risks to the organization steadily grow over time (instead of decreasing). Posture management is a relatively new function that evolved from threat and vulnerability management teams but includes all types of vulnerabilities (including configurations and process/practices) and is focused on enabling operational teams to overcome blockers to remediation (instead of just scanning and reporting). For more information on this critically important security governance function, see the Security Integration section of the CISO workshop at *https://aka.ms/ cisoworkshop-securityintegration*.

- **Security compliance**   This function provides accurate, timely, and complete reporting of compliance and supports remediating noncompliant elements. This helps ensure that the organization meets compliance requirements across the technical estate and processes. Without an effective security compliance function, the organization incurs the risk of noncompliance that can lead to fines, legal restrictions on business operations, and other negative impacts. This chapter discusses various aspects of security compliance and how architects support this function.

Compliance is not security

While compliance provides a consistent required baseline of security best practices and controls, compliance with security standards is insufficient to make an organization "secure." Keeping an organization secure can change dynamically by the week, day, or hour as adversaries learn to exploit different parts of the organization's complex attack surface. This attack surface spans countless thousands of implementation details across an incredibly complex technical estate of IT, OT (operational technology), and IoT (Internet of Things) systems and employees, contractors, partners, vendors, customers, and more. Being compliant with security regulations is important, but it is not enough to be secure.

See Figure 4-2 for an illustration of the relationship between the dynamic discipline of security and the static discipline of compliance.

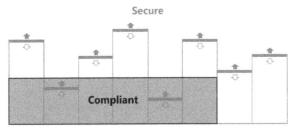

FIGURE 4-2 Compliant is not necessarily secure

For example, very few security regulations require using dedicated privileged-access workstations for IT administrators and other high-impact accounts. This is one of the most effective means of preventing major breaches, but it has not been added to most major security standards.

Security compliance and internal standards

A security compliance strategy can also include internal standards and requirements created by your organization. These internal standards help consistently apply security policy across different business units or technical environments.

Security architects help maintain these standards and update them for the hybrid-of-everything estate that spans multi-cloud, on-premises, IoT, OT, and more. Organizations often adopt Microsoft cloud security benchmarks (MCSB, formerly the Azure Security Benchmarks or ASB) or other benchmarks/frameworks to allow them to report compliance with internal and external compliance requirements.

TIP As you move to the cloud, take a fresh look at all your internal standards and policy because these often have strong assumptions of on-premises technology and operating models. Applying these standards as-is to the cloud often results in failure or friction that slows cloud adoption. This is because most internal standards don't consider the shared responsibility model of cloud services, newer cloud and security capabilities, or other learnings. Updating internal standards (or directly adopting MCSB or similar frameworks) sets your organization up for success rather than slowing down business and technology products without any meaningful increase in security.

Security governance modernization

Security governance is undergoing significant transformation as part of Zero Trust, cloud, and digital business transformations. These transform business processes, technology platforms, and people's daily roles and required skills.

The biggest impact of these transformations is that value delivery and service models are shifting to agile approaches that dynamically change and adjust to external requirements. These approaches replace static "waterfall-style" approaches with long planning cycles that often take months to implement changes.

A lot of change is created when modes are shifted, which can be difficult for people to absorb all at once. Therefore, it's critical to ensure that all teams have a clear direction, guidance, and the support they need to navigate this massive shift. In other words, they need security governance to help lead this change.

Security needs to become more agile because businesses, government agencies, and other organizations today face a world where services are expected to be provided whenever and wherever people want them. People's preferences for delivering these services also continuously evolve as new ideas emerge about their delivery and how competitors implement them in your industry and adjacent industries. Following are the three main drivers for increased organizational and security agility:

- **Business drivers**   This creates pressure to transform business processes to be agile enough to meet these needs before competitors do. Beating your competition also creates pressures to transform technology platforms (cloud) and processes (DevOps/DevSecOps) to support these business processes. And these transformations create pressure to secure all of these technologies and processes.

- **Compliance drivers**   Organizations also often need to rapidly enter new markets and prove regulatory compliance to local standards, putting pressure on security compliance and other governance functions to become more agile. Additionally, the increased regulation of cybersecurity and privacy requires compliance with new frameworks, reporting on new controls, and other changing demands.

- **Security drivers**   And, of course, we can't forget the attackers who only succeed at their jobs if they find a way in, which often requires finding a new approach or a new way to use an older one. These security drivers put pressure on security processes and technology to rapidly become agile.

Security governance functions help lead this change by driving key changes across teams, processes, and capabilities:

- **Continuous improvement culture**   A continuous improvement culture that shifts expectations that change happens fast. Security governance helps people learn how to adapt by focusing on shorter-term, quick wins and incremental progress toward longer-term north star objectives rather than big monolithic projects that take months or years to deliver. Governance helps focus on constant recalibration to new requirements to ensure you stay on the right course. One example of how to do this is to adopt the sprint approach for updating security policy (an agile method), which can result in policy and control procedure updates as frequently as every two weeks in some organizations.

- **Assume-compromise / assume-breach mindset** All governance functions should drive an assume-compromise and assume-breach mindset to ensure that security investments are balanced across identify, protect, detect, respond, recover activities and are continuously evaluated from different perspectives. For example, make sure conversations and thought processes across security and IT teams never end with "it would be blocked at the firewall." Instead, you might ask "what would the attackers try after it's blocked at the firewall?"

- **Asset-centric and data-centric approaches (versus network-centric)** Use asset- and data-centric approaches to ensure that controls can protect assets wherever they are instead of assuming or requiring that assets are always on an internal network. Governance functions should ensure teams are using the best control available (for security and productivity) instead of always trying to use classic network perimeter defenses for all assurances. For example, you should ensure email and user education protections for phishing emails, data protections that follow the data wherever they go, and extended detection and response (XDR) capabilities that detect threats on endpoints and other assets inside and outside the firewall.

- **Automation** Use automation to help reduce repetitive manual tasks that can increase cost and risk from errors, oversights, and gaps.

These changes are implemented into

- Architecture and policy
- How risks are assessed and reported
- New functions for posture management and strategic threat intelligence
- How compliance requirements are assessed and reported

Now that we understand security governance functions and how they are evolving, let's discuss how security architects can effectively support regulatory compliance.

Skill 4-1: Interpret compliance requirements and translate into specific technical capabilities (new or existing)

Security compliance is a partnership between compliance teams and technical teams. Cybersecurity architects support security compliance by helping interpret compliance requirements and translating them into specific technical capabilities. This is illustrated in Figure 4-3.

Security architects ensure that the organization's assessment, monitoring, and remediation of compliance requirements are technically accurate and that all technical elements and controls across the enterprise are considered. Without a cybersecurity architect involved in this process, there is a much higher risk of misinterpreting the compliance requirements or misreporting compliance status to regulators, putting the organization at risk of fines or other negative regulatory consequences.

FIGURE 4-3 Compliance is a team sport, and security architects often play a critical translation role

---

Security Compliance Teams

Security compliance is one type of compliance that an organization may face. Most organizations also must meet financial, health, safety, and other types of regulatory compliance. The security compliance teams responsible for assessing and reporting on security can be part of one or more teams or departments in the organization. Security compliance professionals work in legal, IT, dedicated compliance, or other departments. Or compliance professionals might work in multiple departments.

Security compliance standards often require a people, process, and technology approach. There are three types of actions required for security compliance:

- **Technical resource configurations**   Security architects often assist technical teams with identifying the right technical solutions.

- **Architectural changes**   Many compliance requirements require architectural guidance across technical teams and specialties. Security architects have a key role in identifying these requirements (sometimes implicit) and integrating them into the security, IT, and enterprise architecture.

- **Processes and readiness**   Security architects often have limited interaction with this, but they can be technical advisors to the compliance teams and help identify technical solutions to support or automate these processes.

While many technical elements of different standards are similar, each standard may take a different approach to how compliance is assessed and measured, the scope of the technical estate covered by it, the frequency of reporting, the allowance for exceptions and alternate mitigations, and other aspects.

Your compliance and technical teams should read these carefully (and work with peers in other organizations) to ensure they correctly understand and interpret the controls and how to apply and report them.

Security compliance translation process

Translating compliance requirements into security architectures, policy, and technical capabilities is similar to the translation of security requirements described in Skill 1-3 (Chapter 1).

Figure 4-4 depicts how security architecture and policy meet both security and compliance requirements.

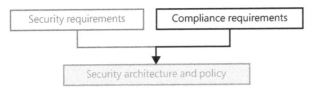

FIGURE 4-4 Compliance and security requirements

Interpreting compliance requirements is similar to translating security requirements into capabilities. Architects work with technical teams across security and IT (and sometimes business teams) to ensure the solutions and technical capabilities are designed and implemented to meet the compliance requirements. One major difference with compliance requirements is that compliance teams (with the appropriate expertise) often lead the processes to identify outcomes and high-level requirements.

Figure 4-5 depicts the process of evaluating and meeting compliance requirements.

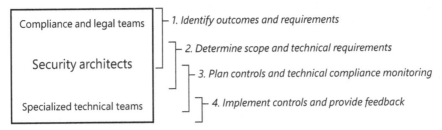

FIGURE 4-5 Compliance requirement translation process

The process of evaluating and meeting compliance requirements includes:

1. **Identify outcomes and requirements**   Identify outcomes and requirements by analyzing the applicable standards and regulations. Compliance teams often lead this, and it should result in a clear requirement for the ultimate outcome.

2. **Determine scope and technical requirements** Translate the requirements into specific technical instructions on which data and systems must meet the requirements.

3. **Plan controls and technical compliance monitoring** Identify and plan how to meet those technical requirements with the technical controls across the platforms you are using and monitor the compliance state.

4. **Implement controls and provide feedback** Implement controls across all applicable resources in the technical estate and continuously improve the process and the controls.

Many organizations need to meet multiple compliance standards related to security. Organizations often need to meet both privacy and security requirements and may handle multiple types of sensitive data (personal information, personal health information, financial information, and so on). Organizations often have employees, operations, or customers in multiple countries with local regulations. Also, some organizations have contractual requirements from their customers to meet regulatory compliance, such as technology outsourcing companies, cloud service providers, and others.

Organizations that must meet multiple compliance standards often use an internal baseline to manage these requirements to minimize duplication of effort (as many standards have similar or identical controls). This internal baseline defines controls mapped to the various compliance standards, so the compliance teams and technical teams can focus on a single set of controls but use that data to assess compliance and report to multiple regulators rapidly. Many organizations start with an existing baseline mapped to multiple compliance standards and then customize it as needed for their organization's unique needs. Some popular existing baselines are the Microsoft Cloud Security Benchmark, the Center for Internet Security (CIS) Benchmarks, and the NIST Cybersecurity Framework (NIST CSF).

Automation is critical to security compliance

Because of the complexity of evaluating and meeting security compliance across a technical estate, it's critical to automate as much as possible. Assessing and reporting on compliance often entailed a lot of work using a manual spreadsheet-based process that could take weeks or months to generate a report. Architects should ensure that the organization is evaluating technologies to automate and simplify these manual tasks, including

- Microsoft Defender for Cloud
- Microsoft Purview Compliance Manager
- Third-party solutions

Resolving conflicts between compliance and security

Security architects also play a critical role in helping identify and resolve potential conflicts between compliance and security. While compliance regulations and standards are intended to improve security, they can sometimes unintentionally degrade or worsen security. This can happen because the compliance standard is outdated or because of how auditors, non-technical compliance teams, or specialized technical teams interpret the standards.

Some examples of how compliance (or its interpretation) can negatively impact security include:

- **Ineffective controls that waste resources and effort**   These include
  - Renaming administrator accounts
  - Banning password managers
  - Password requirements to mitigate password guessing or cracking (account lockouts, regularly changing passwords, requiring very long passwords or different character sets, and the like)

- **Incomplete compliance requirement**   For example, a requirement (or implementation) for data loss protection (DLP) tools that doesn't include the processes that make the technical control effective.

- **Blocking newer and more effective controls**   For example, newer and more effective controls such as requiring specific (lower security) forms of multifactor authentication (MFA) that exclude modern secure single-device options, forced tunneling of all organizational cloud traffic through on-premises network equipment, or using older on-premises controls (instead of cloud controls) could be blocked.

- **Broad exceptions to strict compliance requirements**   These exceptions undermine the intended effect of the requirements, such as providing broad exemptions of MFA for many physical locations, roles, or activities to enable business processes.

- **Well-meaning but poorly implemented controls**   Controls such as phishing training that punish user mistakes rather than increasing their knowledge, skills, and motivation to help protect the organization and data should be avoided.

Cybersecurity architects must work with compliance teams, auditors, technical teams, and other stakeholders to identify the best way to resolve these conflicts. Depending on the type of conflict and the regulation, the solutions to address these conflicts may include the following:

- **One-time workaround**   A one-time workaround might be used to resolve the conflict temporarily, such as an exception to the policy for a single reporting period.

- **Durable workaround (per organization)**   A durable workaround might be used to resolve the conflict for the organization for the foreseeable future. This can take many forms, including the education of auditors, getting a durable exception from regulators, mapping a legacy compliance control to a more effective modern control, automation to alleviate the burden of manual mitigation or reporting, and more.

- **Durable fix (per standard)**   Organizations can also provide feedback to regulators and standards bodies to help update standards for current platforms, controls, and best practices.

Outdated control

In U.S. government standards, a password complexity policy illustrates the challenges organizations face with keeping up with outdated controls. Attackers have gotten very good at stealing and guessing passwords through many different technical attack techniques. After this problem was observed in practice, the U.S. National Institute of Standards and Technology (NIST) performed research to confirm that password complexity rules can be relaxed if there is a mechanism for blocking weak and compromised passwords. This was published in June 2017 as NIST 800-63B Digital Identity Guidelines: Authentication and Lifecycle Management, but the changes weren't incorporated into NIST 800-53 Revision 5 *Control Requirements (control IA-5(1))* until September 2020— more than three years later. When this book was published in 2023, other derivative standards were still based on NIST 800-53 Revision 4 (the previous version) and did not yet reflect these changes (FedRAMP certification, IRS 1075, CJIS, and more).

While compliance frameworks are an excellent way to communicate and enforce a minimum security baseline, they can't keep up with adversaries that change tactics daily to make their attacks successful. Cybersecurity architects help compliance teams develop effective strategies to maintain compliance without compromising the organization's security while simultaneously advocating for faster standards updates.

Cybersecurity architects play a key role in compliance, helping interpret compliance requirements using their technical expertise and broad technical perspective. Architects also support identifying and resolving potential areas of conflict between security and compliance.

Skill 4-2: Evaluate infrastructure compliance by using Microsoft Defender for Cloud

Infrastructure is often the largest and most complex area of the technical estate and architecture, requiring a detailed approach to assessing and reporting compliance across many cloud providers and on-premises datacenters, operating systems, applications, middleware, software versions, and more. The task of assessing and reporting compliance is typically shared by compliance teams, posture management teams, technical teams, application owners, and cybersecurity architects. Cybersecurity architects also help technical teams and application owners with identifying follow-up actions to meet external and internal standards. Microsoft Defender for Cloud (MDC) can significantly simplify many of these tasks across a multi-cloud and hybrid environment with built-in compliance standards, reports, and recommended next steps.

Microsoft Defender for Cloud helps automate meeting regulatory compliance requirements by continuously assessing your managed resources, analyzing the risk factors from the controls, and recommending best practices to remediate them. The MDC regulatory compliance dashboard allows you to manage compliance policies, explore your current status, and download reports on demand.

Figure 4-6 shows the Regulatory Compliance dashboard.

FIGURE 4-6 Regulatory Compliance dashboard

MDC provides these capabilities for resources across Azure, AWS, GCP, and on-premises datacenters, including VMs, containers, databases, and other technical elements. MDC supports many different regulatory standards, including:

- PCI-DSS v3.2.1:2018
- SOC TSP
- NIST SP 800-53 R4
- NIST SP 800 171 R2
- UK OFFICIAL and UK NHS
- Canada Federal PBMM
- Azure CIS 1.1.0
- HIPAA/HITRUST
- SWIFT CSP CSCF v2020
- ISO 27001:2013
- New Zealand ISM Restricted
- CMMC Level 3
- Azure CIS 1.3.0

- NIST SP 800-53 R5
- FedRAMP H
- FedRAMP M

Organizations may also establish internal security standards to help increase security and meet organizational policy. MDC provides the ability to help teams meet these internal standards. Organizations can use the Microsoft cloud security benchmark (MCSB) as the standards, as a starting point for building these standards, or as a comparison point for updating existing standards for the cloud.

> **MORE INFO** For more information on improving your regulatory compliance with MDC, see *https://aka.ms/ComplianceDashboardDocs.*

Skill 4-3: Interpret compliance scores and recommend actions to resolve issues or improve security

Regulatory compliance standards also require security (and privacy) and control assurances for data and the applications that access that data. Assessing and reporting on compliance for cloud applications can be challenging because many standards and controls haven't been updated for the shared responsibility model of the cloud (which is discussed more in Chapter 1). Because many organizations have a sprawling data estate and might not have a strong information classification program, prioritization of resources is also a key priority. Microsoft Purview Compliance Manager helps organizations with those challenges.

Microsoft Purview Compliance Manager helps organizations assess and report on compliance for data and applications, particularly for Microsoft 365 and other Microsoft cloud services. These capabilities help simplify reporting on compliance through the following:

- Built-in assessments that address common industry and regional standards and regulations, along with the ability to create custom assessments
- Step-by-step recommendations on improvement actions to help comply with standards, including implementation details and audit results for controls that are managed by Microsoft (for Microsoft cloud capabilities)
- A compliance score to help prioritize meeting compliance requirements by risk and help you measure progress for completing improvement actions

Compliance Manager also includes workflows to help teams collaborate on compliance assessment and reporting. As with other aspects of security compliance, cybersecurity architects help with technical expertise across multiple disciplines to ensure that the best controls are selected for the organization.

> **MORE INFO** For more on Microsoft Purview Compliance Manager, see *https://aka.ms/compliancemanagerdocs.*

Skill 4-4: Design implementation of Azure Policy

A cybersecurity architect works with technical teams to design the technical policy that monitors and enforces the implementation of organizational security policy. This ensures that the policy is consistently and accurately applied, helping prevent the organization's security posture from drifting into an insecure state that increases organizational risk.

Azure Policy is an important tool for monitoring and enforcing technical policy and standards on infrastructure and platform resources across a multi-cloud and hybrid estate. Azure Policy can be used to manage resources hosted directly on Azure and resources connected via Azure Arc (on AWS, GCP, on-premises, and more). Azure Policy provides the ability to configure policy, assess resource compliance, and enforce it. Azure Policy includes a set of built-in policies and the ability to customize and create additional policies.

Azure Policy is also the underlying technology that enables Microsoft Defender for Cloud (MDC) to monitor resources and assess compliance.

One of the most important use cases for Azure Policy is configuring consistent security guardrails across environments. This helps increase business, IT, and security agility by ensuring consistency across development, test, production, and application/development environments. Development and DevOps teams don't have to troubleshoot infrastructure and security issues as applications move from environment to environment or connect with other applications with different security settings. This also reduces the risk of security misconfigurations being found and exploited by attackers to cause business damage. Azure Policy checks can also be included in continuous integration and continuous delivery (CI/CD) pipelines to catch and fix compliance violations early.

Azure Policy allows you to take different actions called *effects*, including

- **Append** This adds additional fields to a requested resource during creation or update (such as IP address restrictions while creating a storage resource).
- **Audit** This reports a policy result without blocking the request.
- **AuditIfNotExists** This reports on objects and attributes that are missing (should exist but don't).
- **Deny** This blocks the request before it is sent to the Resource Provider.
- **DeployIfNotExists** This forces the creation of missing objects and resources.
- **Disabled** This assignment of policy is disabled.
- **Modify** This adds, updates, or removes properties or tags on a subscription or resource.

A cybersecurity architect should be familiar with Azure Policy and what it can do so that they can guide technical teams with the design implementation of technical policy.

Skill 4-5: Design for data residency requirements

As part of regulatory compliance, many organizations must meet explicit requirements for data residency and data sovereignty:

- **Data residency** Focuses on the physical location of the data, requiring data to be stored within certain geographic boundaries. This may refer to a particular subset of the organization's data or all of it.

- **Data sovereignty** This concept focuses on the control and legal jurisdiction of the data, ensuring that the data is under the organization's control and governed by laws where the organization is located.

Legal or other compliance teams often lead the interpretation of laws and regulations with cybersecurity architects providing technical expertise, technical implementation options, and technical recommendations.

Planning for data residency and data sovereignty requirements includes the following:

- **Identify data residency and sovereignty outcomes and requirements** Identify these by analyzing the applicable laws and regulations. This should result in a clear translation to specific geographic constraints for specific scopes of data. For example, you may find that all European customer data with personally identifiable information (PII) must stay within the European Union (EU).

- **Identify scope** Translate the requirements into specific technical instructions on which data and systems must meet the requirements. For example, all systems currently hosted in on-premises datacenters in the EU must be restricted to EU-only geography in the cloud.

- **Plan controls and technical compliance monitoring** Identify and plan how to meet those requirements with the controls available in the cloud platforms you are using (Azure, Microsoft 365, Dynamics 365 and Power Platform Infrastructure, and others) and report the compliance state.

> **NOTE** Note that this planning should also consider other geographically related elements, including business continuity/disaster recovery (BC/DR) and performance and latency.

- **Microsoft Azure** The data residency boundary in Azure is the Azure Geography, so you should use this as your primary control for these requirements. Figure 4-7 illustrates the Azure data controls for controlling the physical location of systems and data.

> **MORE INFO** For more information on Azure and the data residency boundary, see "Enabling Data Residency and Data Protection in Microsoft Azure Regions" at *https://aka.ms/datageo-Azure*.

Figure 4-7 illustrates the architecture that Azure uses to provide both high availability and control over the geographic location of workloads and data.

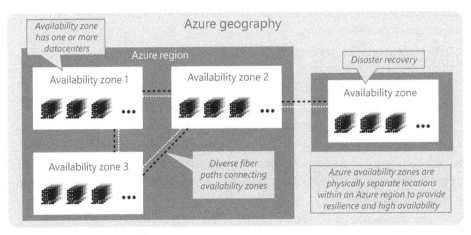

FIGURE 4-7 Azure data controls

- **Microsoft 365** Microsoft 365 offers the ability to specify the physical location of data using geographic areas (each, a Geo). These are datacenters contained within the corresponding physical geography.
- **Dynamics 365 and Power Platform Infrastructure** To keep data within a country in Dynamics 365 and Power Platform, you can use "local cloud" physical datacenters located in specific geographic locales.

> **MORE INFO** You can learn more about the topics described here at the following locations:
>
> - **Global geographies and geos** "Where your Microsoft 365 customer data is stored" at *https://aka.ms/datageo-M365*.
> - **Dynamics 365 and the Power Platform** "Dynamics 365 and Power Platform availability" at *https://aka.ms/datageo-D365*.
> - **Data residency and data sovereignty** "Data Residency, Data Sovereignty, and Compliance in the Microsoft Cloud" at *https://aka.ms/datageo*.

Skill 4-6: Translate privacy requirements into requirements for security solutions

Privacy regulations represent another key source of compliance requirements that must be integrated into the security architecture, policy, and technical solutions. Privacy is an important human right that has been protected by regulatory compliance standards around the world.

Examples include the European Union's General Data Protection Regulation (GDPR), Brazil's Lei Geral de Proteçao de Dados (LGPD), California Consumer Privacy Act (CCPA), and others.

Like in other compliance areas, cybersecurity architects must work with the compliance teams in their organization to help ensure the organization is effectively meeting compliance requirements and accurately reporting status on them to regulators. The interpretation of laws and regulations is often led by legal or other compliance teams. Technical expertise, implementation options, and recommendations are provided by cybersecurity architects or other technical experts.

Like other security and compliance requirements, privacy requirements must be consistently enforced across the technical estate and organization's processes. The controls must be enforced across all platforms you use, such as on-premises datacenters, Microsoft 365, 3rd party SaaS applications, AWS, Azure, GCP, and more.

Privacy assurances are data-centric and will require a combination of the following:

- Controls that are aware of data context (such as data, application, identity, and so on)
- Controls with limited context on data (like storage, infrastructure, network, and the like)

Security and privacy

Security and privacy work together to protect data, but they are two different things, as shown in Figure 4-8.

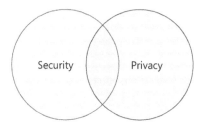

FIGURE 4-8 Security and privacy

Data security is about protecting data from unauthorized access. Privacy is focused on the appropriate handling of data. Privacy relies on data security assurances, but security does much more than this, and there is more to privacy than security.

The processes to identify and evaluate privacy are similar to data residency and other compliance requirements and include:

- **Identify privacy outcomes and requirements**   Identify these by analyzing the applicable laws and regulations. This should result in a clear translation to specific privacy requirements for specific scopes of data, any specific processes that must be executed (such as rapidly reporting incidents to regulators), and any other requirements.
- **Identify scope**   Translate the requirements into specific technical instructions on which data and systems must meet the requirements. For example, all personally identifiable information must be classified, tagged, and protected at an elevated level.

- **Plan controls and technical compliance monitoring** Identify and plan how to meet those requirements with the controls available in the cloud platforms you are using (Azure, Microsoft 365, Dynamics 365 and Power Platform Infrastructure, and others) and report the compliance state.

The controls that architects should be aware of that can help meet privacy requirements are:

- **Microsoft Priva** Priva can help with several aspects of privacy regulations including:
  - Identifying privacy risks such as data hoarding, problematic data transfers, and data oversharing and plan controls to implement mitigations
  - Increasing visibility into how personal data is stored, used, and moved
  - Helping business users more effectively manage data and follow best practices for complying with privacy regulations
  - Enabling processes to manage subject rights requests at scale

> **MORE INFO** For more information on Microsoft Priva, see *https://aka.ms/privadocs*.

- **Microsoft Purview** Purview can help you discover this data across your organization and implement controls to protect it. Some key capabilities include:
  - Microsoft Purview Data Loss Prevention can help protect against unintentional or accidental sharing of sensitive information.
  - Microsoft Purview risk and compliance solutions provide data classification technology, encryption of sensitive documents, and reporting on classified content and activities across clouds, apps, and endpoints.
  - Microsoft Purview Data Lifecycle Management capabilities help you retain and delete content across Microsoft 365 (Exchange, SharePoint, OneDrive, Microsoft 365 Groups, Teams, and Yammer).

> **MORE INFO** For more information on Microsoft Purview, see *https://aka.ms/ purviewdocuments*.

- **Data Discovery & Classification** Built into Azure SQL Database, Azure SQL Managed Instance, and Azure Synapse Analytics, this provides basic capabilities for discovering, classifying, labeling, and reporting on what sensitive data is in your databases.
- **Built-in access controls** These controls are found in Microsoft 365, Azure, and other Microsoft services. These enable you to manage which accounts and groups can access resources, which can help protect data against unauthorized disclosure that could lead to privacy breaches.

- **Microsoft 365**   Access to data in Microsoft 365 is governed by the access control model of each Microsoft 365 application. For more information, see *https://aka.ms/M365Access*.

- **Azure data**   Access to data in Azure is governed by Azure Role Based Access Control (Azure RBAC) and any custom applications and scripts. For more information on Azure RBAC, see *https://aka.ms/azurerbacdocs*.

- **Encryption managed by cloud provider**   Encryption of the cloud service provider platforms can help meet standard compliance requirements. This type of encryption is most useful to protect against the scenario of an attack on the underlying infrastructure of the cloud service provider (CSP).

> **WARNING**   While cloud provider encryption might meet the literal requirement to encrypt data, using only these controls may lead to a false sense of security. Cybersecurity architects should ensure the organization is using additional protections to protect the data (including encryption, access control, and others) to protect against a data breach if an attacker accesses accounts or networks in your organization (which is much more likely than a successful attack on the CSP).

Cybersecurity architects play a supporting role in privacy requirements compliance, helping translate compliance requirements identified by compliance teams into guidance that technical teams can implement.

Thought experiment

In this thought experiment, demonstrate your skills and knowledge of the topics covered in this chapter. You can find answers to this thought experiment in the next section.

Building repeatable technical patterns for security compliance

Fabrikam recently failed a regulatory compliance audit, putting the organization's ability to operate at risk. The board of directors s mandated that the company management focus on rapidly fixing this and implementing mechanisms to adopt the culture, processes, and technical capabilities to ensure a compliance failure doesn't happen again.

You are the cybersecurity architect at Fabrikam, working in a virtual team with compliance team members to plan a strategy that meets leaders' expectations. The compliance team is taking the lead on business process updates and awareness/training elements.

You have worked with the compliance team to identify several requirements requiring a repeatable pattern across the technical teams in the organization.

How would you approach each of these problems?

- Technical enablement of process controls, such as the "right to erasure" in the General Data Protection Regulation (GDPR)

- Specific technical controls, such as "Protect all systems against malware and regularly update anti-virus software or programs"

- Outdated controls, such as password requirements (length, complexity, account lockout, and more) that don't fully apply to Fabrikam, which is nearing completion of deploying passwordless authentication to all users

Thought experiment answers

This section contains the solution to the thought experiment. Each answer explains why the answer choice is correct.

1. The pattern for technical enablement of process controls should include

   - Evaluate technical tooling that meets outcomes required for the processes.

   - Provide valid options and recommendations to the teams operating the processes for consideration in their decision-making.

   - Identify technical processes that may be dependent on the compliance processes and review them to ensure they are aligned to support the compliance processes.

   Regarding the GDPR requirements, you should consider

   - Microsoft Priva for discovering and minimizing risk of private data disclosure, managing business workflows like fulfilling privacy requests from customers, and more.

   - Microsoft Purview to help assess and report on compliance, as well as to discover and mitigate data protection risks.

   - Ensure incident reporting processes and tools are mature enough to provide investigation status and resolutions to regulators (via compliance teams) within the specified deadlines (GDPR requires reporting data breaches if they adversely affect user privacy within 72 hours).

   - Additionally, you should help identify technical controls and processes to support the end goals, such as technical access controls on the data (Microsoft 365, Linux, Windows, AWS, Azure, GCP, Databases, VMware, and so on), as well as Azure Active Directory (Azure AD) access reviews and Entra Permissions Management to discover and contain permission sprawl. You can also use Microsoft Defender for Cloud and Azure Policy to configure, monitor, and enforce policies that help protect your data.

2. The pattern for specific technical controls should include guidance to technical and app teams to do the following:

   - Evaluate control against the current practice and current best practices

- Ensure that the organization is meeting both the intent and the letter of the requirement, such as

  a. Reporting compliance based on the current anti-virus solution that is widely deployed

  b. Accelerating the current pilot program for a new Endpoint Detection and Response (EDR) capability based on Microsoft Defender for Endpoints

- Monitor implementation to ensure that controls don't drift in partnership with security posture management and compliance teams.

3. The pattern for outdated controls like the password requirements should include the following:

- Evaluate control against the current practice and current best practices.

- Analyze and document the original intent of the control and current state, including the following:

  a. Identify the control and why it was included. What underlying risk or threat was this originally designed to mitigate?

  b. How was the control originally expected to be implemented?

  c. How have the assumptions and expectations changed since then?

  d. How can the control be counterproductive to security? Or, how will the control be counterproductive to security?

  e. Document your analysis on how that control is not current or productive (will not meet the current version of the threat, a newer threat has replaced the original threat, a newer best practice meets the threat better than original control, and so on).

- Identify immediate actions to respond to compliance requirements.

- Report on compliance status accurately, including details on the original intent of the control and explanation of how current controls meet or exceed the intended literal outcome of the requirement, for example:

  a. Plan and implement any related mechanism to help meet the original intent with useful controls / effort. This should include who maintains those controls over time (IT Operations, DevOps/DevSecOps team(s), and the like).

  b. Educate auditors and other business stakeholders on how you are working to meet the intent of the control with the best available current controls.

- Advocate for regulatory standard updates. Communicate your concerns and reasoning directly to the regulators through approved feedback mechanisms. You should also work with your peers in the community and common vendors to collectively advocate for updates to regulatory standards. This requires building expertise on compliance frameworks at Fabrikam to effectively navigate the requirements and influencing the regulatory bodies, either via full-time employees or contracting consultants with this expertise.

For the password requirements example, your analysis and documentation should include these elements:

- The original intent of password controls is to prevent unauthorized personnel from using an account to access the organization's resources, private data, and more. The controls in the recommendation are focused on mitigating this risk from older attacks like brute force password guessing.

- Compare original intent to current threats and current practices. Document current controls at your organization that meet (and exceed) the original intent of protecting accounts against unauthorized usage, including

  a. Passwordless authentication that provides strong multifactor authentication via Windows Hello for Business, Microsoft Authenticator app, FIDO keys, and more.

  b. Azure AD Conditional Access and Azure AD Identity Protection that measure user risk like leaked credentials, sign-ins from anonymous IP addresses, impossible travel to atypical locations, sign-ins from infected devices, and more.

  c. You should also include evidence on how Fabrikam's configuration has stronger security assurances than a "strong" password using evidence, such as

     i. Microsoft Password Guidance   *https://aka.ms/PasswordGuidance*

     ii. Microsoft Digital Defense Report   *https://aka.ms/MDDR*

     iii. NIST 800-63B and NIST 800-53 Revision 5

- Plan and implement compliance controls that don't disrupt business operations or negatively impact security posture, including

  a. Extend Azure AD Password Protection to on-premises Active Directory Domain Services. You can find more information at *https://aka/ms/AADPasswordProtectionDocs*.

  b. Implement Azure AD Access Reviews to provide workflows for reviewing access by high-impact accounts. More information can be found at *https://aka.ms/azureadaccessreviewdocs*.

- Document the negative impact of disruptive or nonproductive compliance controls. Follow regulatory processes for documenting and reporting exceptions for:

  a. Some regulations require automatically locking out accounts after a fixed number of authentication attempts with an incorrect password. Fabrikam should push back because implementing this in Fabrikam's passwordless configuration would cause a greater risk of disrupting user access and have little or no effect on protecting the accounts. You can find more information at *https://aka.ms/ALO*.

  b. Fabrikam will configure smart account lockout to manage the risk of invalid sign-in attempts. More information can be found at *https://aka.ms/smartlockout*.

c. Some regulations require limiting users to a specific number of simultaneous sessions (such as NIST 800-53 AC-10). Fabrikam should push back because this leads to a degraded user experience and provides limited security value compared to the Zero Trust security posture that Fabrikam has already established. Today, users connect from multiple devices in multiple physical locations to get their job done (including maintaining security), sometimes connecting from multiple devices simultaneously.

To mitigate controls, Fabrikam will

- Cite the use of conditional access policies that explicitly validates security before a session is created and continually validates them throughout the life of a session. More information can be found at *https://aka.ms/CAE*.

- Expand the use of Conditional Access policies to require compliant devices. Fabrikam will require endpoint integrity in Conditional Access using Intune and Microsoft Defender for Endpoint signals. This reduces the risk of attackers getting control of accounts through compromised endpoints. See *https://aka.ms/AADMDE*.

- Fabrikam should push back on a policy to change a password regularly because changing passwords too frequently increases the chances users will pick easily guessable passwords. Implementing this in Fabrikam's passwordless environment would increase risk instead of decreasing it. Currently, more than 95 percent of Fabrikam users are passwordless, so forcing users to change their passwords would increase the exposure of passwords to theft by attackers. This additional use of passwords will also increase the likelihood that users will disclose passwords to an attacker in a social engineering attack (because passwords are "sometimes used in special cases" instead of "never being used").

- Fabrikam will continue monitoring the use of password authentication to find and address any remaining blockers for passwordless.

- Identify and implement additional best practices related to the original intent of the control, including:

  - Workload identities to reduce the number of service accounts using human-set passwords. More information can be found at *https://aka.ms/AADworkloadidentitiesdocs*.

  - Increased security for privileged accounts by following Microsoft's securing privileged access (SPA) guidance at *https://aka.ms/SPA*. This includes the use of Privileged Access Workstations (PAWs), Azure AD Privileged Identity Management, and other means to restrict and control privileged accounts.

- Advocate with regulators with explicit recommendations on improving the regulatory standards to include current threats and best practices.

- Monitor implementation to ensure controls don't drift in partnership with security posture management and compliance teams.

Chapter summary

- **Security governance** Cybersecurity architects should be familiar with security governance functions to effectively support regulatory compliance and security goals. Security architects should know the major functions of security governance, how architects support these functions and key relationships between these functions.

- **Security compliance** Security compliance is an important function of security governance that ensures the organization meets regulatory standards and reports compliance to avoid fines, loss of approval to operate the business, and other negative consequences.

- **Compliance with internal and external standards** Organizations are often required to meet regulatory requirements for security standards, and many organizations also choose to adopt internal security standards based on best practices like Microsoft Cloud Security Benchmarks.

- **Compliance is not security** Security compliance provides a consistent required baseline of security best practices and controls, but compliance is not enough to keep up with evolving security threats and requirements.

- **Security compliance modernization** Security compliance and other security governance functions have a key role in the Zero-Trust Transformation of security, helping modernize security controls, practices, and culture. Key modernization elements include adopting an assume compromise / assume breach mindset, adopting an agile approach to security focused on continuous improvement, adopting asset-centric and data-centric approaches, and prioritizing automation of manual tasks.

- **Security compliance is a team sport** Meeting security compliance requirements requires a partnership with compliance, security, and technical teams.

- **Resolve conflicts** Conflicts between compliance and security requirements can happen, and cyber architects help discover and resolve these conflicts.

- **Automating and planning** Microsoft Defender for Cloud is a powerful tool for automating the evaluation of compliance requirements and planning for mitigations. It supports many common regulatory standards and the Microsoft Cloud Security Benchmarks with Microsoft's recommended security best practices.

- **Assess and report on complicance** Microsoft Purview Compliance Manager helps organizations assess and report on compliance for data and applications, particularly for Microsoft 365 and other Microsoft cloud services.

- **Monitoring and enforcing** Azure Policy is an important tool for monitoring and enforcing technical policy and standards on infrastructure and platform resources across a multi-cloud and hybrid estate. Azure Policy provides the ability to configure policy, assess resources against the policy, and enforce it.

- **Data residency** Many organizations must meet explicit compliance requirements for data residency, ensuring certain data and systems stay within a geographic area. Architects should be familiar with the types of controls in Azure, Microsoft 365, Dynamics 365, and other platforms to help achieve these goals.

- **Privacy** Many organizations must meet explicit compliance requirements for privacy. While security and privacy share many common controls, privacy requirements often go beyond security requirements to safeguard this important human right.

CHAPTER 5

Evaluate security posture and recommend technical strategies to manage risk

When it comes to governance of workloads in the cloud, security posture management is the mechanism that will enable the team to answer the question, "how secure is the environment?" Security posture management provides on-demand visibility and asset coverage, including vulnerability management and security compliance reporting.

To drive a continuous improvement of your cloud security posture, you need to utilize tools that can perform ongoing assessments using different industry standards and bring visibility to the current security state of each workload.

Skills covered in this chapter:

- Skill 5-1: Evaluate security posture by using benchmarks (including Azure security benchmark for Microsoft Cloud security benchmark, ISO 27001, etc.)
- Skill 5-2: Evaluate security posture by using Microsoft Defender for Cloud
- Skill 5-3: Evaluate security posture by using Secure Scores
- Skill 5-4: Evaluate security posture of cloud workloads
- Skill 5-5: Design security for an Azure Landing Zone
- Skill 5-6: Interpret technical threat intelligence and recommend risk mitigations
- Skill 5-7: Recommend security capabilities or controls to mitigate identified risks

Skill 5-1: Evaluate security posture by using benchmarks (including Azure security benchmark for Microsoft Cloud security benchmark, ISO 27001, etc.)

To improve your security posture, you can leverage benchmarks to give you tangible actions based on industry standards. Using benchmarks helps improve benchmarks over time. This section covers the skills necessary to evaluate security posture by using different benchmarks according to the Exam SC-100 outline.

Microsoft cloud security benchmark

Microsoft cloud security benchmark (MCSB) includes a collection of security recommendations that can be used to help secure Azure workloads. MCSB is usually utilized in the following scenarios:

- **New Azure deployments (greenfield)** When organizations first adopt cloud computing and use Azure as their cloud platform and need to follow security best practices to ensure a secure deployment of their Azure workloads.

- **Improve security posture of existing workloads in Azure (brownfield)** When organizations already have workloads deployed in Azure and want to improve the security posture by prioritizing top risks and mitigations.

- **Cloud evaluation** When organizations are evaluating the security features/capabilities of Azure services before onboarding/approving an Azure service(s) into the cloud service catalog.

- **Compliance requirements** When organizations need to meet compliance requirements in highly regulated industries like government, finance, and healthcare. These organizations need to certify their workload's configurations in Azure meet the security specification defined in a specific framework, such as CIS, NIST, or PCI.

MCSB was created with the idea of providing a canonical set of Azure-centric technical security controls based on controls defined by the Center for Internet Security (CIS), the National Institute of Standards and Technology (NIST), and the Payment Card Industry (PCI). By the time this chapter was written, the latest ASB version was 3 (v3), which considered CIS v8 and v7, NIST SP800-53 Rev4, and PCI-DSS v3.2.1.

When planning your MCSB adoption, you must understand that MCSB comprises security controls and a service baseline. A security control (also called compliance control) specifies a feature or activity that needs to be addressed but is not necessarily related to a technology or implementation. For example, network security is one of the security controls available in MCSB. It contains specific actions that must be addressed to help ensure that the network is more secure. A service baseline is basically the implementation of the control in individual Azure service. For example, an organization needs to improve its database security posture, and implementing an Azure SQL security baseline is one action that can be taken.

Monitoring your MCSB compliance

Using the Microsoft Defender for Cloud regulatory compliance dashboard, you can monitor your MCSB compliance status (and other control sets). Defender for Cloud leverages MCSB for its own set of security recommendations, which means that as you remediate security recommendations in Defender for Cloud, you are automatically improving your level of ASB compliance.

Follow these steps:

1. To access the regulatory compliance dashboard and see the MCSB assessment, open Defender for Cloud in Azure portal and click **Regulatory Compliance** in the left navigation, as shown in Figure 5-1.

FIGURE 5-1 MCSB assessment in Defender for Cloud

2. On this page, you can see the list of security controls; if you expand a security control, you will see a list of controls that belong to that category. For example, by expanding **NS. Network Security**, you will see **NS-1: Establish Network Segmentation Boundaries**. This security control's principle is to ensure that your virtual network deployment aligns with your enterprise segmentation strategy by ensuring that any workload that could incur higher risk for the organization should be in isolated virtual networks.

3. By expanding the control (in this case, **NS-1**), you will see the mapping of security recommendations for which the customer is responsible for addressing under Customer Responsibility. To the right of the recommendations are two columns: **Resource Type** and the number of noncompliant resources (**Failed Resources**). See Figure 5-2.

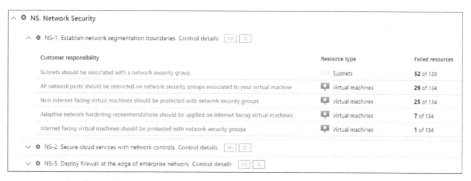

FIGURE 5-2 List of security recommendations belonging to the control

4. For the SC-100 exam, review all compliance controls in MCSB, so you have a basic understanding of the items covered by each. For example, on the exam, you might have scenarios requiring you to know which compliance control has an assessment to determine whether the Web Application Firewall is enabled. In this case, the answer is **NS. Network Security**. For your reference, MCSB contains the following compliance controls:

- Network Security
- Identity Management
- Privileged Access
- Data Protection
- Asset Management
- Logging and Threat Detection
- Incident Response
- Posture and Vulnerability Management
- Endpoint Security
- Backup and Recovery
- DevOps Security
- Governance and Strategy

> **NOTE** For more information about each compliance control assessment, see *https://docs.microsoft.com/en-us/security/benchmark/azure.*

Industry standards

While using MCSB will improve the security posture of your workloads in Azure, some scenarios might require you to use a different benchmark to measure compliance. This usually happens when an organization must comply with a certain standard based on the industry. For example, if the organization is part of the financial industry, it might need to be compliant with Payment Card Industry (PCI) Data Security Standard (DSS) standard.

You can leverage the same regulatory compliance dashboard in Defender for Cloud when you need to monitor your Azure workloads based on an industry standard. Remember that some controls will appear unavailable (grayed out) in the dashboard. This means these controls don't have any Defender for Cloud assessments associated with them, which could happen because some controls may be procedure- or process-related. Other controls don't have any automated policies or assessments implemented yet. An example of the compliance dashboard is shown in Figure 5-3.

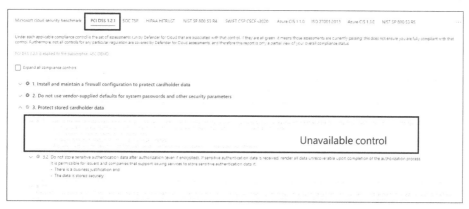

FIGURE 5-3 Example of an unavailable control in the PC DSS 3.2.1 standard in Defender for Cloud

When designing your security posture enhancement strategy based on industry standards, consider the standards supported by Azure that are reflected in Defender for Cloud.

> **MORE INFO**   For a complete list of standards supported in Azure, visit *https:// docs.microsoft.com/en-us/compliance/regulatory/offering-home.*

Skill 5-2: Evaluate security posture by using Microsoft Defender for Cloud

Defender for Cloud offers security posture management capabilities for Azure and other cloud providers such as Amazon Web Services (AWS) and Google Cloud Platform (GCP). This section covers the skills necessary to evaluate security posture by using Microsoft Defender for Cloud according to the Exam SC-100 outline.

Defender for Cloud

Microsoft Defender for Cloud gives organizations complete visibility and control over the security of cloud workloads located in Azure, on-premises, or another cloud provider. By actively monitoring these workloads, Defender for Cloud enhances the overall security posture of the cloud deployment and reduces the exposure of resources to threats. Defender for Cloud also uses intelligent threat detection to assist you in protecting your environment from rapidly evolving cyberattacks.

Defender for Cloud also assesses the security of your hybrid cloud workload and provides recommendations to mitigate threats. In addition, it provides centralized policy management to ensure compliance with company or regulatory security requirements. When you access the Defender for Cloud dashboard, you will see the Overview page, which provides a comprehensive layout that lets you quickly see important indicators. When looking from the top down, you will see which cloud providers are currently configured (Azure subscriptions, AWS account, and GCP Projects), followed by the number of assessed resources, the total of active recommendations, and security alerts. An example is shown in Figure 5-4.

FIGURE 5-4 Defender for Cloud Overview page

When planning to adopt Defender for Cloud, you must first consider the adoption scope. In other words, are you going to adopt this product as the centralized dashboard for cloud security in Azure only, or do you plan to connect with other cloud providers? One of the challenges of multi-cloud adoption is ensuring that you have security posture visibility for all clouds in a single dashboard. That is a big advantage of using Defender for Cloud.

Once you define the scope of the adoption, you need to start thinking about the use case scenario. Are you planning to use Defender for Cloud as your cloud security posture management (CSPM) and cloud workload protection platform (CWPP)? There are two major use case scenarios: CSPM and CWPP. If you plan to use both scenarios, you should always start with CSPM because you first need to ensure that you have good security hygiene and a high Secure Score. In this case, a high Secure Score means reaching 100 percent.

> **NOTE** You will learn more about Secure Score later in this chapter in Skill 5-3: "Evaluate security posture by using Secure Scores."

Security posture management

One of the challenges that many organizations face when trying to improve the security hygiene of their cloud workloads is the lack of privileges to harden workloads based on the recommendations provided by Defender for Cloud.

Security recommendations in Defender for Cloud are organized in security controls containing multiple recommendations. Once you remediate all recommendations within a security control, you earn points that will be added to the Secure Score. Figure 5-5 shows an example of the **Recommendations** page.

FIGURE 5-5 Security recommendations page in Defender for Cloud

For example, let's say the Contoso CSPM team reviews the security recommendations for a SQL Database and identifies the recommendation shown in Figure 5-6; this figure lists unhealthy resources that need attention.

FIGURE 5-6 Security recommendations for SQL database

When the Contoso CSPM team tried to remediate the recommendation, they received a message saying they didn't have the privileges to remediate this resource. Now, the questions are as follows:

- Who should they contact to remediate this resource?
- Who is the owner of this resource?
- Is the owner the same person who maintains this database?

That's when the CSPM team puts aside recommendations they can't remediate and focuses on the ones they can. The problem with this approach is that they are not prioritized by the level of criticality and potential Secure Score improvement.

For this reason, it is imperative to establish an action workflow that must be followed to ensure the workload owner is notified when open security recommendations need to be remediated. Consider the following actions (in this order) as part of your plan:

1. Identify the workload owners.

2. Train workload owners about how to use Defender for Cloud (100-level basic training is enough). The goal is to help them at least navigate through the recommendations and follow the remediation steps.

3. Create governance rules for these owners and establish a timeline for remediation. This is an important step to ensure accountability.

4. Create automations to notify workload owners about new open recommendations.

 TIP As you continue this journey to improve your security hygiene, you will notice that the Secure Score will continue to grow. To avoid sudden drops in Secure Score, make sure the CSPM team has a close relationship with the cloud governance team.

Considerations for multi-cloud

Multi-cloud deployments continue to grow as many organizations adopt different cloud providers to store different workloads. Defender for Cloud supports integration with AWS and GCP, allowing the CSPM team to have full visibility of the Azure, AWS, GCP, and on-premises resources' security posture in a single dashboard.

When planning for multi-cloud adoption, you need to make sure that you have the right teams engaged because, in many organizations, the team managing Azure is not the same team managing AWS and GCP. If this is the case, you must ensure everyone is on the same page regarding security posture management across different cloud providers. To finalize the multi-cloud considerations, ensure that you have a clear answer to the following questions:

- What are the current cloud providers that are used in the organization?
- Who manages each cloud provider account?
- Who owns the workloads on each cloud provider?
- Which workloads are deployed on each cloud provider?
- Is there any tool currently in use that provides centralized management of all cloud providers?

EXAM TIP On the SC-100 Exam, you may see scenarios describing an AWS environment with different types of workloads, and you will need to choose the best solution to monitor the security posture of those workloads. It is important to remember that Microsoft Defender for Cloud supports monitoring AWS EC2 instances, SQL Servers running on AWS EC2, AWS RDS Custom for SQL Server, and Amazon EKS clusters. These capabilities are enabled once you upgrade from the free tier (default Defender for Cloud mode) to Defender for Server plan.

Considerations for vulnerability assessment

Vulnerability assessment (VA) is another key area for security posture improvement. This wasn't covered in the CSPM section of this chapter because large organizations usually have a separate team that handles vulnerability assessment across endpoints and servers. This means the CSPM team needs to engage with the VA team to ensure they can take advantage of Defender for cloud-native VA solutions, which can be either based on Qualys or Microsoft Threat Vulnerability Management (TVM).

If the organization is already using Qualys as their main VA solution, they can also use the bring their own key (BYOK) to deploy the Qualys agent to all VMs in Azure via Defender for Cloud. However, they will have to manage two different dashboards if they want to use their current Qualys VA to monitor only Endpoints and take advantage of the free VA integration for servers enabled by Defender for Cloud. This is because the results for Qualys VA in Defender for Cloud are exposed as security recommendations and will not integrate with the Qualys VA dashboard used by the endpoints.

Figure 5-7 shows the vulnerability assessment presented in a recommendation.

FIGURE 5-7 Recommendation to remediate vulnerability found by Qualys

As shown in Figure 5-7, the results presented in the recommendation will list the findings, and once you click a finding (which, in this case, is ID 91785), another blade opens up on the right side, showing more details about that finding. This example shows the high-severity CVE-2021-34527 vulnerability and the vulnerable machines.

If your organization does not already have a VA solution, you will need to deploy Qualys or TVM. Both are fully integrated with Defender for Cloud, though TVM doesn't require an additional agent because it is part of MDE. However, Qualys requires the installation of an additional agent. The deployment experience is similar since Defender for Cloud will flag machines that don't have a VA installed, and from there, you can deploy the desired solution, as shown in Figure 5-8.

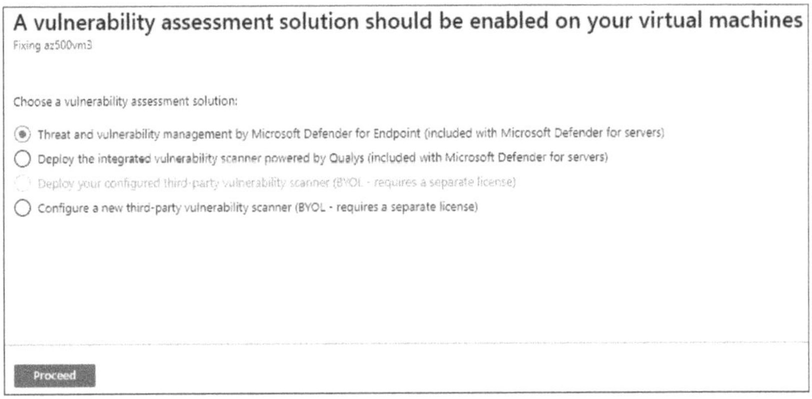

A vulnerability assessment solution should be enabled on your virtual machines
Fixing az500vm3

Choose a vulnerability assessment solution:

◉ Threat and vulnerability management by Microsoft Defender for Endpoint (included with Microsoft Defender for servers)

○ Deploy the integrated vulnerability scanner powered by Qualys (included with Microsoft Defender for servers)

○ Deploy your configured third-party vulnerability scanner (BYOL - requires a separate license)

○ Configure a new third-party vulnerability scanner (BYOL - requires a separate license)

Proceed

FIGURE 5-8 Selecting the appropriate VA solution to deploy

While the example shown in Figure 5-8 is a deployment for just one VM, you can select and deploy multiple VMs simultaneously. If you plan to deploy at scale for the entire subscription, you can also use Azure Policy.

Skill 5-3: Evaluate security posture by using Secure Scores

Using Secure Score to monitor security posture enhancement over time is a growing trend in the industry because it enables decision-makers to better understand their current state, evaluate trends, and identify areas of improvement. This section covers the skills necessary to evaluate security posture using Secure Scores according to the Exam SC-100 outline.

Secure Score in Defender for Cloud

When working in a cloud environment, monitoring the security state of multiple workloads can be challenging. How do you know your security posture is at the highest possible level across all workloads? Are there any security recommendations you are not meeting? These are hard questions to answer when you don't have the right visibility and tools to manage your cloud infrastructure's security aspects.

Defender for Cloud reviews your security recommendations across all workloads, applies advanced algorithms to determine the criticality of each recommendation, and calculates the Secure Score. The overall Secure Score shown in the main Defender for Cloud dashboard (see Figure 5-4 as an example) is an accumulation of all your recommendation scores. Remember, this score can vary because it reflects the currently selected subscription and its resources.

The calculation will be for all subscriptions if you have multiple subscriptions selected. The active recommendations on the selected subscription also make this score change. Recommendations are aggregated in *security controls*, which impact the Secure Score. A Secure Score increase will only occur if all recommendations within a security control that apply to a particular resource are remediated.

The **Security Posture** page in Defender for Cloud shows the Secure Score for Azure and other cloud providers that have connectivity with Defender for Cloud. In Figure 5-9, you can see the Secure Scores for Azure, AWS, and GCP.

FIGURE 5-9 Security posture page in Defender for Cloud

To see individual Secure Scores per cloud provider, you can use the toggle in the top-right corner to select the cloud provider you want to see. If all three (Azure, AWS, and GCP) are selected, the Secure Score reflects an aggregated Secure Score. If you want to improve the Secure Score for only one cloud provider, we recommend that you focus only on that cloud provider. This gives you better visibility of the current state and the areas you can improve. Use the following guidelines when planning your Secure Score improvement over time:

- When reviewing recommendations to remediate, use the top-down approach on the **Recommendations** page to prioritize the security controls that improve your Secure Score by more points.

- Create and assign governance rules to workload owners to make them accountable for remediating recommendations.

- Public Preview recommendations don't affect the Secure Score; only General Available (GA) recommendations improve your Secure Score.

- Use the Secure Score Overtime workbook to track progress and identify potential drops in the Secure Score.

- To avoid potential drops in Secure Score, ensure that you are working closely with the Azure Governance team to include guardrails at the beginning of the pipeline to force workloads to be deployed securely by default. You can use Azure Policy to deny the creation of resources that are not secure.

 TIP While Office 365 has its own Secure Score, the SC-100 Exam is focused on the Defender for Cloud Secure Score, which reflects the security state of Azure workloads.

Skill 5-4: Evaluate security posture of cloud workloads

Workloads deployed in Azure must be hardened to reduce the likelihood that a threat actor will be able to exploit that workload. From configuration improvement to ensuring the workload is up to date, the workload's security hygiene is imperative and must be continuously monitored. This section covers the skills necessary to evaluate the security posture of cloud workloads based on the Exam SC-100 outline.

Workload security

Azure Security Benchmark for Microsoft Cloud Security Benchmark provides security recommendations for different Azure workloads, which are reflected in Defender for Cloud. This means once you start improving the Secure Score for your Azure subscription, you automatically improve the security posture of your Azure workloads.

Workload owners can also benefit from the native integration of an Azure service with Defender for Cloud to gain visibility of the workload's security posture. For example, if you are the workload owner for an Azure Storage account and you want to see the open security recommendations for a specific Azure Storage account, you can open the Azure Storage dashboard and click the storage account to see a summary of Defender for Cloud recommendations, as shown in Figure 5-10.

The advantage of this approach is that the workload owner can focus only on the relevant recommendations for this workload (in this case, an Azure Storage account). Defender for Cloud supports security recommendations (part of the free tier), alerts (which require a paid plan), and vulnerability assessment (VA) for the workload described in Table 5-1.

FIGURE 5-10 Native integration with Defender for Cloud

TABLE 5-1 Defender for Cloud Recommendations and Alerts per Workload

Service	Recommendations	Alerts	VA	Required plan
Azure App Service	✓	✓	–	Defender for App Service
Azure Automation account	✓	–	–	–
Azure Batch account	✓	–	–	–
Azure Blob Storage	✓	✓	–	Defender for Storage
Azure Cache for Redis	✓	–	–	–
Azure Cloud Services	✓	–	–	–
Azure Cognitive Search	✓	–	–	–
Azure Container Registry	✓	✓	✓	Defender for Containers
Azure Cosmos DB	✓	✓	–	Defender for Cosmos DB
Azure Data Lake Analytics	✓	–	–	–
Azure Data Lake Storage	✓	✓	–	Defender for Storage
Azure Database for MySQL	–	✓	–	Defender for Open-Source relational database
Azure Database for PostgreSQL	–	✓	–	Defender for Open-Source relational database
Azure DNS	✓	✓	–	Defender for DNS
Azure Event Hubs namespace	✓	–	–	–

Service	Recommendations	Alerts	VA	Required plan
Azure Functions app	✓	–	–	–
Azure Key Vault	✓	✓	–	Defender for Key Vault
Azure Kubernetes Service	✓	✓	–	Defender for Containers
Azure Load Balancer	✓	–	–	–
Azure Logic Apps	✓	–	–	–
Azure SQL Database	✓	✓	✓	Defender for SQL
Azure SQL Managed Instance	✓	✓	✓	Defender for SQL
Azure Resource Manager	–	✓	–	Defender for Resource Manager
Azure Service Bus namespace	✓	–	–	–
Azure Service Fabric account	✓	–	–	–
Azure Storage accounts	✓	✓	–	Defender for Storage
Azure Stream Analytics	✓	–	–	–
Azure Virtual Machine	✓	✓	✓	Defender for Servers
Azure Virtual Network (including subnets, NICs, and network security groups)	✓	–	–	

When designing your solution to improve your workload's security posture, make sure you understand the supported services in Defender for Cloud and the level of support (recommendations, alerts, and VA).

 EXAM TIP On the SC-100 Exam, you might have scenarios that will lead you to suggest an upgrade to a specific Defender for Cloud plan to fulfill the scenario's requirements. For example, Contoso is currently using the free tier of Defender for Cloud, but now the company needs to improve its container's security posture by implementing a vulnerability assessment solution. In this case, it will be necessary to enable the Defender for Containers plan.

Skill 5-5: Design security for an Azure Landing Zone

Azure Landing Zone is an environment to host Azure workloads pre-provisioned through code. It uses a set of defined cloud services and best practices to add foundational capability while providing cloud adoption teams with a well-managed environment to run their workloads. This section covers the skills necessary to design security for an Azure Landing Zone according to the Exam SC-100 outline.

Design principles

Everything starts with a subscription, which can be considered a management unit for new application development and accelerating the migration of existing applications. It is important to align the subscription with business needs. Even if you have multiple subscriptions, they should be provided to support existing and new workloads. When necessary, you can also decide to aggregate multiple subscriptions into a single Management Group (MG). Using an MG, you can easily scale while keeping centralized management for multiple subscriptions.

When designing your landing zone, you must consider scenarios where workload owners need more control and autonomy on their workloads within the guardrails established by the platform foundation. For this type of scenario, you will use decentralized operations.

Azure landing zone conceptual architecture design presumes that a specific MG and subscription hierarchy are available for all operations management subscriptions, which may not be aligned with your operating model. As your organization grows and continues to evolve, your operational model may change. This can lead to another resource migration into separate subscriptions, which, in turn, can lead to technical migration challenges.

> **EXAM TIP** On the SC-100 Exam, you may see scenarios that present the business requirements and the Azure Landing Zone requirements. Make sure that as you review both, you choose a solution that can fit both requirements. For example, one of the business requirements may be to minimize the operational cost associated with administrative overhead, while the technical requirement for the Azure Landing Zone is to meet a certain Secure Score level per subscription. In this case, you can use an MG to reduce the administrative overhead because all policies established in the MG level will be inherited by the subscriptions while keeping the Secure Score per subscription.

Enforcing guardrails

Regarding guardrails, Azure Policy is the primary tool enabling organizations to deploy compliant workloads during provisioning time. Organizations adopting Azure without using Azure Policy are increasing their operation and management overhead to maintain compliance.

In Azure Policy, you can prevent workloads from being provisioned by using `DeployIfNotExists (DINE)` or `Modify` policies. DINE and Modify policies are part of the Azure landing zone reference implementations. They ensure that your landing zones (also known as subscriptions) and workloads within the subscription comply with certain pre-established parameters. For example, suppose the organization decides that no Azure Storage account should be exposed to the Internet. In that case, you need to have a policy that immediately remediates the workload once it finds that this workload doesn't meet the policy's requirements. To ensure that multiple subscriptions comply with certain requirements, you need to assign the policy to the MG containing the subscriptions.

Single management plane

Avoid multiple tooling that challenges organizations to have visibility across the resources in the landing zone. A consistent experience for the operations team and workload owners is highly recommended. When it comes to visibility and security posture across resources within the landing zone, Defender for Cloud is the recommended solution.

A multi-vendor approach to managing resources is not the best experience and can cause unintended errors due to inherent dependencies. Even when the organization already has a set of tooling used on its on-premises workloads, we recommend reviewing the dependencies.

Application-centric

If an application requires separate landing zones (for example, Dev, Test, and Production), use a separate subscription for each one. Ensure that all environments are secure according to technical requirements and business needs.

While there may be legitimate scenarios where lift-and-shift migrations can occur—such as moving virtual machines—always prioritize application-centric migrations.

Security considerations

When considering the overall security of a landing zone, you use many native capabilities and add on top of that security posture management and threat mitigation layer for the workload. The scenario's requirements will dictate which options should be utilized, but here are some common strategies that enhance the security posture in Azure landing zones:

- **Segmentation** Isolation through segmentation can be utilized to create boundaries between resources from other parts of the organization. This is an effective strategy to detect and contain threat actors' movements. When it comes to segmentation, you should minimize operational friction by aligning the segmentation with the business practices and applications, which is done by using the following guidelines:
  - Isolate sensitive workloads
  - Isolate high-exposure systems from being used as a pivot to other systems
- **Governance** By having consistent cloud adoption via Azure Policy across multiple subscriptions, you can harden deployments and identify weaknesses that need to be addressed.

- **Configurations aligned with Zero Trust** Consider using Zero Trust for all resources you are deploying within the landing zone.
- **Automations using Blueprints** Automations of deployments using Azure Blueprints help prevent human errors and harden resources at scale.
- **Enforce policy compliance** Organizations of all sizes must comply with different industry and government compliance regulations.

Skill 5-6: Interpret technical threat intelligence and recommend risk mitigations

Threat intelligence (TI) is used as a tool to understand threats and uses this learning experience to assist in mitigating risks. TI provides context and relevance and helps prioritize proactive actions to improve an environment's security hygiene and reactive responses to attacks. This section covers the skills necessary to interpret technical threat intelligence and recommend risk mitigations according to the Exam SC-100 outline.

Threat intelligence in Defender for Cloud

Different Defender for Cloud plans leverage threat intelligence to increase the certainty that an alert is a true-positive and enrich the alert with more detailed information regarding the event, threat actor, and other insights that can be useful during an investigation.

Depending on the alert, a threat intelligence report is provided to facilitate your investigation. These reports contain information about the detected threats, including the following:

- Attackers' identity or associations (if this information is available)
- Attackers' objectives
- Current and historical attack campaigns (if this information is available)
- Attackers' tactics, tools, and procedures
- Associated indicators of compromise (IoC), such as URLs and file hashes
- Victimology, which is the industry and geographic prevalence to assist you in determining if your Azure resources are at risk
- Mitigation and remediation information

Keep in mind that this information is not always available for all types of alerts. Figure 5-11 shows an example of an alert that contains a threat intelligence report.

On the **Alerts** details tab, there is a link for the report, which in this case is **Report: Shadow Copy Delete**. By clicking this hyperlink, you can download the PDF containing detailed information about this threat, as shown in Figure 5-12.

FIGURE 5-11 Alert with enrichment from a threat intelligence report

FIGURE 5-12 Threat intelligence report

 EXAM TIP On the SC-100 Exam, you might be asked to select which Defender for Cloud capability can be used to help you triage an alert requiring additional information about security events, including suggestions to remediate the issue. In that case, you can utilize the threat intelligence report available for the alert.

Threat intelligence in Microsoft Sentinel

Threat intelligence in Microsoft Sentinel can be integrated through multiple platforms, including

- Trusted Automated Exchange of Intelligence Information (TAXII) protocol
- Threat Intelligence Platforms (TIP) data connector
- Built-in threat detections using Microsoft Threat Intelligence Analytics
- Threat intelligence workbooks

The most widely adopted industry standard for sending threat indicators is a combination of the Structured Threat Information Expression (STIX) data format and the TAXII protocol.

When planning your adoption to use TI with Microsoft Sentinel, the first step is configuring the TAXII Connector. Microsoft enriches all imported TI indicators with GeoLocation and WhoIs data, which is displayed in conjunction with other indicator details.

> **MORE INFO** For guidance on configuring the TAXII data connector, see *https://aka.ms/SentinelSetupTAXIIdataconnector.*

Interactive dashboards and visualizing data in different dimensions are important components of every security operation and threat-hunting discipline. Another way to consume the TI in Microsoft Sentinel is by leveraging the Threat Intelligence dashboard, as shown in Figure 5-13.

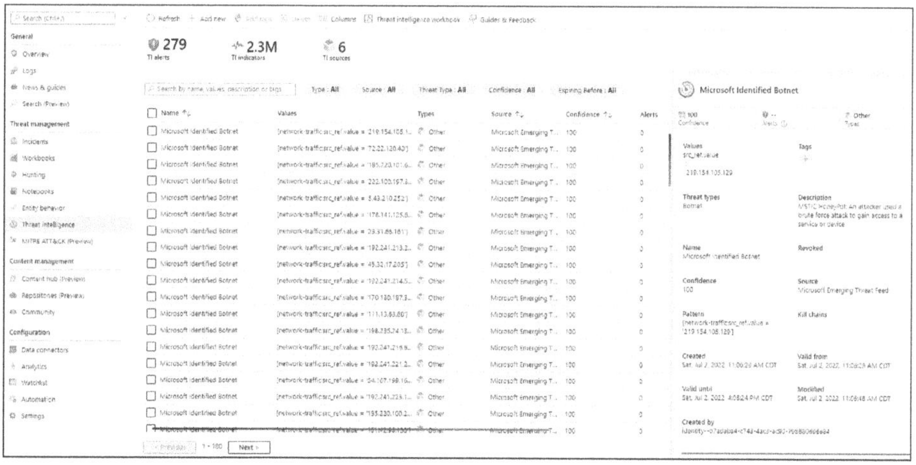

FIGURE 5-13 Threat Intelligence dashboard in Microsoft Sentinel

Skill 5-7: Recommend security capabilities or controls to mitigate identified risks

As a cybersecurity architect, you must recommend the appropriate security capability for a given risk. In some cases, you might conclude that the desired security capability requires adding a new service to mitigate the risk. This section covers the skills necessary to recommend security capabilities or controls to mitigate identified risks according to the Exam SC-100 outline.

Identifying and mitigating risk

When driving security posture enhancements across different workloads, you will face the challenge of identifying a series of risks and evaluating which ones you should prioritize mitigation. When evaluating a vulnerability, you need to consider the risk on the workload itself and what could happen if the threat actor can exploit that vulnerability successfully. What is the attacker able to do at that point? Can the attacker move laterally to another workload and escalate privileges? In addition to the chain of effects that could happen, the other important consideration is the type of data that can be exploited if a certain vulnerability is not remediated. Is the attacker able to access Personal Identifiable Information (PII)? What is the potential cost if the attacker can access PII data?

As you can see, many important questions must be answered before you start taking remediation actions. So, it is important that you can leverage a platform that provides visibility of the security improvements that can be applied to different workloads and helps you to make decisions that can enhance the overall security posture of your environment.

Another important consideration when designing your solution is the capability to have multiple sources of insights about a workload to facilitate the prioritization order. For example, if you have multiple storage accounts exposed to the Internet, which one should you remediate first? If you have insights into each storage account, you will have more evidence about which one is more critical for the organization. Then, you can make a smart decision about prioritization. By leveraging Microsoft Purview integration with Defender for Cloud, you will have data classification information about the storage account, and you can use this insight to make a better decision.

The security posture management team needs to establish a closer relationship with the governance team and feed them with lessons learned to avoid deploying resources that are not secure by default. In the example shown in Figure 5-14, a series of storage account–related recommendations are currently open because the necessary security controls were not implemented at the beginning of the pipeline.

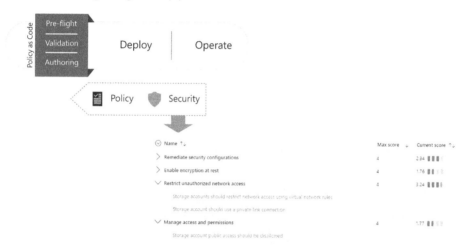

FIGURE 5-14 Security recommendations to mitigate risk

This is a typical scenario where the security controls to remediate them do not require adding a new service because the remediation is solely based on built-in settings to harden the storage account. However, to enforce these settings to be automatically deployed as a new Azure storage account is provisioned, you will need to use another service, which, in this case, is Azure Policy. With that, we can conclude that Defender for Cloud is the tool that will give you visibility of a risk. However, it won't necessarily be the tool that will be used to mitigate the risk because you might need to just harden some workload settings, or you will need to add a new service to mitigate that risk.

The **Defender for Cloud Management Ports Of EC2 Instances Should Be Protected With Just-In-Time Network Access Control** recommendation is an example of how Defender for Cloud gives you visibility of a risk, and another service is needed to mitigate it. In this case, you need to enable Defender for Cloud plan to implement just-in-time (JIT) VM access to secure those EC2 instances in AWS.

EXAM TIP On the SC-100 Exam, you might have scenarios in which a list of Defender for Cloud recommendations will be surfaced as the risks are identified. You will need to select a service that can be utilized to mitigate these recommendations.

When you need to add another service to mitigate the risk, you also need to evaluate the cost of that service compared to the cost of the asset that you are trying to protect. If the cost to protect the asset is higher than the asset itself, you might have to find alternatives to protect the asset, transfer the risk (for example, to an insurance company), or assume the risk.

Thought experiment

In this thought experiment, demonstrate your skills and knowledge of the topics covered in this chapter. You can find answers to this thought experiment in the next section.

Monitoring security at Fabrikam Inc

You are the Cybersecurity Architect for Fabrikam, an online general store specializing in various home products. Fabrikam has an on-premises environment using Active Directory Domain Services (AD DS) called corp.fabrikam.com. Fabrikam also has a single-tenant Azure AD environment with a single subscription. Fabrikam also has some workloads (EC2 instances) in AWS.

You are working on a project to improve Fabrikam's security posture, and you need to provide quarterly reports to upper management showing evidence that the overall security posture is improving. Fabrikam's CISO decided to use NIST SP 800 171 R2 as its main framework. In this initial phase, Frabrikam wants you to ensure that the ID NIST SP 800-171 R2 3.1.13 control—specifying cryptographic standards, including FIPS-validated cryptography and NSA-approved cryptography—is remediated.

Another important requirement for this project is that Qualys vulnerability assessment needs to be implemented in all Azure VMs and AWS EC2 instances. Also, you need to suggest a solution to help the SOC team to investigate incidents.

Based on this scenario, respond to the following questions:

1. Which solution should be utilized to allow you to show evidence of security posture improvement over time?

2. Which solution should be used to track NIST compliance?

3. Which solution should be used to enable Qualys vulnerability assessment in Azure and AWS?

4. Which solution should you suggest for the SOC team?

Thought experiment answers

This section contains the solution to the thought experiment. Each answer explains why the answer choice is correct.

1. Based on this scenario, you should utilize the Secure Score capability in Defender for Cloud. With Secure Score, you can track security posture enhancement over time.

2. In this case, you should utilize the Regulatory Compliance feature in Defender for Cloud.

3. Vulnerability assessment is available in Defender for Servers, which supports workloads in Azure, AWS, and GCP.

4. For this scenario, the Threat Intelligence capability in Microsoft Sentinel can be used to help during the investigation.

Chapter summary

- Microsoft cloud security benchmark (MCSB) was created with the idea of providing a canonical set of Azure-centric technical security controls based on controls defined by the Center for Internet Security (CIS), the National Institute of Standards and Technology (NIST), and the Payment Card Industry (PCI). When this chapter was written, the latest ASB version was 3 (v3), which considered CIS v8 and v7, NIST SP800-53 Rev4, and PCI-DSS v3.2.1.

- Microsoft Defender for Cloud gives organizations complete visibility and control over the security of cloud workloads located in Azure, on-premises, or another cloud provider. By actively monitoring these workloads, Defender for Cloud enhances the overall security posture of the cloud deployment and reduces the exposure of resources to threats. Defender for Cloud also uses intelligent threat detection to assist you in protecting your environment from rapidly evolving cyberattacks.

- Multi-cloud deployments continue to grow as many organizations adopt different cloud providers to store different workloads. Defender for Cloud supports integration with AWS and GCP, allowing the CSPM team to have full visibility of the security posture of Azure, AWS, and on-premises resources in one dashboard.

- Defender for Cloud–native vulnerability assessment solutions include Qualys and Microsoft Threat Vulnerability Management (TVM).

- Azure Security Benchmark for Microsoft Cloud Security Benchmark provides security recommendations for different Azure workloads, which are reflected in Defender for Cloud. Once you start improving the Secure Score for your Azure subscription, you automatically improve your Azure workloads' security posture.

- When designing your landing zone, you must consider scenarios where workload owners need more control and autonomy on their workloads within the guardrails established by the platform foundation. For this type of scenario, you will use decentralized operations.

- Threat intelligence is leveraged by different Defender for Cloud plans to
    - Increase the level of certainty that an alert is a true-positive
    - Enrich the alert with more detailed information regarding the event, the threat actor, and other insights that can be useful during an investigation
- The security posture management team needs to establish a closer relationship with the governance team and feed them with lessons learned to avoid deploying resources that are not secure by default.

CHAPTER 6

Design a strategy for securing server and client endpoints

To ensure that resources are secured, organizations must put the proper security controls in place from the start, meaning security baselines should be implemented to ensure that the server or client has the security capability to withstand most malicious attacks.

However, attackers are persistent, and with enough time, they will find ways to circumvent the built-in protections. Therefore, organizations must enable multi-layer defenses to take over when other layers have failed. Also, organizations must enable the generation of signals needed for the machine learning and behavior analysis workloads to perform proper analyses and take the proper actions to protect the environment. Because of the diversity of applications, endpoints, servers, and other environmental resources, a single strategy might not be feasible. Exceptions will always exist. The outcome should be to mitigate as many risks as possible with a centralized architecture and deal with the exceptions separately from the general implementation.

In the next few sections, we describe the capabilities that can be implemented to deal with the security requirements in an environment. Also, you learn those capabilities can be used together to provide a layered, end-to-end approach to secure your organization's resources.

Skills covered in this chapter:

- Skill 6-1: Specify security baselines for server and client endpoints
- Skill 6-2: Specify security requirements for servers, including multiple platforms and operating systems
- Skill 6-3: Specify security requirements for mobile devices and clients, including endpoint protection, hardening, and configuration
- Skill 6-4: Specify requirements to secure Active Directory Domain Services
- Skill 6-5: Design a strategy to manage secrets, keys, and certificates
- Skill 6-6: Design a strategy for secure remote access

Skill 6-1: Specify security baselines for server and client endpoints

Since Microsoft's Trustworthy Computing initiative from the early 2000s, Microsoft has focused on delivering solutions that are secure by default, including the Windows and Windows Server. However, although many controls provide good security for organizations, those security controls can also affect the functionality of applications. Microsoft provides guidance for implementing those controls through baselines that can be modified to meet the organization's requirements.

Because Microsoft has many products and services, different baselines have been released to meet organizational needs. A baseline is a group of Microsoft-recommended configurations explaining the impact these settings might have. The baselines might contain settings that enable organizations to comply with security standards while other settings mitigate threats. Depending on the product/service you want to configure, you can decide which tool best suits your needs.

The next few sections explain the available tools and how you can use them to implement baselines across the whole digital estate. We also explain where you can access and customize these baselines for deployment to the environment.

Be aware that although the main purpose of these tools is to help you create and implement configuration baselines, they generate alerts and events, such as whether a system is compliant, which are then fed to other services, such as conditional access and threat protection.

Group Policy Objects (GPO)

Group Policy enables you to manage Active Directory Domain Services (AD DS) joined user and computer configurations. You can configure the settings using the Group Policy Management Console (GPMC)—commonly called the *policy editor*—or PowerShell cmdlets. GPMC is an easy user interface that allows you to create policies and provides reporting capabilities that allow you to review a list of enabled policies, calculate an effective configuration for a user or computer after applying all inherited policies, and more.

To configure the GPO, the policy editor displays settings defined as part of the ADMX templates imported into the tool. ADMX templates are files containing

- The setting name
- A brief description of the setting
- The registry location that will be changed after the configuration is set
- Values that can be set
- Other control-required information

By default, Group Policy can configure user- or Windows-related settings. However, more ADMX templates can be added to extend the number of configurable settings, including Office products and even third-party applications like Google Chrome browser. Based on its extensibility—and to reduce performance issues created by a conflicting or erroneous configuration—Microsoft began releasing baselines and guidance for customers to use when implementing different configurations.

Security Compliance Toolkit (SCT)

You can use the Security Compliance Toolkit (SCT) to help select the proper baseline to use for clients and servers to customize the controls that will be implemented. SCT allows you to download, analyze, test, edit, and store baselines for all Microsoft products, including the Windows client and server.

The SCT also allows customers to compare existing Group Policy Objects (GPOs) with the baseline recommended by Microsoft to help quickly align with the requirements and apply the changes. You can download SCT (and find more information) at *https://aka.ms/sct*.

When you download SCT, you will have the option to download the Policy Analyzer, Local Group Policy tools, and several newer baselines, such as Windows 10, Windows 11, and Microsoft 365 Apps for Enterprise. The Policy Analyzer tool allows you to compare GPOs against baselines. It highlights possible conflicts or configuration erros. You can even export to Excel to perform further analysis and comparisons.

To start comparing GPOs in your AD DS environment, follow these steps:

1. Under the Group Policy Management Console (GPMC), save a backup of your domain policies to a folder. You can select one or all domain GPOs.
2. To load the domain GPO that you want to compare, click **Add > File > Add The File From GPOs** in the **Policy Analyzer**.
3. Select the GPO folder location.
4. Click **Import**.
5. Add the baseline template to compare by clicking **Add > File > Add The File From GPOs.**
6. Select the folder where the baseline is stored.
7. Select the two baselines you want to compare, and click **View/Compare** to see a comparison of them.

The Local Group Policy (LGPO) allows you to verify the effect of GPOs by importing settings into the local registry. In addition, it helps manage non-domain-joined systems. The LGPO can also export settings into a backup location.

Both GPMC and the Security Compliance toolkit can help implement the configuration using GPOs. You can also use Microsoft Endpoint Manager (MEM), which is discussed below. We recommend that you select the appropriate platform to implement and manage your settings because having multiple platforms can cause unpredictable systems behavior.

Azure Security Benchmark (ASB)

ASB was discussed in detail in Chapter 5, but it is important to emphasize that ASB can help define and enforce security and compliance requirements consistently. ASB includes baseline recommendations that are applicable across the Azure tenant and other services using guidance that maps to standards such as the Center for Internet Security (CIS), the National Institute of Standards and Technology (NIST), and the Payment Card Industry Data Security Standard (PCI-DSS).

Microsoft Endpoint Manager (MEM)

Microsoft Endpoint Manager is an enterprise suite of products that also can help implement baselines for clients and servers. MEM can check for compliance and deploy OS updates, applications, drivers, configuration settings, and more. For example, you could implement compliance or configuration policies to either check or implement configurations on platforms such as Android (AOSP), Android Enterprise, iOS/iPadOS, macOS, Windows 10, and Windows 11.

MEM combines services like Microsoft Intune, Configuration Manager, Desktop Analytics, and Windows Autopilot to deliver modern management capabilities to support all those platforms in the cloud and on-premises. Because of the integration of products, no matter where the client or server is located, the suite of products can manage the configuration. Also, the integration allows you to deploy more than just settings.

Many other capabilities can be integrated with Microsoft Endpoint Manager to deploy secure configurations to servers and clients. One is Microsoft Intune, which provides features and settings to help configure Android, iOS, macOS, and Windows devices. Configuration Management is an on-premises solution that enables you to support Windows Clients and Servers. You can integrate Configuration Management with Microsoft Intune to enable co-management from both services, which, in turn, extends configuration verifications to be used with conditional access. This is important if you want to enable configuration compliance as part of the conditional access verifications for on-premises systems.

Desktop Analytics is another MEM integration that provides insight into your clients by creating reports to help speed up OS deployment. These insights include things such as application inventory, application compatibility, and OS version. This helps with baseline deployment plans since you can tell which version of Windows your systems are running and select the proper Microsoft baseline to implement. Figure 6-1 shows one of the reports that can be used to determine baseline implementation and upgrade planning.

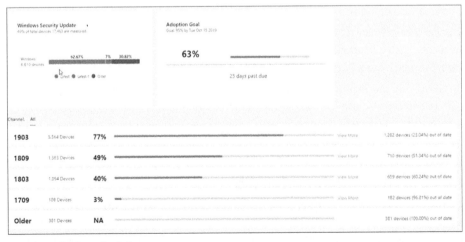

FIGURE 6-1 Desktop Analytics

Windows Autopilot integration with MEM helps pre-configure new Windows client devices or reset them to a default business-ready state by deploying Windows images, applications, and baseline configurations to them. It also automatically joins devices to Azure AD or Active Directory and auto-enrolls devices into MDM services like Intune. By using this capability, devices are provisioned automatically and securely.

PowerShell DSC

PowerShell DSC is a configuration management platform that supports Windows client and server, Linux, Nano, Azure Guest Configuration, and Azure Automation. This platform enables you to use PowerShell scripts to configure something as simple as a feature within a client or server to something as complex as an environment with several computers and services running in them.

The benefit of DSC is that it simplifies the amount of code needed with PowerShell, allowing users to focus on the deployment structure instead of the details of the implementation of individual features. It does this by letting the user declare how they want the configuration to be, and the code knows how to get there without explicit coding from the user.

> **MORE INFO** For more detailed code samples and resources, visit *https://aka.ms/ DSCOverview.*

Azure Automation

Azure Automation is a centralized platform where you can run different automation jobs or runbooks. It provides many different automations, including configuration and update management.

Change Tracking and Inventory allows you to track Linux and Windows virtual machines and server changes. It supports change tracking across services, the software registry, files, and more.

State Configuration allows you to manage your DSC resources from Azure Automation.

> **NOTE** This section does not explain how the automation is created and executed to perform configuration or update management. The key is understanding that this is a platform you can use to build and execute your own configuration and update management automation. For more information, see *https://AzureAutomation.*

Azure Policy

Azure Policy was already discussed in Chapter 4. However, in this section, we briefly summarize how it helps enforce security and compliance settings by first evaluating the environment with best practices and compliance requirements and providing an overview of the environment with the ability to drill down per-resource, per-policy.

Similar to MEM, Azure Policy goes beyond configuring client and server settings. It can deploy updates, applications, and other services to ensure compliance. For example, it might deploy Log Analytics to a resource if it is a VM and does not have Log Analytics already deployed. Also, Azure Policy can configure settings within the OS, such as configuring the User Rights Assignment to some defined values. It does this using PowerShell DSC and Chef InSpec.

> **MORE INFO** For more information about Chef InSpec, visit *https://docs.chef.io/azure_portal/.*

Since Azure Policy works directly with Azure Resource Manager, Azure Policy has a few extra capabilities that MEM does not provide for client and server configuration. It can look at how those resources are configured at the SKU level. For example, Azure Policy can provide a configuration to control the selected platform options, such as allowing the deployment of any SKU except Premium_ZRS Storage accounts. Additionally, Azure Policy can configure other Azure Services like Arc, Key Vault, Kubernetes, Internet of Things (IoT), and many others.

You can create a policy definition using JSON format by either importing a sample policy from GitHub or creating a custom one. However, Microsoft already provides many predefined policy definitions. If you want to apply several policy definitions, you can create a policy initiative to track a full resource configuration or compliance rather than tracking individual controls. This means you would group a set of policy definitions into a policy initiative. Microsoft has already predefined many policy initiatives (or baselines) to help customers to align to NIST SP 800 171, NIST SP 800-53, PCI v3.2.1.201, Microsoft Cloud Security Benchmark recommendations, and many others. Once you have a policy initiative, you assign it to a management group, subscription, or resource group, which enables the settings to be inherited by every resource under those levels.

We recommend that even if you assign just one policy definition, create a policy initiative to do the assignment since you'll likely need to implement other settings for those resources in the future. You can lump those policy definitions together.

> **CAUTION** When planning your policy assignments, be aware of the resources you are working with. Some settings in the policy definition might not be suitable for some of the resources inheriting the assignment. If the wrong configuration is enabled, it is hard to overwrite settings.

You can define exclusions in the policy assignment, define parameters, and add JSON designating that certain defined settings should not be applied if a particular configuration value is found. Be aware that when you have many policy initiatives applying to the same set of resources and use enforcement to exclude the policy configuration, it will make it more difficult to figure out what might be affecting the resource.

Also, we recommend you apply new policy definitions to existing infrastructure with the definition's effect set to **Audit**. Doing so allows you to analyze the policy definition's effects and understand its possible impact before it is applied. Be aware that you can apply these policy assignments in several ways, including Blueprints and Terraforms. Finally, be aware that Azure Policy has limits. For example, a management group or subscription has a maximum of 500 policy definitions, 200 initiative definitions, and 200 policy or initiative assignments.

> **MORE INFO**   For more information about other limitations, see *https://aka.ms/ AzurePolicyObjects*.

Azure Resource Manager (ARM) templates

ARM templates allow you to manage your infrastructure using JSON format. As discussed in the next section, you can deploy Blueprints as code. Some other benefits include built-in validation, modular files, tracked templates, and many authoring tools such as the Template Editor in Azure Portal, Visual Studio, and Visual Studio Code to help create templates and deliver consistent results.

In addition, the ARM Template Viewer allows you to view templates as an interactive map, where you can inspect the deployment visually and document your deployment much more easily. All deployments are logged in the **Deployments** section. When you click the deployment you want to review, you can see deployment details, such as what was deployed, the input providers, and even the template itself.

> **MORE INFO**   If you want sample templates, see the GitHub repository at *https://aka.ms/ ARMQuickStart*.

Blueprints

Azure Blueprints is a collection of artifacts that orchestrates the deployment. These artifacts can include definitions for creating role assignments, policy assignments, resource groups, and other resources defined within Azure Resource Manager templates.

One of the benefits of using Azure Blueprint is that the blueprint is "stamped" to the deployment, meaning the auditing and tracking mechanisms can compare deployments with the current configuration.

Also, you can assign environment control options to the Blueprint:

- You can choose to have the environment always meet the configuration definition and never be changed (**Read Only**).
- You can choose to have the environment allow changes but never allow deletion (**Do Not Delete**).
- You can allow any changes, including deletion (**Don't Lock**).

If you enable the first two options and want to change something that is not permitted, you either must change the Blueprint or unassign it from the target subscription.

Microsoft Defender for Cloud (MDC)

Microsoft Defender for Cloud was discussed in Chapter 5, but it is important to highlight how it helps implement security baselines for servers. As mentioned earlier in this chapter, MDC is a cloud security posture management (CSPM) and cloud workload protection (CWP) solution that finds areas of improvement in your configuration and helps protect workloads across on-premises and multi-cloud environments.

MDC continuously discovers newly deployed resources, assesses whether they meet the security best practices, and flags them to be fixed. To implement configurations, MDC takes advantage of the Azure Policy's REST API to apply configurations with policy initiatives. Then, you can decide whether to apply those settings to a management group, subscription, or resource group. You can use similar steps to remediate compliance issues because MDC provides capabilities to align with compliance requirements such as NIST 800-53.

Microsoft Defender for IoT (MDIoT)

MDIoT is an agentless device monitoring tool that helps discover IoT/OT devices, assess risks, and manage vulnerabilities by identifying unpatched devices, open ports, unauthorized applications, unauthorized connections, and other issues. It also helps detect advanced malware like fileless and zero-day malware using machine learning, threat intelligence, and behavioral analytics.

Baseline configuration

Previous sections focused on the different solutions provided to deploy baseline configurations. This section discusses some key configurations that need to be set in your enterprise resources, including the following:

- Enable firewalls, antivirus, and other built-in security capabilities
- Enable EDR Solutions
- Configure the following on Windows devices:
  - Windows Defender Credential Guard reduces the chances of credentials being stolen from memory. It also prevents using older NTLM credentials, unconstrained Kerberos delegation, or DES encryption. Because some older legacy applications might use these older types of credentials, enable Credential Guard on desktops that do not have applications with older credential dependencies and work toward modernizing those older applications.
  - Windows Defender Application Control allows list/block list applications.
  - Windows Defender SmartScreen protects against phishing, malware sites, and applications by blocking access to potentially malicious content.

- Windows Defender System Guard protects and maintains the system's integrity as it starts up and validates that the system integrity has been maintained through local and remote attestation.

- Windows Defender Exploit Guard provides attack surface reduction, controlled folder access, and exploit and network protection.

Key Recommendations

The following list summarizes tools to help drive end-to-end seamless and consistent configuration. It is important to select only the required medium to deploy configuration since configuring from different toolsets and services might have conflicting configurations, which, if implemented, can open doors for attacks. Also, the continuous configuration change can also cause performance issues in the clients and servers.

When deciding which toolset to use, consider the different outcomes you are trying to achieve:

- Consider using Windows Autopilot and MEM if you regularly deploy Windows client devices.

- If you currently own Configuration Manager or another similar on-premises configuration management solution and are planning some upgrade or new OS deployment, use MEM with Desktop Analytics.

- If you currently have on-premises or multi-cloud IaaS servers and want to implement settings to improve the environment's security, consider using Defender for Cloud to manage your configurations.

- If you have Configuration Manager for on-premises systems and want to use Conditional Access, configure co-management so you can manage the systems from both the cloud and on-premises, and Intune can share the proper signals to the conditional access engine.

- If you need to have regulatory compliance, use Defender for Cloud and Azure Policy to ensure that your workloads comply with the different requirements.

- Use ARM templates or Azure Blueprints if you deploy multiple environments that need consistent configuration.

- Use Azure Blueprints if you want to prevent configuration changes from being made or the environment from being deleted.

Skill 6-2: Specify security requirements for servers, including multiple platforms and operating systems

While Microsoft automatically enables many security configurations by default, some configurations might affect the operation of certain applications. To understand what foundational security requirements you can implement, you need to understand the server role.

For example, a domain controller configuration will differ from a SQL Server. The easiest way to start building the proper security configuration is to understand the current state, the expected behavior of the OS and applications installed in the server, and what behavior you should never see. However, this is often difficult to do on a scale unless you have the proper tool/services to help you automate the build.

As mentioned in Skill 6-1, "Specify security baselines for server and client endpoints," the following tools and services can provide a lot of information about the current state and the normal behavior of servers and clients.

- Security Compliance Toolkit (SCT)
- Microsoft Endpoint Manager (MEM)
- Microsoft Defender for Cloud (MDC)
- Microsoft Defender for IoT

The information provided by these tools can help you develop the proper configuration.

Shared responsibility in the cloud

Attackers have had 20 years to learn the different types of vulnerabilities the different protocols and OS have, and they use the knowledge and OS capabilities to extend their attacks without going unnoticed. This is why you may have heard people saying that attackers live out of the land. In other words, they use OS files, processes, native applications, and other capabilities to drive the attack forward. Can you imagine how much risk you could reduce and the time you could save if you could make all your applications SaaS and PaaS applications?

Also, you will save a lot of money in management and personnel by not having to deal with hardware, OS, and application management, and your organization could redirect those funds to deal with security operations and environment governance.

Figure 6-2 shows the shared Microsoft and Customer responsibilities for each SaaS, PaaS, IaaS, and on-premises environment. For example, when using on-premises, the customer is still responsible for information and data, mobile devices and PCs, and identity objects but is no longer responsible for physical host hardware, network, and datacenter. This means the customer no longer has to worry about purchasing the hardware, upgrading the hardware firmware, or implementing processes to minimize hardware security-related risks.

For PaaS, in addition to Microsoft taking over physical host hardware and the physical network and datacenter, Microsoft takes over operating system management. This means the customer no longer must take care of upgrading, patching, and implementing policies and other services to secure the OS. It also means, as mentioned above, the attacker has no access to the files and capabilities provided by the OS.

For SaaS, the customer's only responsibility is the information and data, mobile devices and PCs used to access that data, Identity objects that provide access, and portions of the identity and access infrastructure used to govern the identity objects and configuration.

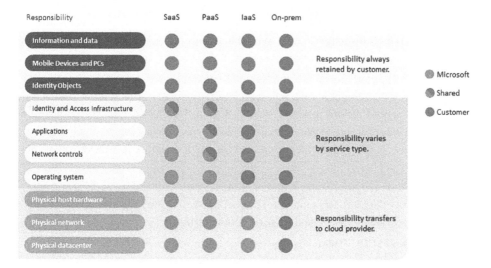

FIGURE 6-2 Microsoft and customer responsibilities

Legacy insecure protocols

Another very important part of securing servers is making sure legacy protocols are disabled:

- **Server Message Block (SMB) v1**   SMB is normally used for file shares, printers, scanners, and email servers. It does not support encryption. SMB 3.0 provides many features, including encryption, transparent failover, PowerShell capabilities, and insecure guest authorization blocking. This helps prevent tampering and eavesdropping. Also, you can have Pre-authentication Integrity and Secure Dialect Negotiation with SMB 3.1.1+, which protects against security downgrade attacks.

- **LAN Manager (LM) or New Technology LAN Manager (NTLM) v1**   We recommended that you disable NTLM authentication.

  - Although the main settings are managed from the domain controllers, if **Network Security: Restrict NTLM: Outgoing NTLM Traffic To Remote Servers** is set to **Deny All**, the client device can't authenticate identities to a remote server.

  - Also, the **Network Security: Restrict NTLM: Add Server Exceptions In This Domain** setting allows you to deny or allow incoming NTLM traffic from clients or other servers.

  - The **Network Security: Restrict NTLM: Outgoing NTLM Traffic To Remote Servers** setting allows you to deny or audit outgoing NTLM traffic.

  - You also should review any configurations under the **Network Security: Restrict NTLM: Add Remote Server Exceptions For NTLM Authentication** and **Network security: Restrict NTLM: Add Server Exceptions In This Domain** settings that might be configured in any GPOs in the domain and Forest.

- Before setting these to **Deny All**, we recommend you use Audit All first and review the generated event log in `Applications And Services Log\Microsoft\Windows\NTLM` to understand the possible impact. With this setting, you eliminate malicious attacks on NTML authentication traffic that results in a compromised server.

- **TLS V1.1**   This is another protocol that should be updated to the latest possible version, especially since RDP Negotiation Request and Response uses it. The modern TLS capabilities remove obsolete and insecure features, such as SHA-1, RC4, DES, 3DES, MD5, and others. TLS 1.3, supported on Windows Server 2019+, requires servers to cryptographically sign the entire handshake, reducing the chances of downgrade attacks from earlier versions.

- **SSL 3.0**   You should disable this protocol because of the vulnerabilities discussed at *https://aka.ms/3009008*. The same is true for wDigest, unsigned Lightweight Directory Access Protocol (LDAP) Binds, and weak ciphers in Kerberos.

- **FTP, FTPS, and SFTP**   These have become major targets for attackers. FTP is more than 30 years old and was not designed for the modern threats we deal with today. It lacks privacy and integrity mechanisms, so it is easy for data to be intercepted and modified. Although FTPS and SFTP add encryption to their capabilities, each creates security risks. For example, FTPS underlying transport uses the legacy FTP protocol and needs a secondary data channel, making it difficult to use behind a firewall. SFTP doesn't have controls for cross-script vulnerabilities, doesn't stop unauthorized transfers, and it is hard for logs to be correlated to show threats.

Using Microsoft Cloud Security Benchmark in Microsoft Defender for Cloud or Microsoft Sentinel can help you discover the use of these protocols. In addition, Microsoft Defender for Identity has a security assessment that checks for Legacy protocol usage.

Threat protection

Defender for Server is one of the enhanced capabilities provided by Microsoft Defender for Cloud security features that should be required for all Windows and Linux environments located on-premises and multi-cloud (Azure, AWS, GCO). It includes a license to run Microsoft Defender for Endpoint and adaptive application hardening, which creates an allowed list based on what it has learned the server runs. Then, if something outside of that allowed-list attempts to run, its execution is denied.

Defender for Server also includes File Integrity Monitoring, which monitors changes happening on critical files. Also, it monitors the registry for changes; if those changes seem abnormal, it blocks them. It provides recommendations for adaptive network hardening based on observed traffic in and out of the server.

Also, Defender for Server provides Docker-hardening guidance for containers running on Linux machines based on the Center for Internet Security (CIS) Docker Benchmark. Also, it provides detection against fileless attacks. More importantly, all this information is shared with the services to enable cross-service workloads to execute to provide further protection, detection, and response. These services include Microsoft Defender for Cloud and Microsoft Sentinel.

Local Administrator Password Management (LAPS)

Often, customers create Windows Server images with similar security configurations. This also means that when those images get deployed, every single server created from that image has a local administrator account configured with the same password. If an attacker compromises one server, they can extract the password for that administrator account and use it to gain access to the rest of the environment servers.

To minimize the risk and simplify password management for the local administrator account, you can use LAPS. LAPS randomizes the local administrator password and creates a plan to reset the password on a scheduled basis. Only one local administrator account is managed per server. We recommend that you select the built-in Administrator account for management. If you use the built-in account—even if the account is renamed—the system can continue managing the account since the account is auto-detected using the well-known SID assigned to the account.

For this functionality to work, the Active Directory Schema gets updated to have two additional attributes as part of the endpoint object. One object stores the account password, while the other stores the password's expiration date, enabling the password to be reset after the expiration.

You must download the LAPS MSI and install it on a server or workstation to enable this functionality. Installing this MSI provides you with the necessary files for updating the schema, setting the proper permissions for administrators to read the schema values, creating the GPOs, and accessing the password when needed.

User rights assignments

One of the problems—especially in ADDS environments—is the number of accounts that have privileged rights across the ADDS environment. Most of those rights are defined on each device using the Group Policy Management Console (GPMC) under `Computer Configuration\Windows Settings\Security Settings\Local Policies\User Rights Assignment` or on the local device using Local Group Policy Editor (`gpedit.msc`). Although we recommend that you review the permissions provided to all the settings under this GPO hive, these are the most important settings we recommend you control:

- **Access This Computer From The Network**
- **Allow Log On Locally**
- **Allow Log On Through Remote Desktop Services**
- **Deny Access To This Computer From The Network**
- **Deny Log On As A Batch Job**
- **Deny Log On As A Service**
- **Deny Log On Locally**
- **Deny Log On Through Remote Desktop Services**
- **Log On As A Batch Job**
- **Log On As A Service**

For example, when configuring the **Allow Log On Locally** setting, the client computer's effective default values are **Administrators**, **Backup Operators**, and **Users**. When analyzing the membership to determine, keep the following points in mind:

- Be aware that because the Administrators group is a local group, domain groups and other local accounts might be added to this group. Review this group membership and try to reduce the number of assigned accounts assigned. We recommend removing all local accounts, besides the default local administrator, from the local Administrator group because most monitoring services tend to monitor only domain account access instead of local accounts. Also, it's harder to manage local accounts at an enterprise level.

- Many domain groups and domain accounts might be assigned membership to this group. Monitoring solutions tend to use accounts that are then assigned Administrator membership instead of the least-privilege access needed. Be aware that if the monitoring applications with this right are compromised, the attacker will essentially have administrator rights to all monitored systems. Hence, it might be more beneficial to have a cloud service to provide that service instead of having these services, which might extend the attack surface.

- **Allow Log On Through Remote Desktop Services** and **Remote Desktop Users** are another example of access that should be reviewed because these access types might have many groups and accounts assigned to them. You might want to remove all access to this and use one of the following since they enable all the cloud protections, such as MFA and conditional access, to be executed before the user attempts to connect via RDP to the server:

  - Azure Bastion to allow RDP from the Azure portal. However, this works only for Azure VMs.

  - Azure AD Application Proxy provides secure remote access to on-premises web applications, including Remote Desktop Gateway.

- For **Deny Log On Locally**, we recommend that you assign the local guest account as part of the configuration of this setting.

Microsoft Cloud Security Benchmark within Defender for Cloud can help automate and comply with these recommendations.

Network-based controls

Although we want to minimize the use of the network to mitigate issues like lateral movement, many organizations still have lots of on-premises or IaaS-related workloads. Hence, the recommendation is to provide defense-in-depth, but we must be careful not to add too many layers because it adds complexity and increases the attack surface.

So, it is important to balance the number of layers used but not at the expense of opening doors for simple types of attacks. After all, many people question the value antivirus software brings since most attacks are no longer detected through signatures. However, although everyone agrees that attackers have changed to more advanced tactics, everyone also understands that removing antivirus capabilities will only open the door for attackers to revert back to using simpler and more affordable methods.

When using Azure, there are several network securities that can be used to protect servers, such as:

- **Azure Front Door** A Cloud Content Delivery Network (CDN) that provides secure connection between users and applications. Front Door is protected by the default Azure infrastructure DDoS protection, but because it only accepts traffic on the HTTP and HTTPS protocols with requests that have valid known host headers, it helps mitigate other common DDoS attack types, including volumetric attacks.

- **Web Application Firewall** Centralized inbound application protection from common exploits and vulnerabilities. It utilizes a managed rule set that is updated by Azure as needed to protect against new attack signatures. It can provide geo-filtering, which can block traffic from outside a defined geographic region. It can block IP addresses identified as malicious, block HTTP/HTTPS attacks with known signatures, and prevent certain IP addresses from calling your service too frequently.

- **DDoS Protection** Tunes to your applications' traffic patterns by automatically performing traffic scrubbing to ensure only legitimate traffic reaches the service.

- **Virtual Network Isolation** There are several ways to provide network isolation, including

  - Deploying dedicated instances of a service into a virtual network, so the services can be privately accessed within a virtual network or on-premises.

  - Using a private endpoint to connect you privately to a service powered by Azure Private Link. Since Private Endpoint uses a private IP, it brings the service into your virtual network. Azure Private Link enables access to your Azure services using the Microsoft backbone as a private connection.

  - By extending a virtual network using public service endpoints to connect to your virtual network, service endpoints allow private IP addresses to reach an Azure service without needing an outbound public IP.

Service tags Using service tags to allow or deny traffic to your resources:

- **Azure Firewall** Using Azure Firewall Advanced network and application threat protection, your organization can have L3-l7 filtering, outbound SNAT, inbound DNAT, DNS Proxy, and other capabilities.

- **NSG/ASG and UDR** Distributed inbound and outbound network traffic filtering on VMs, containers, or subnets using NSG/ASG and UDR.

Network endpoint micro-segmentation is another control that can be used to control communications between devices. Although firewalls and/or Network Security Groups (NSGs) are used to segment devices, using the endpoint firewall to limit the inbound and outbound communication allowed to certain IPs and ports will provide a more server-targeted set of configurations.

We recommend using an endpoint firewall, at least for on-premises server workloads. Because servers tend to be more static regarding location and set of applications installed, it is easier to define a set of policies that works for those static workloads requirements. This will help reduce the attack surface to a smaller number of IPs and ports.

You can further limit the attack surface by using identity workload micro-segmentation to permission by application or process level. For example, with network micro-segmentation, you can have a policy that enables the IPs for your Configuration Manager Servers to talk to Wkst01 via ports 445, 443, and 135. With identity workload micro-segmentation, you can further segment by drilling down to the application level and specifying the processes to be involved. This makes it harder for attackers to discover avenues for compromise and provides more opportunity for the different services to generate events triggering protections, detections, and response workloads to stop attacks.

Several capabilities can be used to help gather information necessary to implement micro-segmentation tactics and implement policies. For example, Defender for Cloud Adaptive Network Hardening uses a machine learning algorithm to analyze normal traffic patterns. Using threat intelligence and other information can provide hardening guidance. Microsoft Defender for Cloud Network Map, Topology View, and Traffic View can help you understand traffic between your endpoints. Defender for IoT provides a device view, where you can also understand the traffic between IoT devices.

Governance

You can create security initiatives and policies or use built-in ones using Defender for Cloud for your on-premises and multi-cloud servers. Although custom initiatives are not taken into consideration when calculating the Secure Score, recommendations will be provided if your environment doesn't follow the policies you create. When you remediate your custom initiative, you will still manage the implementation of the recommendations using Azure Policy applied to a management group or subscription.

Built-in initiatives will help you improve your regulatory compliance. One of the built-in initiatives is the Azure Security Benchmark, which builds on the Center for Internet Security (CIS) controls and the National Institute of Standards and Technology (NIST). As seen by Figure 6-3, besides the Azure Security Benchmark, other regulatory standards that can be used as part of the Microsoft Defender for Cloud Regulatory Compliance dashboard include the following:

- PCI-DSS v3.2.1:2018
- SOC TSP
- CMMC Level 3
- NIST SP 800-53 R4
- NIST SP 800-53 R5
- NIST SP 800 171 R2
- FedRAMP H
- FedRAMP M
- HIPAA/HITRUST

- SWIFT CSP CSCF v2020

- Azure CIS 1.1.0

- Azure CIS 1.3.0

- UK OFFICIAL and UK NHS

- Canada Federal PBMM

- New Zealand ISM Restricted

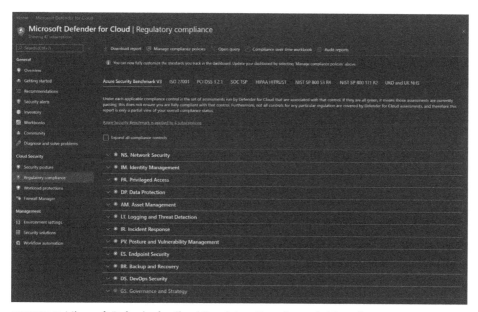

FIGURE 6-3 Microsoft Defender for Cloud Regulatory Compliance dashboard

The AWS Foundational Security Best Practices is automatically assigned for AWS, but you can add ASW CIS 1.2.0 and AWS PCI DSS 3.2.1. For GCP, the GCP Default is assigned with the capability of adding GCP CIS 1.1.0, GCP CIS 1.2.0, GCP NIST 800 53, and PCI DSS 3.2.1. More standards are added frequently.

To improve your security posture, find the recommendations with a higher Secure Score impact. After you implement the recommendations, you can generate a compliance status report on the Defender for Cloud Regulatory Compliance dashboard; select an initiative (such as **NIST SP 800-53 R4 Framework**), and review the findings. You can also select **Download Report** from the options provided at the top of the user interface. You can also enable continuous export of Regulatory Compliance information by opening **Environment Settings**, selecting the subscription you want the report from, and selecting **Continuous Export**. Then select the desired format (PDF or CSV), the frequency, and the export location. This will help you can see changes happening in the environment over time. Also, you can run workflow automations to email, send an alert, or create an event by triggering a Logic App whenever one of your regulatory compliance assessments changes state.

Skill 6-3: Specify security requirements for mobile devices and clients, including endpoint protection, hardening, and configuration

Users connect to organizations' resources and access sensitive applications and data from everywhere. To address the significant increase in risk brought by this mobility, we recommend that you enable the built-in security capabilities and add configuration management and threat and vulnerability services. This ensures a predictable configuration and set of capabilities that will protect, detect, respond, and help you recover from attacks. The following sections focus on the key capabilities that should be configured to address the security requirements for the mobile world.

Local Administrator Password Management

Like servers, customers create Windows images to be used with deployment tools or manually deploy a computer. As mentioned, each computer created from the image will have a local administrator account configured with the same password across the enterprise.

The configuration of LAPS is the same as the server configuration. You might need to distribute the password extraction tool to the Help Desk. Even though users might want access to this password, we recommend that you don't provide access since that will give access to many users, diluting this solution's benefits. Instead, create a process for users to contact the Help Desk to help with the client device or get the password. Ensure that the help desk sets an expiration date for the password, so once the user finishes their task, the password is reset. To make sure that no changes are made to the Administrators group membership or the User Rights Assignment while the user uses the Administrator account, a GPO should be configured to manage these settings.

Basic Mobility and Security

Basis Mobility and Security, part of the Microsoft 365 plans, allows you to manage mobile devices. It is included in all Office 365 and Microsoft 365 plans except Enterprise Mobility & Security E3/E5 and Microsoft Intune.

Basic Mobility and Security can help you manage devices like iPhones, iPads, Android, and Windows Phones. Basic Mobility and Security enables you to enroll the device, set security policies and access rules, and wipe mobile devices if they're lost or stolen. To enroll the devices, when the user first runs one of the supported Microsoft 365 apps, it will prompt the user to enroll in Basic Mobility and Security. A new mobile device policy will be applied. Depending on how you set up the policy, if the device does not comply, the user might be blocked, or access might be provided, generating an event for policy violation.

Following are a few things to be aware of when using Basic Mobility and Security:

- Basic Mobility and Security for Microsoft 365 Business Standard will overwrite Exchange Active sync mobile device mailbox policies.

- Basic Mobility and Security will not work if using Microsoft Intune. Basic Mobility and Security is a subset of Intune services provided as a benefit to Microsoft 365. Intune provides WiFi profiles, VPN profiles, mobile application management, mobile application protection, managed browser, and zero-touch enrollment (Autopilot).

- The following security settings might block users from accessing Microsoft 365 and corporate data unless the device meets the security compliance requirements: **Require A Password**, **Minimum Password Length**, **Number Of Sign-In Failures Before Device Is Wiped**, **Minutes Of Inactivity Before Device Is Locked**, **Password Expiration**, and **Remember Password History And Prevent Reuse**. Also, other settings that might lock access include **Require Data Encryption On Devices**, **Device Cannot Be JailBroken Or Rooted**, or **Email Profile Is Managed**.

To activate Basic Mobility and Security, go to *https://protection.office.com* and choose **Data Lost Prevention** > **Device Management**.

Threat protection

Microsoft Defender for Endpoint (MDE) provides protection, detection, and response for threats affecting the client. It also can detect endpoints that are not managed, including Linux, IoS, macOS, and IoT devices, and surfaces that information with any known vulnerabilities that might be affecting those devices.

This functionality is part of the Threat Vulnerability Management component of MDE, which provides an exposure score to help understand your entire organization. MDE feeds out the Windows Defender components, such as Credential Guard, System Guard, Exploit Guard, and Application Guard to provide better detections. This includes stopping scripts such as PowerShell, Java, and Python from being executed, USB key usage, lateral movement, credential theft, and process creation behavior.

Also, MDE has collected information from other services like Azure AD Identity Protection and Microsoft Defender for Endpoint, as well as all the internal threat intelligence, and uses AI/ML to generate indicators that enable better protections and detections to be triggered. If suspicious files are detected, they can be uploaded to a sandbox and detonated, inspecting and evaluating the behavior.

And even more importantly, MDE findings are shared with other services to allow them to make further decisions. For example, MDE can share whether it sees some indication of compromise, which, in turn, triggers Azure AD conditional access CAE to revoke the user session. This forces the user to reauthenticate and automation to possibly be triggered to remediate threats affecting the user or their device.

Conditional access

As mentioned in Chapter 3, conditional access is the heart of zero-trust. It is one of the engines that drives many of the session verifications. For devices, you can verify if the device is registered, if it is compliant with the configuration defined by your organization, if it is showing an indication of compromise, and so on. Based on the findings, automated workloads can be triggered to remediate the issues.

Microsoft Intune

In Skill 6-1, we mentioned that MEM is a suite of services that enables client management on-premises and everywhere else the client is at. It brings together Microsoft Intune and Configuration Manager to enable those capabilities. In this section, we focus on Microsoft Intune and how it enables security requirements on mobile devices. When planning the deployment, you first need to determine your objectives:

- **Mobile application management (MAM)** To manage the organization apps and email of mobile devices. This includes deciding which applications you want to be available for your devices and whether they will be deployed as a suite of products or as individual applications. Then, you need to decide which configurations you want to enable, how to enable continuous improvement through updates, and how to retire the application from use. In addition, because the organization's data is the most important thing we must protect, decisions will have to be made about how organizational data will be isolated from personal data and how it will be controlled. For example, depending on the following use cases, you decide what services get enabled:

  - A device is lost, stolen, or no longer being used for organization-related work. Intune can wipe company data and unenroll the device.

  - You can prevent users from copying and taking screenshots and forwarding data by using app-protection policies. The benefits of doing this are that productivity isn't affected, and policies do not apply when the app is used in a personal context. When the app is in work mode, you can require a PIN to open the app, encrypt the work files, block the work files from being backed up to iTunes, iCloud, or Android backup services, require that the files be saved to SharePoint or OneDrive, and the like.

- **Mobile Device Management (MDM)** MDM will help you secure all devices by deploying security capabilities such as threat protection and antivirus, as well as using conditional access and configuring other requirements on the device.

When configuring capabilities to protect mobile devices and the data stored in them, consider enabling the following settings:

- Remove work files if the device is offline for 90 days.

- Encrypt work files.

- Require a PIN to access work files.

- Require the PIN to be reset after five failed attempts.

- Block work files from being backed up in iTunes, iCloud, or Android backup services.

- Require work files to only be saved to OneDrive or SharePoint.

- Prevent protected apps from loading work files on jailbroken or rooted devices.

- Use Office applications and Microsoft Purview Information Protection and Microsoft Purview Data Loss Prevention to monitor and control access to individual files.

Intune can wipe application data by

- Performing a full-device wipe, a selective wipe for MDM, which sets the device to factory-default settings and keeping user data if they choose to retain it
- Performing a retire action, which removes managed data, settings, and email profile and even removes them from Intune.

Another type of wipe is MAM selective wipe, which simply removes company data from the app.

User right assignments

As mentioned earlier in this chapter, one of the problems in ADDS-type environments is the number of accounts that have privileged rights defined across all devices of the ADDS environment. Most of these rights are defined on each device using the Group Policy Management Console (GPMC) under Computer Configuration\Windows Settings\Security Settings\ Local Policies\User Rights Assignment or on the local device using Local Group Policy Editor (gpedit.msc). Although local Windows accounts permissions can be defined using User Right Assignment, these settings tend to be used most on Windows devices that are members of ADDS. Some recommendations for minimizing access include:

By default, the **Allow Log On Locally User Rights Assignment** values are **Administrators**, **Backup Operators**, and **Users**. When analyzing the membership, consider the following:

- Most Windows workstations are not backed up because they are using services like file shares or cloud services like OneDrive, Box, Dropbox, and and so on. Hence, backup operators do not need to be given the **Allow Log On Locally** right assignment.
- The Local Administrators group might have many members. It is recommended that you do the following:
  - Remove all local accounts, besides the default local administrator, from being members of the local Administrators group.
  - Many domain groups and domain accounts might be assigned to this group. Try to configure least-privilege access for these accounts, consider using other monitoring services that can have agents installed by a Configuration Manager service, or use cloud services that do not require accounts. Minimizing the use of service accounts reduces the risk of attackers stealing these account credentials and using them to execute their attacks.
- **Allow Log On Through Remote Desktop Services** rights assignment and the **Remote Desktop Users** group should have no members defined, except in very special cases.
- **Deny Access To A Computer From The Network** should have the following groups defined: Guests; S-1-5-113: NT AUTHORITY\Local account; and S-1-5-114: NT AUTHORITY\Local account.

- **Deny Log-In Through Remote Desktop Services** should have the following groups defined: Domain Users, Guests, S-1-5-113: NT AUTHORITY\Local account, S-1-5-114: NT AUTHORITY\Local account, and Administrators. This prevents local accounts from being used. Again, users should not have any reason to log in remotely on workstations.

Micro-segmentation

There are several micro-segmentation capabilities. Network micro-segmentation is beneficial when you have clients that are not as mobile. With this type of micro-segmentation, you use the endpoint firewall and close all communication to any non-essential IP and ports. This helps make it harder for lateral movement to happen. However, it is still possible for movement to take place since many applications can communicate through the open ports. Hence, as part of your defense-in-depth, you should use an identity workload micro-segmentation. This is where you have rules that allow access only through the open ports if the approved applications/processes are used.

Be aware that this combination of security offerings reduces access and increases the bar of your defense in-depth approach. However, it is not a panacea. This will not stop a supply-chain attack or an attack where one of your on-premises monitoring or configuration management solutions is compromised and used to deliver the malicious payloads. So, you must build a defense-in-depth solution that triggers signals, enabling your threat protection and machine learning models to uncover malicious behavior and have time to protect, detect, and respond.

Governance

Microsoft Purview provides many capabilities to help with your governance requirements. It helps with risk assessments, compliance management, identity governance, information governance, sensitive data discovery, audit and assessment, legal discovery, and so on. Although Microsoft Purview focuses on data governance, securing organizations' applications and data is the major concern and what drives most mobile device security requirements.

When planning to use Microsoft Purview services, you will notice that these services provide a lot of functionality that most companies did not have previously. Hence, to fully take advantage of these, organizations will have to define new roles and responsibilities and devise proper processes to deal with the findings. Also, a proper communication plan must be developed to inform the users about the monitoring capabilities and how they might impact them. Also, you will find that you might have to get your HR, legal, records management, compliance, privacy, audit, unions, and other teams involved in planning the implementations and communication that will be sent to employees. Following are some of the services included as part of Microsoft Purview:

- **Microsoft Purview Audit** Purview Audit helps organizations to have visibility into the activities performed across your Microsoft 365 and effectively respond to security events, forensic investigations, internal investigations, and compliance obligations. Purview Audit (Standard) is turned on by default for organizations with the appropriate licensing. It holds 90-days of logs, while the premium version allows 1-yr audit log with a possible extension to 10-yrs with an add-on license. For both versions, you can search for a wide range of activities that occur within Microsoft 365 services and export to CSV.

- **Microsoft Purview Communication Compliance**   Purview Communication Compliance is an insider risk solution that helps you ensure that users comply with acceptable corporate use and ethical standards when communicating. Policies enable you to scan for communication via email, messages from Teams, Yammer or third-party communications and take action to ensure compliance. It also helps you identify potential legal exposure and risk from unauthorized communications and conflicts of interest regarding confidential projects.

- **Microsoft Purview Compliance Manager**   Purview Compliance Manager helps automatically track multi-cloud compliance by providing-built assessments for more than 350 global standards and regulations, step-by-step guidance on suggested improvements, a compliance score, exporting a report of user history data, and so on. It helps your organization teams understand the criteria required for complying with the specific regulations and work together toward meeting compliance goals using the built-in collaboration platform. For more information, see *http://aka.ms/MPCMMechanics*.

- **Microsoft Purview Customer Lockbox**   Purview Customer Lockbox enables you to control when Microsoft support engineers can access your organization's content and for how long. This is often necessary when troubleshooting an issue with Exchange Online, SharePoint Online, and OneDrive for Business. For the access to take place, the customer must submit a request, the Microsoft engineer requests access, and access request goes through an approval workflow. Once the customer approves, the Microsoft engineer has access for a specific period.

- **Microsoft Purview Data Catalog**   Purview Data Catalog finds data sources and aligns the data into business-related terms and data classification.

- **Microsoft Purview Data Loss Prevention (DLP)**   Purview Data Loss Prevention (DLP) helps define and apply policies to data that match a defined sensitive context and decide if the action the user wants to perform is allowed. For example, a policy might be defined to prevent any documentation containing credit card information from being shared externally. All DLP activity is recorded to the Microsoft 365 Audit Logs and alerts are displayed in the management dashboard.

- **Microsoft Purview Data Map**   Creates a relationship between all the data your organization has based on the metadata of that data.

- **Microsoft Purview Records Management**   Purview Records Management helps you manage regulatory, legal, and business-critical records across your organization. It helps create retention labels to mark content as records, manage your retention requirements with a plan, start different retention periods when a particular event occurs, validate disposition, and the like.

- **Microsoft Purview eDiscovery**   Purview eDiscovery allows you to search and identify electronic information that can be used as evidence in legal cases. It can search for content in Exchange Online, Microsoft Teams, OneDrive for Business, SharePoint Online,

Microsoft 365 Groups, and Yammer. You can mark the information as on hold so even though it gets deleted from the user locations, the system keeps a copy for review. The content can also be exported. The premium version allows you to manage custodians and have better content analysis capabilities.

- **Microsoft Purview Information** Barriers allow you to create policies restricting certain individuals from collaborating or communicating with each other. For example, the trader group should not be talking with the marketing group. Rules that can be set up include searching for a user, adding a member to a team, starting a group chat, inviting someone to join a meeting, sharing a screen, and others.

- **Microsoft Purview Information Protection** Identifies, labels, and encrypts sensitive information on-premises, Microsoft 365, and other cloud services. The label can be automatically assigned or manually assigned from the Microsoft Office Sensitivity icon. It can also be selected from Windows Explorer or from applications that support it like Adobe PDF. When selecting the label, it can apply encryption and allow access to a group of users or the whole organization. These labels can be used with Microsoft Purview DLP and Microsoft Defender for Cloud Apps to reduce the risk of exfiltration.

- **Microsoft Purview Insider Risk Management** Helps investigate and act on inadvertent and malicious activities in your organization. It can interconnect with Microsoft eDiscovery (Premium) to escalate management of cases. It can help identify leaks of sensitive data and data spillage, confidentiality violations, intellectual property theft, fraud, insider trading, and regulatory compliance violations.

- **Microsoft Purview Governance Portal** Is a portal that brings together information from a set of Microsoft Purview services such as Data Map, Data Catalog, Data Estate Insights, and Data Sharing to provide a holistic map of your organization data.

- **Microsoft Purview Compliance Portal** Is a centralized dashboard (see *https:// compliance.microsoft.com*) where information from many other Microsoft Purview services such as Communication Compliance, Insider Risk Management, Data lifecycle management, and Privacy risk management is brought together to provide deep analysis of the organization's compliance. It provides a score card with recommendations to increase compliance and alerts that provide information about the activity happening in your environment.

- **Microsoft Purview Customer Key** Provides control of your organization root encryption keys for your Microsoft 365 data at-rest to help you meet regulatory or compliance obligations. It is not meant to prevent Microsoft personnel from accessing your data when troubleshooting.

Other security controls

To provide defense-in-depth, other security requirements that should not be forgotten include Antivirus, Disk encryption, endpoint firewall, attack surface reduction, OS protections such as Credential Guard, Exploit Guard, and others. Often there is scrutiny about whether Antivirus provides any value in protecting the environment since antivirus cannot detect zero-day attacks or attacks that mutate the code. Security's role is to make life harder for attackers to gain control of the environment. Hence, antivirus still prevents attackers from using cheap signature-based attacks. Therefore, since there is no single silver bullet to properly protect an organization from attacks, the recommendation is still for customers to continue using it.

Skill 6-4: Specify requirements to secure Active Directory Domain Services

Active Directory Domain Services (ADDS) is the on-premises identity solution that Microsoft released back in 1999. Although Microsoft has been providing updates and extra functionality since 1999 as part of the Windows Server releases, the solutions rely on fewer modern protocols and capabilities, which, if not configured and monitored correctly, can open doors to compromise.

Nobody intentionally builds an infrastructure with configurations that expose the environment. However, when organizations have environments originally architected over 20 years ago, the environment they originally planned for is not the same today. Also, the threats they dealt with when they first brought the environment life have changed and become more sophisticated. To deal with these issues, organizations have just added more and more configurations and changes on top of the old configuration creating a lot of complexity which, after a while, exposes misconfigurations. For example, some customers have many thousands of group policies (GPO) linked at many levels of the AD structure. Many of these policies overwrite each other. And the capabilities provided by the platform do not show the resulting configuration for each system when overwrites are performed in the complex way that many customers have configured these policies. Also, many customers have other configuration management solutions that push configuration as well. So, when you have so many competing solutions changing configurations, do you know how everything is really configured? Could it be configured one minute and be different a few minutes later?

Secure the control plane

Many of the security requirements explained in Skill 6-2 apply to domain controllers. Microsoft has released guidance specifically to help secure Active Directory Domain Services (AD DS or AD) and has published under the Securing privileged access documentation at *https://aka.ms/SPA*.

The control plane is one of the most critical systems that need to be secured. These include DCs, certificate servers, federation servers, servers used to sync identities across environments, servers/services that backup, control configuration, and monitor those systems. This is because these systems can perform changes on those servers.

Also, we recommend that you implement the enterprise access model in the production environment to segregate the critical assets, users, and security groups. This separation helps minimize lateral movement and privileged escalation and enables opportunities for the different access checks to generate alerts that help catch suspicious events.

There are three Tiers:

- **Tier 0**   All devices that serve as a control plane to the environment. This includes DCs, certificate servers, federation servers, servers used to sync identities across environments, servers/services that backup and control configuration on those systems, and so on.

- **Tier 1**   Divided into two areas: the administration of the management plane, which configures and monitors the environment, and the administration of the data/workload plane, which includes productivity services like SharePoint, Teams, OneDrive, and the like.

- **User and Application Access**   The ability to move laterally and escalate privileges without being noticed is significantly reduced by creating an OU structure to host each of these resource types and then implementing baselines (as explained in the previous skill), reducing the attack surface, and implementing an identity and access management strategy (as discussed in the Chapter 3).

> **MORE INFO**   For more information about User and Application Access, see *https://aka.ms/eam*.

> **MORE INFO**   To further reduce lateral movement capabilities, review the registry locations for the following User Right Assignments on all endpoints and reduce accounts with that access:
>
> - Deny Access To This Computer From The Network
> - Deny Log On As A Batch Job
> - Deny Log On As A Service
> - Deny Log On Through Remote Desktop Services
> - Access This Computer From The Network
> - Allow Log On Locally
> - Allow Log On Through Remote Desktop Services
> - Log On As A Batch Job
> - Log On As A Service

For example, the domain controller default setting for **Allow Log On Locally** includes Account Operators, Administrators, Backup Operators, Print Operators, and Server Operators. It is a best practice to have the **Print Spooler** service disabled for all DCs.

Therefore, you should also remove **Print Operators** from having access to **Log On Locally** on the DCs. **Print Operators** have other rights for domain controllers, including **Load And Unload Device Drivers** and **Shut Down the System**. Be aware that the spooler service is responsible for removing stale print queue objects from Active Directory, so there is a trade-off between security and the ability to perform print pruning. To address the issue, periodically review and remove stale print queue objects from AD.

Following are some other actions you should perform:

- Move and clean up the membership of the following list of critical security groups and accounts. These groups and accounts have capabilities of modifying critical systems such as the following:
  - Domain controllers within AD DS
  - Enterprise Admins
  - Domain Admins
  - Schema Admin
  - BUILTIN\Administrators
  - Account Operators
  - Backup Operators
  - Print Operators
  - Server Operators
  - Domain controllers
  - Read-only domain controllers
  - Group Policy Creator Owners
  - Cryptographic Operators
  - Distributed COM Users
- Sensitive on-premises Exchange groups (including Exchange Windows Permissions and Exchange Trusted Subsystem)
- Other Delegated Groups
- Custom groups that might be created by your organization to manage directory operations
- Any local administrator for an underlying operating system or cloud service tenant that is hosting the above capabilities, including
  - Members of the local Administrators group
  - Administrators of any management or security tools or applications with agents installed on those systems.

TIP At first, many of these accounts do not seem like they have access to make changes to the domain controllers. For example, you can use GPOs to change DC configuration and provide access to a security group or user. With a backup account, you can build a DC from a backup and read all the account's information offline, and Print Operators can install drivers in any server, which means that malicious payloads can be included within the drivers. Also, monitoring applications can change the systems they monitor.

MORE INFO As discussed in Chapter 3, we recommend that you use a Privileged Access Workstation (PAW) for all privileged users. See *https://aka.ms/paw*.

- You should enforce the use of separate accounts for administration of the environment. Imagine that you use a server administrative account to manage a SQL server used by one of your monitoring applications and somehow that server gets compromised. If you use the same account for cloud administration, the attacker automatically has access to jump and compromise the cloud services.

- Block legacy authentication protocols such as NTLM V1 and TLS V1. Once you completely disable NTLM, perform a full password hash synchronization in Azure AD Connect to remove all the password hashes from the managed domain. Skipping this step will cause NTLM password hashes for a user account not to be removed until the next password change and will allow a user to continue to sign in if they have cached credentials on a system where NTLM was used for authentication.

- Disable Kerberos unconstrained delegation from being used in the environment, as it allows the services/computer to impersonate any user authenticated against it without limitations. It might allow attackers to extract Kerberos keys from the isolated LSA process.

- Enable endpoint firewall micro-segmentation to enforce least-access. For example, most workstations do not need to communicate with other workstations and will only need to communicate with servers. Using the firewall to control communication this way can reduce lateral movement and reduce the chances of an attacker finding an endpoint where a privileged user had logged in.

- Remove custom-created local accounts from all devices. This is important because many on-premises monitoring capabilities do not monitor these accounts. Also, these accounts are harder to manage and secure since they are not managed centrally but on each endpoint where the account is created.

- Utilize passwordless solutions like Windows Hello for Business to remove passwords from being stolen.

- Implement Windows Defender capabilities on all endpoints.

- Implement Defender for Endpoint, which prevents, detects, investigates, and responds to advanced threats in real-time. It uses threat intelligence provided by partners and generated by Microsoft services to uncover threats and risks. It also shares health change information, which might trigger Azure AD to revoke a user session if the session is deemed risky (Conditional access Continuous Access Evaluation).

Privileged Access Management

Microsoft Identity Manager (MIM) has a functionality called Privileged Access Management (PAM) that helps organizations isolate privileged accounts using a Bastion environment. This Bastion environment is a separate AD Forest, normally 2-3 DCs, where the Privilege Users log in and use the MIM server to request time-bound privileges to the main production environment. The benefits of having this separate environment are:

- Hardened security could be enforced via GPOs to all machines in this Bastion forest because no production application, except for MIM, will run in this forest.

- Older configurations from the production environment will not impact this environment.

- The users that login into this Bastion forest do not have privileges within the Bastion forest. They only obtain privileged access upon using MIM PAM to request Just-in-Time privileges to the production environment.

- It is recommended that users also use PAWs and MFA. Combining PAW and MIM PAM makes it difficult for attackers to harvest those users' credentials since they will be logged in from an isolated environment.

- If the customer is re-establishing control over a compromised AD environment, this separation will keep the Bastion environment unaffected by the attack.

- There are some drawbacks which include:

  - It requires an infrastructure that needs to be managed.

  - Some legacy applications might not be able to work as expected when users are logged in from a trusted domain (Bastion Forest) to the trusted domain (Production), which might lead users to use remote desktop services to connect to the servers. Unfortunately, that bypasses the solution and leaves credentials on the server to which the user is connected.

  - There are capabilities for MIM to provide availability, but the synchronization of data can sometimes take a bit of time, impacting end-user operations. In addition, organizations that have users all over the world will need to reach the MIM portal, which might be in another country.

Figure 6-4 shows a highly available configuration of the MIM PAM environment. Smaller environments that might not be too concerned about availability might be able to use this environment with only 1 DC and 1 MIM Server running all the roles. To protect the privileged user (referred to as Priv user in the image), the user logs into the Bastion forest with normal user rights. Then, they access the PAM user interface to request privileged access to the production server. A special object representing the user that logged in from the Bastion forest is given membership in the production's privileged group requested for a predefined amount of time. This object is referred to as a shadow principal. When the time expiration is reached, the user is removed from the group.

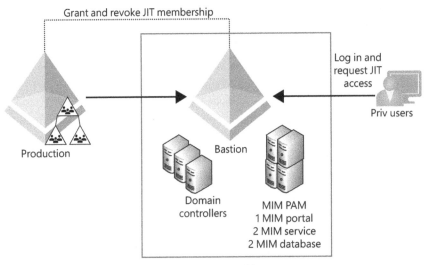

FIGURE 6-4 Privileged Access Management (PAM) architecture

Key recommendations

- Implement the enterprise access model explained in the **Secure The Control Plane** section.
- Apply the Secure Baselines defined in Skill 6-1.
- Enable updates to applications and devices to be installed as soon as possible.
- Enforce MFA for all users.
- Enable only a one-way trust between the Bastion Forest and the Production Active Directory domain.
- Whenever possible, use cloud monitoring and configuration management capabilities. With threat intelligence, cross-service collaboration, and AI and ML capabilities, cloud services can offer much more orchestration, automation, and reporting than on-premises services. Also, cloud services are easier and faster to adopt, require less maintenance, and there is continuous improvement of capabilities happening all the time.

Microsoft Defender for Identity

Microsoft Defender for Identity (MDI) is a cloud security solution that monitors, detects, and helps remediate on-premises Identity-based threats. It monitors DCs and AD FS infrastructure for reconnaissance events such as account enumeration, attributes reconnaissance, network mapping reconnaissance, security group reconnaissance, user and IP address reconnaissance, and so on.

It also checks for compromised credentials activities such as suspicious modification of the sAMNameAccount attribute, honeytoken activity, brute-force attack, Kerberos SPNexposure, Netlogon privileged elevation attempt, Metasploit framework, VPN connections, WannaCry attack, and others. As discussed above, we are

- Limiting the lateral movement, so Defender for Identity alerts us to attempts to perform the lateral movement to exploit Windows Print Spooler.
- Executing remote code over DNS.
- Performing pass-the-hash, passing-the-ticket, or overpassing-the-hash attacks.
- Tampering with NTLM authentication and Rogue Kerberos certificate usage.
- And lastly, it has domain dominance workloads to detect attacks using Golden Ticket, DCShadow, and exfiltration over SMB and DNS.

A few things to know when architecting this solution include:

- Microsoft Defender for Identity (MDI) protects against Active Directory Domain Services (ADDS) type of attacks. It is recommended for all DCs, AD FS, certificates, and other servers to also have Microsoft Defender for Endpoint (MDE) installed since it extends the checks to include server threats.
- MDI does not work for Nano servers.
- Although there are capabilities to protect AD FS, Microsoft recommends replacing the AD FS infrastructure, if possible, to reduce the surface area of attack that might be used to compromise your organization's on-premises environment and be used as a jumping point to the cloud. Azure AD now supports smart card authentication, one of the leading reasons organizations use AD FS.
- When looking at the different attack chains, attackers tend to move from using identity techniques to endpoint techniques and vice versa. By having MDI and MDE together, you can gain more visibility on the tactics and techniques used in an attack and address them holistically. Other services like Defender for Office, Defender for Cloud Apps, and Defender for Cloud extend the visibility of the attack chain, especially when an attacker tries to get a hold of the organization's applications and data. Be aware that when you integrate all the Defender Services, Microsoft brings all the signals from all these products into a centralized user interface named Microsoft 365 Defender. The integration and cross-service collaboration between all these products is the Microsoft XDR experience.
- When integrating all these services, each of them has endpoint requirements that must be met for the services to work properly. Endpoints are a set of IP addresses, DNS domain names, and URLs required for proper communication with Microsoft services. The requirements change depending on the cloud that you are connecting to.

MORE INFO   For more information, see *https://aka.ms/MsEndpoints*.

- MID sensor requires a minimum of 2 cores and 6GB of RAM installed on the server, and time should be synchronized within five minutes. The Sizing Tool can help with this task. The time synchronization is a requirement for Kerberos to work correctly. Also, the MDI sensor is not supported on DCs running Windows 2008 R2 with Broadcom Network Adapter Teaming enabled.

- MDI relies heavily on collecting Windows Event logs to perform the required analysis. The server's auditing level on AD FS needs to be set to Verbose.

- MDI requires a minimum of one domain service account to work. We recommend that the account be a Group Managed Service Account (gMSA) since Active Directory will manage the account automatically. This account needs read permissions for all the domains in the forest. If the service has the option to use multiple domain service accounts, which might be needed for multi-domain architecture, MDI has a process to figure out which domain service account to use.

Active Directory Federation Services (AD FS)

AD FS extends web single sign-on (SSO) functionality across enterprise boundaries to enable customer and partner collaboration when accessing claims-based applications or resources in a partner organization. Organizations tend to use AD FS if there is a sign-in requirement that is not natively supported by Azure AD, including requiring sign-in using on-premises MFA Server or using a third-party authentication, or needing multi-side on-premises authentication. For example, smart card use was one of the reasons many organizations used AD FS. Azure AD recently added support for X.509 certificates on smart cards, so we recommend that you use Azure AD for smart card authentication instead.

 TIP   Detailed design and deployment considerations will not be discussed in this chapter since that should have been covered as part of the SC-300: Microsoft Identity and Access Administrator exam. See *https://docs.microsoft.com/en-us/learn/certifications/exams/sc-300*.

Following are some design considerations that will help secure your ADDS environment:

- Consider upgrading your AD FS environment to Windows Server 2019, if not done already, since it provides many SSO improvements, SAML updates, authentication/policy, and protected login capabilities.

- Remember that this is considered a Tier-0 device. Therefore, all recommendations provided in the "Secure the control plane" section earlier in this chapter should be followed, including the installation of MDI, MDE, audit, and monitoring of local accounts and User Right Assignment registries.

- Reduce administration via agents.

- Reduce monitoring from on-premises monitoring systems.
- Place the AD FS servers in a brand-new top-level OU that does not have other servers, which minimizes delegation issues.
- When configuring GPOs to manage AD FS configuration, those GPOs should be solely used for AD FS. This minimizes extra permissions given to support other applications or devices.
- Logging should be in verbose mode.
- Use Group Managed Service Account (gMSA) for the AD FS Service.
- Remove any unnecessary protocols, Windows features, and applications from these servers to reduce the attack surface.
- The AD FS Servers should be placed on-premises, while the Web Application Proxy (WAP) should be placed in the DMZ, both protected by firewalls in the middle.
- AD FS and WAP should always be current with updates.
- Use Azure AD Connect Health for AD FS, which provides alerts that trigger if an AD FS or WAP is missing updates.
- Monitor the AD FS trust with Azure AD for changes made to the federation configuration. You can do this by Configuring Azure AD audit logs to flow into an Azure Log Analytics Workspace and creating an alert rule that triggers based on the log.
- Consider using a hardware security module (HSM) to protect the keys AD FS uses to sign tokens.
- Require MFS to be used and enable protection to prevent the bypassing Azure AD MFA when federated with Azure AD. This is done by configuring a new security setting named `federatedIdpMfaBehavior` using the `Update-MgDomainFederationConfiguration` PowerShell cmdlet.
- Monitor and block suspicious IP addresses by using the Azure AD Connect Health for AD FS and Risky IP Reports.
- Move toward passwordless.
- Use Attack Simulator to evaluate your AD FS security posture and adjust accordingly.

Skill 6-5: Design a strategy to manage secrets, keys, and certificates

The best way to authenticate services is by using a managed identity. However, there are scenarios you will have to use secrets, access keys, or certificates. When designing a strategy to manage secrets, keys, and certificates, several considerations must be reviewed before looking at a technical approach.

You will need to take into consideration your business requirements, countries where your organization operates, limitations, and exceptions you need to incorporate to meet legal, compliance, supportability, and user requirements. All these are very important since they might change the architecture of your solution. For example, there is a list of countries where the U.S. export of cryptography technology is prohibited. There are many countries that are tougher than the U.S. regarding what they let corporations do with encryption, which just adds to the complexity.

Geographical location is also important because of the backup and restore behaviors of Azure Key Vault. You can only restore to a vault that is part of the same geographical location and subscription where the backup was performed. This means that you will want to ensure that applications and resources that use Azure Key Vault are within the same region as the Vault. Otherwise, there might be country compliance and legal requirements that those resources outside the region might need to comply.

Some services only use Azure Key Vault if they are in the same region as the resources, such as storage accounts, SQL Transparent Data Encryption (TDE), and others. But services like SQL can have replicas in other regions, and you need to ensure that the keys can work accordingly on each of the Key Vaults in other regions.

Another consideration that needs to be considered as part of the strategy for managing secrets, keys, and certificates is the personas needed for managing, using, and reading the different secrets, keys, and certificates. For example, developers might need secrets for an application, server administrators might need certificates for a server they administer, and Certificate administrators might need access to everything. So, there will be different permissions and requirements for data plane operations versus management plane operations, which will require different role assignments.

Azure Key Vault provides centralized secrets, key, and certificate management services. This means that Azure Key vault can securely control access to tokens, passwords, certificates, encryption keys, and so on. It lets you provide TLS/SSL certificates for using Azure and internal connected resources. It helps eliminate having to store credentials in your applications by having the applications authenticate to Key Vault at runtime and retrieve credentials. Because it centrally manages secrets, keys, and certificates, you can monitor usage by enabling logging on to your vaults.

Access control

Azure Key Vault gets automatically associated with the Azure AD tenant of the subscription used to create it. All identities that manage or use the data within Key Vault must be registered within this tenant. To provide access to Azure Key Vault, applications must have a managed identity or a service principal so access can be provided to the service principal. There are two ways to provide access:

- **Key Vault access policy** defines the different operations a security principal, such as a user, application, or user group, can perform on all instances of vault secrets, keys, and certificates. For example, you can assign Joe get, list, set, delete, recover, backup, and restore permissions on keys, which will provide access to those operations for all keys in the vault. Because Key Vault supports up to 1024 access policies, it is recommended that the policies are assigned to groups of users rather than individual users.

- **Azure RBAC** enables centralized management of individual keys, certificates, and secrets' permissions on different scope levels, including management group, subscription, resource group, or individual resources. You can administer main access via role assignments using the Access Control (IAM) blade in the main Key Vault portal or be more granular and use the IAM for each secret, key, or certificate shown in the vault.

Configuration control

Azure Key Vault has configurations that can be enabled within each vault. However, it is recommended that you use Azure Policy to standardize the configuration to ensure that Key Vault is configured exactly as you want and standardized across all Key Vaults.

For example, as shown by Figure 6-5, you can configure settings that are Vault related, such as configuring purge protection enabled, soft delete enabled, firewall enabled, etc. Other settings control the secrets, keys, and certificates, such as

- Keys should have the specified maximum validity.
- Keys should have expiration dates.
- Keys using RSA should have a specified minimum key size.
- Secrets should have a content type set.
- Certificates should have the specified lifetime action triggers.

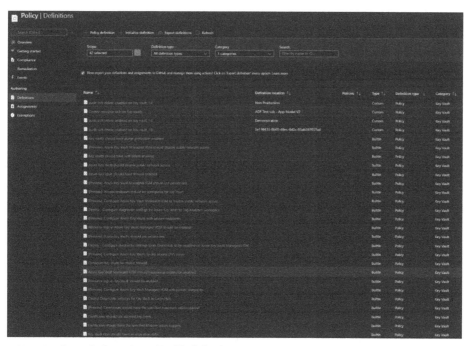

FIGURE 6-5 Azure Policy – Azure Key Vault Settings

Key management

Encryption keys can be either platform-managed (PMK) or customer-managed (CMK). PMKs are managed entirely by Azure, while CMKs can be administered, read, created, deleted, and updated by a user. Keys created by services such as Azure Data Encryption-at-Rest is an example of PMK, while Bring Your Own Key (BYOK) is an example of CMK.

Services such as storage accounts can use a Microsoft Managed Key (MMK) or PMK but can be changed to CMK. The main advantage of PMK or MMK is that the platform does the rotation management, while with the CMK, you are responsible for the rotation of the Key. Azure Policy can be used to remind you about the rotation timelines. Services like Azure Storage, Data Encryption Set, SQL, and others can see that new versions of the keys rotate the keys automatically.

There are different ways to manage these types of keys:

- **Azure Key Vault (Standard Tier)**   Can store software-based secrets, software keys, and certificates. It is FIPS 140-2 Level 1 multi-tenant cloud management service.

- **Azure Key Vault (Premium Tier)**   Can store software-based secrets, keys, and certificates. It can also store Keys in HSM. It is FIPS 140-2 Level 2.

- **Azure Managed HSM**   Only allows you to create Keys. In other words, you cannot create software-based secrets, certificates, or keys. You need a different vault for that. It only works in a single-tenant setting, provides customers with a pool of three HSM partitions, and offers FIPS 140-2 Level 3 validation. Although Microsoft takes care of provisioning, patching, maintenance, and failover, it does not have access to the keys stored in it. It supports Keyless SSL and is integrated with Azure SQL, Azure Storage, and Microsoft Information Protection.

- **Azure Dedicated HSM**   Is a leased appliance where the customer is not sharing hardware with other customers. The customer is responsible for patching and updating firmware since Microsoft has no permission on the device or access to the key material. Provides FIPS 140-2 Level 3.

- **Azure Payments HSM**   Provides FIPS 140-3 Level 3 PCI HSM v3, PCS DSS, and PCI 3DS compliant for payment operations. Microsoft has no access to the data.

Key recommendations

Following are some key recommendations:

- Implement Security baseline for Azure Key Vault using Azure Policy
- Enable Microsoft Defender for Key Vault
- Enable logging for Azure Key Vault
- Enable rotation where possible
- Use a managed identity for applications deployed to Azure. If you are using an Azure service that doesn't support a managed identity or is on-premises, use a service principal with a certificate as an alternative. The only issue is that you will need to store that

certificate (or secret) in an on-premises vault since you cannot store it in Azure Key Vault because it will be needed to authenticate to the Key Vault. (This is a chicken and egg issue.) Don't put this authentication information in code or a configuration file. Another option for on-premises or multi-cloud is to use Azure Arc, which creates a managed identity for the resource.

- Use RBAC to lock down access to your Key Vaults instead of the vault access policy.

- Use a service principal with a secret only for local development and testing.

- Only use Azure Key Vault to store secrets for your application, such as client application secrets, connection strings, passwords, shared access keys, and SSH keys.

- Use a vault for each environment (such as Development, Pre-Production, and Production). The outcome you are trying to achieve is not to share secrets across environments and regions. This helps reduce the blast radius by segmenting in case of a breach. Also, because of performance or compliance requirements, you might have to store the secrets near where the application resides.

- Turn on the firewall and virtual network service endpoints.

- Reduce exposure to your vaults by specifying which IP addresses, service endpoints (such as a subnet), or private endpoints can access the vault. After these firewall rules are in place, users can only access Key Vault from requests originating from allowed virtual networks. This also applies to Azure portal.

- Individual keys, secrets, and certificates permissions should only be used for specific scenarios, such as sharing keys, secrets, and certificates between multiple applications or providing cross-tenant encryption.

- Turn on soft delete and purge protection for each vault.

- When architecting a solution that requires replicas in several regions that use encryption, create the key locally and then ensure that you import the key to every Key Vault used in all the regions that host a replica, such as SQL replicas.

- Make regular backups of your vault, especially when you update, delete, or create objects. Be aware that restores can only be done to a vault in the same geographical location and subscription. Retain backups for as long as you have the data. For example, be aware that certain services might encrypt data with a key; the service might be configured to use a different key, but the data that was already encrypted using the previous key might continue to remain encrypted with the old keys. One example is Microsoft Information Protection Sensitive Labels. So, if you delete those keys, you might lose access to the data encrypted with those old keys.

- You might want a Vault for Microsoft Information Protection Sensitive Labels and configure different policies to ensure that you do not delete keys in this vault, so you always have access to the data encrypted with those keys. You might want to align your encryption keys with your data retention policies since your policies might delete data after a certain amount of time, so losing access to that data might not impact the organization.

- Be aware of the Key Vault limits and plan accordingly.
- Use Key Vault SDK version 4 (.NET, Python, Java, Javascript) Azure Identity in your applications.
- Ensure that the users performing operations in Azure Key Vault use MFA. In addition, ensure that conditional access applies to these users and that they require PIM for enabling role assignments.
- Use Dedicated HSM when performing legacy lift-and-shift using PKI, SSL Offloading, and Keyless TLS (supported integrations include F5, Nginx, Apache, Palo Alto, IBM GW, and more), OpenSSL applications, Oracle TDE, and Azure SQL TDE IaaS.
- Plan for key rotation for your services. Some Microsoft cloud services (such as Azure Storage and SQL) automatically detect new versions and use those new versions. However, other services and applications might need to be manually rotated. When you first assign the key to the service, one way to know whether a key needs to be rotated manually. When you assign it, if it does not ask which version of the key needs to be used, the service, in general, will auto-detect and rotate.

Skill 6-6: Design a strategy for secure remote access

New guidance is released frequently, recommending that organizations progressively de-emphasize network-level authentication and safely make applications Internet-accessible— without relying on a virtual private network (VPN).

Gartner's SASE, NIST, and many other services recommend using identity-based Internet workloads to secure remote access because it enables constant capabilities, regardless of where the user or endpoint is located. Also, it automatically mitigates legacy risks. For example, the number of accounts providing access across many devices is reduced. This, in turn, mitigates lateral movement. The following sessions will focus on other approaches that can help your organization start aligning with the different remote access requirements.

Key configurations to enable secure remote access

There is a misconception that single sign-on (SSO) is a security weakness, when, in fact, it strengthens it. When the applications and services support one identity, your monitoring services can see and analyze end-to-end the behaviors of the identity. Risk-based authentication can be used to verify if the identity is authenticating from an unusual IP, if it has had multiple failures across the infrastructure, if the password seems to have been compromised, and others. Also, users do not have to remember multiple passwords and store them in a location where they can be accessible for others to reach. Hence it is recommended to interconnect and authenticate as many services as possible using SSO.

Using Cloud Authentication makes it easier to use SSO since it is reachable to many applications. Microsoft has made it easy to integrate by providing connectors for many applications. Visit the Azure Marketplace at *https://azuremarketplace.microsoft.com/* to get a list of applications that already have pre-built connectors. Besides enabling SSO, Cloud Authentication enables you to use other security services like Microsoft Entra Azure AD Identity Protection which, as mentioned in Chapter 3, allows you to use insights for risky users and risky sign-ins and past historical signals to uncover risks. If any concern is found, steps are necessary to ensure the requested authentication is authentic.

MFA is one of the capabilities that can be used to verify authenticity. A password-less approach like Windows Hello for Business or using Microsoft Authenticator with number match, as shown in Figure 6-6, which prompts you to enter the number shown on the authenticator app and then asks you to enter a PIN or biometric as a second factor. This helps prevent token theft, phishing, or brute-force attacks.

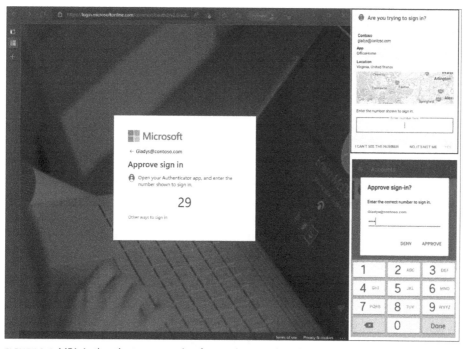

FIGURE 6-6 MFA Authenticator prompting for number match and pin

Risk-based sign-in might trigger a password prompt action if signs of leaked credentials are found. Of course, this only happens if the user can perform MFA authentication first. For this capability to be available, you must have configured Azure AD Self-Service Password Reset (SSPR) and enabled a user risk policy for password change. Enabling the risk policy is done under **Azure AD Identity Protection > User risk policy > All Users > Assignments**. Under **Conditions**, select a risk level; under **Access**, select the desired control. For SSPR, all the steps are performed under **Azure AD > Password Reset Section**.

MORE INFO   For step-by-step instructions, see the video at *https://aka.ms/configureSSPR*.

The heart of making those verifications and triggering the actions is conditional access. This is a must-have for enabling secure remote access. Not only for enabling user verifications but also for enabling verification for the device being used by the user. For example, you might require Intune enrollment to proactively manage updates and compliance with your device's configuration and then use conditional access to check the compliance of that configuration as part of the authorization process. If using Microsoft Endpoint Manager (MEM) Configuration Manager, you can extend those checks to on-premises devices.

The following functionalities should be implemented to provide the proper verifications at authentication and authorization time:

- SSO
- Cloud Authentication
- MFA
- Azure AD Identity Protection risk-based policies
- SSPR
- Conditional access
- MEM/Intune enrollment

The next sections discuss securing access for specific services.

Remote access to desktop, applications, and data

As customers continue to modernize their environments, they still want to reach any applications that haven't yet been migrated to a modern solution. How do you make that happen while reducing the risk brought by interconnecting to those legacy workflows?

At first, administrators might think about implementing Remote Desktop Protocol (RDP)/ Secure Shell (SSH) to virtual machines. However, attackers continue to target RDP/SSH, and any vulnerabilities in the OS and/or application running on those systems make the decision very risky. Instead, you should aim to use the zero-trust principles and ensure proper authentication, verifications, and authorizations before getting access to the resources.

Azure Virtual Desktop uses many built-in security capabilities before providing access to the virtual environment. Unlike RDP and SSH, when the user tries to access the Virtual Desktop, they get redirected to Azure AD to start all the authentication and verification process. Once all the checks are performed, the user gets redirected back to the Virtual Desktop. By using Azure Virtual Desktop, you can use:

- Cloud authentication then allows you to use Azure AD Identity Protection risky sign-ins and risky-users workloads.
- MFA and conditional access to reduce the risk of lost or stolen credentials.
- Reverse Connect, which instead of using a TCP listener to receive incoming RDP connections on the specified IP and port, it utilizes outbound connectivity to the Azure Virtual Desktop infrastructure over HTTPS.

Figure 6-7 shows how the Azure Virtual Desktop connection works. The following steps show the sequence for the client connection:

1. The user selects the resource to connect and tries to establish a secure TLS 1.2 connection with the closest Azure Virtual Desktop gateway instance.

2. The user gets redirected to Authenticate to Azure AD.

3. User requests authentication.

4. Azure AD triggers conditional access, where you might enforce MFA, compliance checks, and so on.

5. When verifications are completed, the findings are sent to Azure AD.

6. Azure AD then either authorizes or denies the connection. If the connection is authorized, the user receives the session token.

7. The token is presented to the Gateway, which validates the token and asks the Azure Virtual desktop broker to orchestrate the connection.

8. The broker identifies the host and initializes a connection between the host and the previously established Gateway connection.

9. The host RD stack initializes a TLS 1.2 session with the gateway, and the gateway starts relaying raw data between the endpoint, causing the Reverse Connect to be established for the RDP.

10. The client starts the RDP connection.

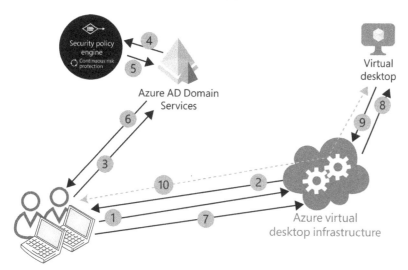

FIGURE 6-7 Virtual Desktop

Figure 6-7 shows that many checks happen before the client touches the virtual desktop. Although quite a lot of security is enabled, we still recommend that you collect audit logs to view user and admin activity related to Azure Virtual desktop, including Azure Activity logs, Azure AD Activity logs, Session hosts, and Key Vault logs.

In addition, you should

- Install an endpoint detection and response (EDR) solution like MDE and a Vulnerability Management solution like MDE Plan 2.

- Make sure that you enable policies to control maximum inactive time and disconnection.

- Lock the screen for idle sessions.

- Redirect drives, printers, and USB to the user's local devices.

- Hide local and remove drive mappings.

Azure Virtual Desktop also supports Trusted Launch, which, as with Gen2 VMs, allows you to take advantage of Windows built-in protections for rootkits, boot kits, and kernel-level malware, such as Secure Boot, vTPM, virtualization-based security, Credential Guard, and others.

Remote access to on-premises web applications

As mentioned in Chapter 3, Azure AD Application Proxy enables secure access to on-premises web applications. This configuration reduces the complexity of managing the applications. It makes it easier for users to find all the applications they have access to since they can see them as part of the Application Portal; see *https://myapps.microsoft.com*. Figure 6-8 illustrates how the Azure AD Application Proxy works.

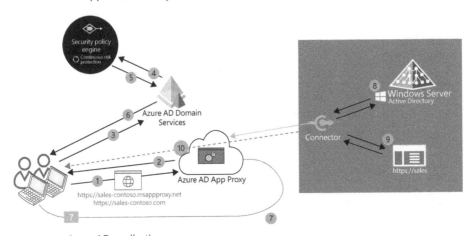

FIGURE 6-8 Azure AD application proxy

Figure 6-8 illustrates the process of connecting an application published via an external URL or through the Application Dashboard:

1. The user tries to gain access.

2. The user is redirected to authenticate to Azure AD.

3. The user tries authenticating.

4. Conditional access verifications are performed

5. The results of the verifications are returned.

6. If the conditional access verifications are acceptable (defined by the conditional access policy), Azure AD provides a session token to the user.

7. Azure AD Application Proxy service gets the token, and after evaluating it, a connection is established through the Azure AD App Proxy connector.

8. The connector goes to AD to exchange the token for Kerberos tickets.

9. With the ticket, the connector goes to the application and authenticates as the user.

10. The content passes back through the connector and the app proxy service to the user and now the user can work with the application.

Azure AD Application Proxy enables your organization to use Identity-based workload micro-segmentation and reduces the need for relying on VPN connections. This, in turn, increases the security of your on-premises servers and clients since not having those VPN network connections mitigates possible lateral movement that might have otherwise been introduced by those connections.

RDP/SSH connectivity

Another way to secure remote connectivity is using Azure Bastion to provide secure and seamless RDP/SSH connectivity to your Azure virtual machines by using the Azure portal over TLS rather than configuring a public IP and port and exposing it to the Internet.

We recommend that you don't configure public IPs just to enable an RDP/SSH connection. Instead, make sure that RDP/SSH is not allowed in the Network Security Group (NSG) configuration and that you use Azure Bastion instead. Figure 6-9 shows how the connection works using Azure Bastion.

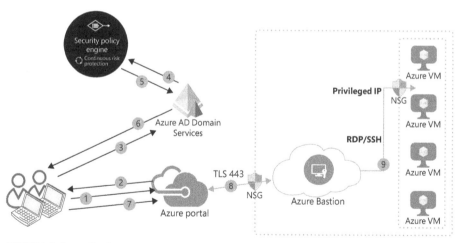

FIGURE 6-9 Azure Bastion

Follow these steps to gain RDP/SSH access to a VM:

1. Connect to the Azure portal.

2. The user is redirected to authenticate to Azure AD.

3. The user tries authenticating.

4. Conditional access verifications are performed.

5. Results of the verifications are returned.

6. Azure AD provides a session token to the user.

7. The user provides the session token to Azure Bastion.

8. Token gets redirected to the Azure Bastion.

9. Azure Bastion sets the connection with the proper VM using the defined Private IP.

Remotely provisioning new devices

Many customers tend to use DVDs or USB devices to provide remote provisioning of images to different devices. However, images delivered that way tend to get stagnant. Also, these images are difficult to manage as applications, drivers, and security settings get implemented directly into the OS, making changes difficult to track and perform.

With Intune Autopilot self-deployment, your IT team doesn't need to touch the device, so the configuration can be done from anywhere. It just selects the OS, applications, and configurations. Then the users just turn on the device, connect it to the network, and wait for the configuration to be deployed remotely. Because everything is automated, your devices will be fully updated, configured, secured, and compliant before any employee begins using them. Some configurations that can be enabled include Bitlocker, Credential Guard, Defender for Endpoint, and many others discussed in Skill 6-1. This process can be used for more than deploying new devices. It can also easily reset, repurpose, and recover devices.

B2B collaboration

In the past, to collaborate with partners, either new accounts had to be created for the partner users or a trust relationship had to be set up with the organization's on-premises Active Directory, which opens the environment for wide access unless explicitly denied.

As described in Chapter 3, B2B Collaboration enables partners to use their own credentials to access your company's resources. The comprehensive settings let you control your inbound and outbound collaboration. You can use conditional access to enforce the use of MFA and other security requirements and Azure AD entitlement management to manage access. Because the accounts show external identities and there are many Governance services to manage external access, it is much easier to control access across the environment than before.

Key recommendations

As you can see, there is a pattern where cloud services are used to perform the proper authentication, verification, and session before the resource connection is established. Using Azure AD in combination with SSO, MFA, conditional access, and Azure AD Identity Protection will provide the most verifications and machine learning analytics to reduce user risk. By enabling Microsoft Defender for Endpoint, you can use Conditional Access Continuous Access

Evaluation, discussed in Chapter 3, to flag when an indication of compromise is seen in an endpoint and trigger a need for re-evaluation of the session.

The benefits are that there is no public exposure of the resource, and the user and device are authenticated and verified before even attempting to provide resource access. Also, because the resource is not publicly exposed, it limits exposure to threats such as port scanning, DDoS, and other malware-related attacks.

Thought experiment

In this thought experiment, demonstrate your skills and knowledge of the topics covered in this chapter. You can find answers to this thought experiment in the next section.

You are one of the Azure administrators for Tailwind Traders, an online general store specializing in various home and office products. Tailwind Traders' employees are now working at least 60 percent of their time from home. Although Tailwind Traders has been migrating its applications to the cloud, many applications are still on-premises. The company has VPN capabilities, but the hardware is not keeping up with the demands.

Tailwind Traders has purchased Microsoft 365 E5 and wants to provide the most secure remote configuration for new desktops and protect existing applications and data. The company wants to modernize applications and slowly reduce access without interfering with current on-premises operations. Tailwind Traders also has some partners they collaborate with and want to remove the federation services that use and enable collaborations using Teams and SharePoint Site. Some of their sellers carry small mobile devices that cannot run some of the applications they need. Also, they handle customer contracts that contain sensitive information that needs to be protected. Because of the amount of customer information that is being handled in the field, there are concerns about how this information is being used and shared. How would you architect the solution to address the organization's concerns?

Thought experiment answers

This section contains the solution to the thought experiment. Each answer explains why the answer choice is correct.

- Based on this scenario, you will need to enable Defender for Endpoint and Microsoft Endpoint Management to provide threat and vulnerability protection and manage the compliance and vulnerability requirements.
- Configure baselines using Intune and Microsoft Endpoint Protection.
- For on-premises endpoints, enable LAPS.
- Configure on-premises client and server firewalls to limit incoming and outgoing traffic.
- Disable any legacy on-premises protocols.
- Configure SSO by registering applications into Azure AD.

- Enable conditional access.

- Enable Identity Protection User Risk and Sign-in risk to uncover account risk and require an additional Factor for Authentication when using conditional access.

- Use Continuous access evaluation with Microsoft Endpoint Protection to make sure that the user session is re-evaluated when risk changes are detected.

- Use Identity workloads micro-segmentation capabilities provided by Azure AD Application Proxy to enable connectivity of on-premises web applications that cannot yet be migrated into a cloud solution. This will reduce dependency on VPN and reduce lateral movement risks.

- Enforce password-less phone sign-in using Authenticator with number match and pin to reduce the risk of phishing and password attacks.

- Because some non-web on-premises applications will take some time to upgrade to the cloud, use a VPN solution that can interact with Azure AD conditional access, such as Aruba Clearpass or any of the other Microsoft Intelligent Security Association (MISA) partners that can interconnect with Microsoft offerings.

- Use B2B to collaborate with partners and use Azure AD Entitlement Management to assign permissions.

- Configure Azure Virtual Desktops for personnel in the field to connect to and run applications from it. This will minimize the data exfiltration concerns since the data will always be in the Virtual Desktops instead of the mobile device.

- To address data concerns, implement Azure Purview capabilities such as DLP and Information Protection to ensure that sensitive information is protected. Also, use Azure Purview to analyze usage and perform audits of how the information is being used. Use Defender for Cloud Apps to monitor and manage cloud applications and their data.

Chapter summary

This chapter provides recommendations to strengthen your server and client endpoints security strategy. For the most part, it is assumed that you understand the basics of Microsoft and Azure Security.

> **MORE INFO** For more information, see the AZ-500 Microsoft Azure Security Technologies Learning paths provided at *https://aka.ms/AZ500* and the Microsoft 365 Security Administration Learning path at *http://aka.ms/ms500*.

Below are some key recommendations provided in each skill:

- Consider using MEM for endpoint management, including on-premises.
- Use MDE to uncover endpoint vulnerabilities and discover any IoT Devices in the environment.
- Use Defender for Cloud to manage your on-premises and multi-cloud Server workloads.
- Implement Microsoft-defined baselines for all your endpoints and put special effort into enabling the Windows Defender capabilities in Windows 10 and 11, including Credential Guard, System Guard, Exploit Guard, Application Guard, and so on.
- Consider using Azure Benchmarks to ensure that your servers have the best-practiced and defined security configuration.
- Azure Purview Sensitive Labels enables you to label and encrypt your files. This encryption will follow the file no matter where it is stored.
- Implement identity-based workload segmentation when possible. However, there might be situations where network-based security configurations might be needed.
- If using Azure ADF, consider removing it and using Azure AD capabilities instead.
- Try to use capabilities such as Azure Bastion and Azure Application Proxy to reduce the number of exposed RDP/SSH connections to the Internet.
- To enable full visibility for both Microsoft and third-party resources, use Azure Arc and Azure Sentinel.

CHAPTER 7

Design a strategy for securing SaaS, PaaS, and IaaS services

When designing a cybersecurity architecture solution for cloud services, you need to consider the different cloud computing service models. Each service model will present different requirements to ensure that workloads that use those models are properly secure. To increase the security hygiene of the workloads deployed in the different service models, it is important to use a common set of security configurations tailored for the specific service you are planning to deploy, and that's where you will leverage security baselines.

To design a strategy to secure Software as a Service (SaaS), Platform as a Service (PaaS), and Infrastructure as a Service (IaaS) service models in Azure, you will need to understand the different security requirements for Azure workloads and address them as part of your adoption plan.

Skills covered in this chapter:

- Skill 7-1: Specify security baselines for SaaS, PaaS, and IaaS services
- Skill 7-2: Specify security requirements for IoT workloads
- Skill 7-3: Specify security requirements for data workloads, including SQL, Azure SQL Database, Azure Synapse, and Azure Cosmos DB
- Skill 7-4: Specify security requirements for web workloads, including Azure App Service
- Skill 7-5: Specify security requirements for storage workloads, including Azure Storage
- Skill 7-6: Specify security requirements for containers
- Skill 7-7: Specify security requirements for container orchestration

Skill 7-1: Specify security baselines for SaaS, PaaS, and IaaS services

In modern organizations, the security threat landscape is constantly evolving, and security professionals must keep up with security threats and make required changes to security settings to help mitigate these threats. To improve your workload's security posture, you need to implement security baselines created according to the service model and constraints of the service. This section covers the skills necessary to specify security baselines for SaaS, PaaS, and IaaS services according to the Exam SC-100 outline.

Specify security baselines for SaaS services

With SaaS solutions, the security options you can control are only a subset of the entire stack, which is usually targeted to the application level only. In a Public Cloud scenario, this requires a high degree of trust in the cloud provider because they have complete control of the infrastructure and platform layers.

Although the cloud provider has its responsibilities, the hardening of the application is part of your (customer) responsibility when it comes to SaaS. Using security baselines can help mitigate threats, enable faster and more secure deployments of workloads, and make it easier to manage SaaS applications.

In an Azure infrastructure using IaaS and PaaS service models, you can utilize Microsoft Defender for Cloud Secure Score to assist you in improving the Azure workloads' security posture. For a SaaS environment (in this case, Microsoft 365), you can utilize the Microsoft Secure Score available in Microsoft 365 to help you with the security posture of your applications. Microsoft Secure Score can help organizations to assess their current security state and improve their security posture by providing discoverability, visibility, guidance, and control. Microsoft Secure Score provides security recommendations for the following products:

- Microsoft 365 (including Exchange Online)
- Azure Active Directory
- Microsoft Defender for Endpoint
- Microsoft Defender for Identity
- Defender for Cloud Apps
- Microsoft Teams

To continuously drive the improvement of your Microsoft Secure Score, you need to ensure that remediations to recommendations are implemented and that security best practices are applied across all SaaS applications. Cloud Policy service for Microsoft 365 enables you to enforce policy settings for Microsoft 365 Apps for enterprise on a user's device, even if the device isn't domain joined or otherwise managed. When creating policy configurations, you can review and apply policies recommended by Microsoft as security baseline policies. These recommendations are marked as *Security Baseline* when selecting policies.

 EXAM TIP When analyzing a case study on the SC-100 exam, ensure that you pay close attention to the requirements. In a scenario where you need to configure security baselines for devices running Windows, macOS, iOS, and Android, you should use Cloud Policy service for Microsoft 365.

Skill 7-2: Specify security requirements for IoT workloads

When designing a cloud solution that includes IoT workloads, it is imperative to understand the potential threats to these workloads and ensure that you use the defense-in-depth approach as part of your design and architect it. By ensuring that security is part of the design phase, you create mitigations for potential attack scenarios. These mitigations are usually identified in the designing phase when you use threat modeling, which provides you with the greatest flexibility to make changes to eliminate threats.

Security requirements

An important consideration when analyzing an IoT scenario is the type of adoption device that needs to be monitored: greenfield or brownfield.

- **Greenfield devices**   Can be managed and configured using agents
- **Brownfield devices**   Legacy IoT devices that cannot be managed with agents and cannot directly communicate with external networks, such as a cloud environment

For example, these could be shopfloor devices, such as manufacturing robots that run an operating system as old as Windows NT 4.0 and aren't connectable to IT networks for a variety of other reasons. However, to communicate with each other, brownfield devices are usually connected using network switches that do not have external access. Defender for IoT can monitor their communication by connecting with a Defender for IoT sensor, which can be a hardware appliance or a server, such as a virtual machine, to the network switch's SPAN port (Switch Port Analyzer) or a TAP (Test Access Point). Once connected, the Defender for IoT sensor will immediately start analyzing network traffic using passive monitoring on IoT devices.

Another important consideration when designing IoT solutions is incorporating Zero Trust principles. This includes explicitly verifying users, having visibility into the devices they're bringing onto the network, and making dynamic access decisions using real-time risk detections. Security requirements for IoT workloads must be aligned with key security principles that inform a strong security posture, which, in this case, includes:

- **Enforce strong identity**   Make sure to register IoT devices, have an infrastructure that enables you to issue renewable credentials, and employ strong authentication (including MFA) for personnel.
- **Apply least-privilege access**   To reduce the likelihood that IoT devices can be compromised, make sure to implement device and workload access control based on least-privilege access.
- **Ensure device health**   By flagging unhealthy devices and applying remediations to bring them into a state of compliance, you are reducing the risk of compromise.
- **Continuous update**   Make sure to have a centralized configuration and compliance management solution that can use an update mechanism to ensure devices are up-to-date and healthy.

- **Security monitoring and response** Proactive and reactive monitoring is a pivotal part of the continuous monitoring strategy for IoT devices. This is a critical step in identifying unauthorized or compromised devices.

How IoT workloads are distributed in the network is another important security aspect that needs to be considered. You should design your IoT architecture into several components/zones. Zones are used to segment IoT workloads by allowing each zone to have its own data and authentication and authorization requirements. Also, zones allow you to isolate damages and restrict the impact of low-trust zones on higher-trust zones. While the number of zones can vary according to the organization's needs and requirements, you will typically have two major zones: device/field gateway and cloud gateway/services.

- **Device/field gateway zone** You will use the device/field gateway zone to establish the immediate physical space around the device and gateway where physical access and/or peer-to-peer digital access is feasible. This zone type is used in scenarios involving industrial organizations leveraging the Purdue model. This method ensures their process-control networks are protected from the network perspective's limited bandwidth and the ability to offer real-time deterministic behavior.

- **Cloud gateway/services zone** Cloud gateway/services zones are used for any software component or module running in the cloud in scenarios that need to interact with devices and/or gateways for data collection, analysis, or command-and-control.

> **NOTE** The Purdue model is included in the ISA 95 standard. For more information, see *https://www.isa.org/store?query=isa95*.

Security posture and threat detection

As part of the security requirements for IoT workloads, you need to adopt a solution that can continuously monitor the network traffic using behavioral analytics tailored to IoT scenarios to help identify unauthorized or compromised IoT devices. Microsoft Defender for IoT is an agentless solution that can be used to accomplish that goal and provide asset inventory, identify potential vulnerabilities on IoT devices, and risk-based mitigation recommendations.

Defender for IoT aims to enable you to see the security state of your IoT solution with end-to-end analysis and management of security posture. Defender for IoT provides actionable recommendations to reduce the attack surface, and it provides real-time threat detection. Defender for IoT unifies security posture and threat detection across an entire IoT solution, from low-resource leaf devices, field gateways, and all the way to the service side of cloud gateways and applications. It delivers unified visibility and control, adaptive threat prevention, and intelligent threat detection and response across IoT workloads that run on Edge, on-premises, Azure, and other clouds.

Defender for IoT can leverage patented, IoT-aware Layer-7 Deep Packet Inspection (DPI) and behavioral analytics that allow you to immediately detect advanced IoT threats based on activities instead of relying on signature-based solutions. Within this context, Defender for IoT covers two different scenarios:

- **Cloud-connected deployment**   The Defender for IoT sensor (VM or appliance) is connected to the network switch or Test Access Point (TAP) and Azure Portal for cloud management and integration with Microsoft Sentinel. For local-site management, there is an on-premises management console.

- **Air-gapped deployment (offline)**   There is no connection between the Defender for IoT sensor and Azure. Air-gapped deployments only use an on-premises Defender for IoT sensor device and a local management console.

Air-gapped deployments are possible because data collection, processing, analysis, and alerting take place on the sensor itself without having to send metadata to Azure. This is a huge deal, making Defender for IoT suitable for any scenario in which you are facing low bandwidth or high latency connectivity, pre-historic operating systems on devices, high-secure environments, and others.

 EXAM TIP   On the SC-100 exam, you might have scenarios involving IoT devices. Pay close attention to the requirements and always recommend Defender for IoT if the requirement is security posture and threat detection from a single solution.

Skill 7-3: Specify security requirements for data workloads, including SQL, Azure SQL Database, Azure Synapse, and Azure Cosmos DB

Data workloads will have different security requirements according to the type of data that resides on the workload. Some data workloads may be more critical than others and require more protections. While database technology on its own offers many built-in security features, when it comes to security requirements for data workloads, it is important to consider the different layers of protection for the data, as shown in Figure 7-1.

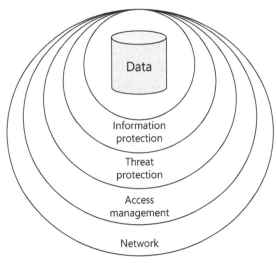

FIGURE 7-1 Multiple layers of protection for the data

When you think about a defense-in-depth approach for data workloads, you should always ensure that the security requirements include these four layers of defense. The list below includes examples of security recommendations for each layer:

Network

- Use IP firewall rules to grant access to databases based on the originating IP address of each request
- Use virtual network firewall rules only to accept communications that are sent from selected subnets inside a virtual network
- Minimize the attack surface by enforcing connection to the database using a private endpoint

Access management

- Make sure to always authenticate the user when trying to connect to the database. For Azure SQL Database or Azure SQL Managed Instance, you can use SQL Authentication
- When available, leverage directory service to authenticate the user. Azure Active Directory authentication is a mechanism of connecting to Azure SQL Database, Azure SQL Managed Instance, and Azure Synapse Analytics by using identities in Azure Active Directory (Azure AD)
- Enable Multi-Factor Authentication (MFA) in Azure AD and use Azure AD Interactive authentication mode for Azure SQL Database and Azure SQL Managed Instance
- Enforce authorization by assigning permissions to a user within a database. You can leverage the different database roles available to facilitate the authorization management process
- Use SQL authentication for legacy applications

- In SQL Databases use granular permissions and user-defined database roles
- When deeper control in the database row level is required, you can utilize row-Level security to enable you to use group membership or execution context to control access to rows in a database table
- Make sure to monitor who accesses sensitive data and capture queries on sensitive data by ensuring that database logging and auditing are enabled

Threat protection

- Use cloud workload protection capabilities available in Defender for SQL to detect unusual behavior and potentially harmful attempts to access or exploit databases.

Information protection

- Use Transport Layer Security (TLS) to encrypt data in transit.
- Use Transparent Data Encryption (TDE) to encrypt data at rest.
- Use the **Always Encrypted** option in SQL in conjunction with TDE and TLS for comprehensive data protection at rest, in transit, and in use.
- Use column-based encryption to encrypt a column of data by leveraging symmetric encryption in SQL Server using Transact-SQL.
- Use dynamic data masking to limit sensitive data exposure by masking it for non-privileged users.
- Remember that the **Always Encrypted** option does not work with Dynamic Data Masking. In other words, it is not possible to encrypt and mask the same column. Suppose these two options are stated in the same question in the SC-100 exam. In that case, you need to review the design and technical requirements to understand which one you need to prioritize, data in use vs. masking the data for your app users via Dynamic Data Masking.

> **IMPORTANT** Dynamic data masking automatically discovers potentially sensitive data in Azure SQL Database and SQL Managed Instance and provides actionable recommendations to mask these fields.

In addition to the security considerations mentioned previously, you must implement security management to manage your database's security posture. While Defender for Cloud includes security recommendations to improve the database's security posture, when you enable Defender for SQL, you also get SQL Vulnerability Assessment (VA). SQL VA scans your database and gives you a comprehensive list of items that need to be addressed. SQL VA employs a knowledge base of rules that flag security vulnerabilities. It brings awareness of deviations from security best practices, such as misconfigurations, excessive permissions, and unprotected sensitive data. Figure 7-2 has an example of the type of recommendation generated by SQL VA.

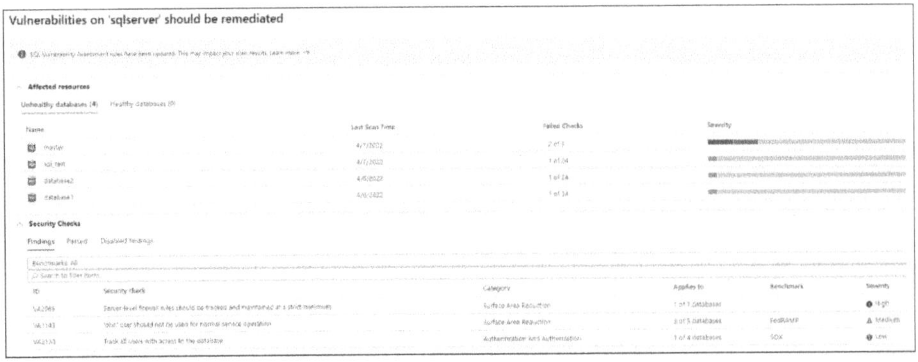

FIGURE 7-2 List of affected databases

Security considerations for Azure Cosmos DB

Azure Cosmos DB is a fully managed NoSQL database for modern, fast, and flexible app development, capable of having single-digit millisecond response times, automatic and instant scalability, and multiple SDKs and APIs to support a variety of non-relational data models.

While many of the security recommendations previously stated also apply to Azure Cosmos DB, there are a few differences. For example, data stored in your Azure Cosmos account is automatically and seamlessly encrypted with keys managed by Microsoft using service-managed keys. When it comes to authorization, Azure Cosmos DB uses hash-based message authentication code (HMAC).

When analyzing a question in the SC-100 that requires the database workload to have automatic backups, you can leverage this native capability in Azure Cosmos DB. Automated online backups can be used to recover data you may have accidentally deleted up to 30 days after the deletion.

When it comes to threat protection, you can enable Defender for Azure Cosmos DB to monitor your Azure Cosmos DB accounts. It also detects various attack vectors, such as attacks originating from the application layer, SQL injections, suspicious access patterns, compromised identities, malicious insiders, and direct attacks on the database.

Continuous monitoring is also an important aspect of security hygiene, and Azure Cosmos DB can monitor different scenarios using different experiences, as shown in Table 7-1.

TABLE 7-1 Monitoring scenarios

Scenario	Monitoring location	Other options available
Monitor the throughput	Azure Cosmos DB Portal	Availability, storage, latency, consistency, and system
Monitor request rate	Azure Monitor metrics	Request charges, control plane metrics, and other metrics
Changes in the Cosmos account	Azure Monitor logs	Cosmos activities visible in Activity Logs, overall diagnostics logs, and query logs

Skill 7-4: Specify security requirements for web workloads, including Azure App Service

When considering the security requirements for web workloads, you need to include Azure App Service. Azure App Service is an HTTP-based service that hosts web applications, REST APIs, and mobile backends. Azure App Services includes the following components that are hardened by default:

- Virtual machine
- Storage
- Network
- Web framework
- Management
- Integrated features

Microsoft performs ongoing compliance checks in Azure App Service to ensure that these components stay secure and up to date. However, since Azure App Service is a PaaS service, the shared responsibility model is applicable, which means the customer also needs to ensure that the components controlled by the customer (mostly the configuration) are also secure. One example is using insecure protocols, such as HTTP, to access the web application.

Network communication

All Azure App Service tiers run your apps on the shared network infrastructure in App Service, except the isolated pricing tier. The advantage of using the isolated pricing tier is that you have complete network isolation achieved by running your apps inside a dedicated App Service environment. Also, you can also use network security groups (NSG) to restrict network access by controlling the number of exposed endpoints.

Network communication also includes access to your apps. By default, when you create an app under Azure App Service, a domain name with the following structure is created: `<app_name>.azurewebsites.net`, and it is accessible via HTTPS. If you need to customize the domain, you must ensure that you secure it with a TLS/SSL certificate to enable client browsers to make HTTPS connections. While by default, the app you create under Azure App Service will accept requests coming from all Internet IP addresses, you can create restrictions if there is a technical or strategic requirement for that. You can create an *allow list* (by individual IP or range) to define the IP addresses permitted to access your app.

In addition to that, you should also ensure that the following security best practices are applied:

- Always redirect HTTP requests to HTTPS.
- When communicating with other Azure resources, such as Azure SQL, ensure that the communication is encrypted.

- Always use the latest version of TLS unless there is a technical justification (legacy application would be an example) not to use the latest version.

- If file transfer is required and you need to use legacy protocols such as FTP, always prioritize the use of FTPS instead of FTP.

- Avoid storing application secrets, such as database credentials or private keys, in your code or configuration files.

Authentication and authorization

Another option to improve security is to leverage one of the principles of Zero Trust (verify explicitly) to enable authentication and authorization of users or client apps. While you can implement your own authentication and authorization solution, you can also leverage App Service native authentication and authorization modules to handle web requests. The advantage of using this native capability is that it can deny unauthorized requests even before the request reaches the code itself. These native modules support different authentication providers, such as Azure Active Directory, Microsoft accounts, Facebook, Google, and Twitter.

While the option previously explained is available for users or client apps, you also have the service-to-service authentication scenario, which occurs when the authentication is done against a backend service. In this scenario, you can use service identity, which can be implemented by signing in to a remote resource and leveraging the app's identity. In this case, App Service allows you to create a managed identity that you can use to authenticate with other services, such as Azure SQL Database. Another option is to use on-behalf-of (OBO), which is basically delegated access to remote resources on behalf of the user. You can use Azure Active Directory as the authentication provider, and your app can perform delegated sign-in to a remote service.

EXAM TIP When reading the SC-100 scenarios involving Azure App Service, make sure to disable anonymous access unless it is explicitly required in the technical or business description of the question.

Security posture and threat protection

Attackers probe web applications to find and exploit weaknesses. Before being routed to specific environments, requests to applications running in Azure go through several gateways, where they're inspected and logged. For continuous monitoring of your Azure App Service security posture and active threat detection, you should use Microsoft Defender for App Service.

Defender for App Service detects many threats by continuously monitoring the VM instance in which the App Service is running and its management interface. It also monitors the requests and responses sent to and from your App Service apps and the underlying sandboxes and VMs.

Defender for App Service can identify attacks targeting applications running over App Service, and once it detects a threat, it triggers an alert. One attack that Defender for App Service can detect is the Dangling DNS attack. This attack usually occurs when a website is removed, but the custom domain from the DNS registrar is not. In this case, the DNS entry points to a non-existent resource, which means the domain is vulnerable to a takeover. Although Defender for Cloud does not perform a scan DNS registrar for existing dangling DNS entries, it will still trigger an alert when an App Service website is decommissioned, and its custom domain (DNS entry) is not deleted. This Dangling DNS alert is available whether your domains are managed with Azure DNS or an external domain registrar. It applies to App Service on Windows and Linux.

Skill 7-5: Specify security requirements for storage workloads, including Azure Storage

When designing your Azure storage account security strategy, it is important to understand that threat actors targeting cloud storage will initially perform reconnaissance to enumerate storage account names to find active accounts. For this reason, it is important to ensure proper security hygiene of your storage account, including implementing security recommendations such as disabling anonymous public read access to containers and blobs. Security requirements for storage workloads are divided into the following categories:

- Data protection
- Identity and access management
- Networking
- Logging and monitoring

 EXAM TIP While the options available in each category are important security require-ments to have in place, the technical and business requirements presented in the SC-100 exam scenario ultimately dictate which options will be selected.

Data protection

Data protection in Azure Storage starts by ensuring that you choose the most secure method to provision your storage account from the beginning. When you create a new storage account using the Azure Resource Manager (ARM) deployment model, you take advantage of the security enhancements capabilities such as the superior Azure role-based access control (Azure RBAC) model and auditing capabilities. Another advantage of using an ARM-based deployment is the option to use managed identities, access to Azure Key Vault for secrets, and Azure AD-based authentication and authorization for access to Azure Storage data and resources.

If you are designing a solution for an existing environment with storage accounts that were not created using ARM, consider migrating existing storage accounts that use the classic deployment model to use ARM. Another advantage of using the ARM deployment model is that you can lock the storage account to prevent accidental or malicious deletion or configuration changes.

 TIP On the SC-100 exam, you will have different scenarios, and each scenario may have different types of requirements. For data recovery scenarios in storage accounts, consider enabling soft delete for blobs and soft delete for containers, allowing you to recover blob data and containers after they have been deleted.

For data protection scenarios where you want to ensure that the in-transit data is secure, make sure to avoid pre-shared key usage in direct mode and ensure that the following storage account options are enabled:

- **Require Secure Transfer (HTTPS) To The Storage Account**
- **Limit Shared Access Signature (SAS) Tokens To HTTPS Connections Only**

Exposed storage containers are a typical scenario targeted by threat actors utilizing custom scanners built specifically to identify public containers. Microsoft Defender for Storage is an Azure-native layer of security intelligence that detects unusual and potentially harmful attempts to access or exploit your storage accounts.

Defender for Storage can be enabled for data stored in Azure Blob Storage (Standard/ Premium StorageV2, Block Blobs), Azure Files, and Azure Data Lake Storage (ADLS) Gen2. You can enable Defender for Storage on the subscription level just like any other plan, but you can also enable it only on the storage accounts you want to protect.

Defender for Storage works by continually analyzing the telemetry stream generated by the Azure Blob Storage and Azure Files services. If a potentially malicious activity is detected, a security alert is generated. Defender for Storage provides alerts based on different types of threats, as shown here:

- **Unusual Access To An Account** Alerts that fit this category include threats such as access from a TOR exit node.
- **Unusual Behavior In An Account** These alerts indicate when the behavior deviates from a learned baseline, such as an unusual deletion of blobs or files.
- **Hash Reputation-Based Malware Detection** As files get uploaded to the storage account, it gets analyzed by the hash reputation system, which looks into Microsoft Threat Intelligence to determine if the file is suspicious. It is very important to understand that this is not an antimalware feature because it only looks into the file hash and does not scan the file.
- **Unusual File Uploads** Alerts that fit this category are the ones where upload deviates from the normal pattern, such as uploading cloud service packages and executable files.
- **Public Visibility** Alerts in this category relate to break-in attempts using public scanners.

- **Phishing Campaigns** Alerts in this category are related to scenarios where a piece of content hosted on Azure Storage was identified as part of a phishing attack impacting Microsoft 365 users.

While our general recommendation is to keep Defender for Storage enabled across every type of storage account at the subscription level, some organizations that need to save costs might need to prioritize what is most critical to them and only enable those things on the storage account level.

There is also a misunderstanding that storage accounts behind private links don't pose a risk and therefore don't need to have Defender for Storage enabled. The reality is that several threats still threaten the storage account behind private links. The most prominent threats are

- Malicious insiders
- Compromised identities
- Lateral movement within the private network when a resource has been compromised and access keys or access tokens have been compromised
- Identity has been compromised, and access privileges have been escalated

For this reason, using exclusively this rationale is not a recommended approach.

Before making this decision, your organization needs to perform a risk assessment that considers the following factors:

- The type of information stored in the storage account
- The potential impact if this data is compromised
- Whether an attacker can leverage the storage account as an entry point into your organization

Based on this assessment and the cost estimation that you found using the estimation workbook, you can decide if you want to keep Defender for Storage enabled in the entire sub-scription or if you want to enable it only on critical storage accounts. Another outcome of this risk assessment is that you always want to have threat detection for all storage accounts but want to exclude storage accounts that don't have critical data that needs to be monitored.

Identity and access management

An important consideration when hardening your Azure storage account is ensuring that only authorized users can access it. Azure Active Directory (Azure AD) should be your primary choice to handle access to the blob data. In addition, make sure to use the principle of least-privilege when assigning a role to a user, group, or application and granting access to the blob data. Limiting access to resources helps prevent both unintentional and malicious misuse of your data.

While Azure AD is the primary choice to authorize access, there are some scenarios in which you won't be able to use this option, for example, if the scenario requirements dictate that you need to use shared key authorization. In this case, consider securing your account access keys using Azure Key Vault. In addition, make sure to regenerate your account keys periodically to reduce the likelihood of exposing your data to threat actors.

Networking

Network security considerations for Azure storage accounts can ensure that the in-transit data is secure, including the basic security hygiene recommendation for ensuring the minimum required version of Transport Layer Security (TLS) for a storage account is used and enabling firewall rules in the storage account.

These two options are imperative for client access to storage account communication. However, enabling firewall rules for your storage account blocks incoming requests for data by default unless the requests originate from a service operating within an Azure Virtual Network (VNet) or from allowed public IP addresses. This means access from other Azure services that send legitimate access requests to your storage account will also be blocked. To avoid this behavior, enable the option to allow trusted Microsoft services to access the storage account.

Also, consider the following network security best practices to improve the security posture of your storage account:

- Limit network access to specific networks
- Use VNet service tags
- Use private endpoints
- Enable the **Secure Transfer Required** option on all your storage accounts

Logging and monitoring

While enabling Defender for Storage will provide the level of monitoring you need, it will only give you visibility for potential threats identified based on the threat analytics for this plan. If you need to track how each request made against Azure Storage was authorized, you need to consider enabling Azure Storage logging to track how requests are authorized.

Optionally, you can configure Azure Monitor alerts to evaluate resource logs at a specific frequency and then configure alerts to be triggered based on the results.

Skill 7-6: Specify security requirements for containers

Containers in Azure use the same network stack as the regular Azure VMs; the difference is that in the container environment, you also have the concept of Azure Virtual Network container network interface (CNI) plug-in. This plug-in is responsible for assigning an IP address from a virtual network to containers brought up in the VM, attaching them to the VNet, and connecting them directly to other containers.

One important container concept is that the pod represents a single instance of your application and typically has a 1:1 mapping with a container. However, some unique scenarios exist when a pod might contain multiple containers. A VNet IP address is assigned to every pod, which could consist of one or more containers.

When planning the security requirements for your containers, make sure to include requirements that fulfill the following best practices:

- Ensure that containers are operating with the lowest privilege and access required possible to perform the job to reduce your exposure to risk
- Within the same principle, make sure to remove unnecessary privileges to reduce the attack surface
- Use preapproved or safe listed files and executables to limit exposure to risk
- Monitor container activity and user access
- Log all container administrative user access for auditing purposes

Hardening access to Azure Container Registry

Azure Container Registry (ACR) is a private registry of Docker and Open Container Initiative (OCI) images based on open-source Docker Registry 2.0. Developers can pull (download) images from an Azure container registry and push (upload) to a container registry as part of a container development workflow. ACR pricing tiers are

- **Basic**   More suitable for developers that are learning about ACR
- **Standard**   Increased storage and image throughput, which is more suitable for a production environment
- **Premium**   More suitable for high-volume scenarios and high image throughput

Using the defense-in-depth approach, you should maintain network segmentation (or nano-segmentation) or segregation between containers. Creating network segmentation may also be necessary to use containers in industries that are required to meet compliance mandates.

Vulnerability management is another important security recommendation for your container environment. Defender for Containers leverages the built-in integration with Qualys. With Defender for Containers, the vulnerability assessment solution scans all pushed images and shows the vulnerability assessment result in the dashboard.

To manage access to your Azure Container Registry (ACR), you must add a user to a specific role that will allow the user to perform certain tasks. Table 7-2 provides the mapping of the roles for the allowed tasks that can be executed in the ACR:

TABLE 7-2 Azure Container Registry RBAC roles

Role	Tasks that can be executed
Owner	Access resource manager; create and delete registry; push images; pull images; delete image data; change polices
Contributor	Access resource manager; create and delete registry; push images; pull images; delete image data; and change policies
Reader	Access resource manager and pull images
ArcPush	Push and pull images
ArcPull	Pull images
ArcDelete	Delete image data
ArcImageSigner	Sign images

For CI/CD automation scenarios, you need Docker push capabilities. For this type of scenario, we recommend assigning the **AcrPush** role. This recommendation comes from applying the principle of least-privilege because this role, unlike the broader **Contributor** role, prevents the user from performing other registry operations or accessing Azure Resource Manager. Using the same rationale, nodes running containers need the **AcrPull** role but shouldn't require Reader capabilities.

To pull or push images to an Azure container registry, a client must interact over HTTPS with the Registry REST API endpoint and the storage endpoint. By default, an ACR accepts connections over the Internet from hosts on any network. If you are using ACR Premium, you can leverage Azure VNet network access rules to control access to your ACR.

Skill 7-7: Specify security requirements for container orchestration

Azure Container Instances enables a layered approach to container orchestration. It provides all scheduling and management capabilities necessary to run a single container, allowing the orchestrator platforms to manage multi-container tasks. When planning your security requirements for container orchestration, you need to ensure that you have access control management in place to reduce the likelihood that over-privileged accounts can successfully perform attacks over the network and start potential lateral movement operations from there.

When using Azure container registry with Azure Container Instances, make sure to create procedures to enable the built-in admin account of a container registry and disable the account when not in use. In addition to that, consider also:

- Use dedicated administrative accounts
- Use single sign-on (SSO) with Azure Active Directory
- Use multi-factor authentication (MFA) for all Azure Active Directory–based access

- Regularly review and reconcile user access
- Monitor attempts to access deactivated credentials

Threat detection

Another important part of security for orchestration is the capability to detect attempts to compromise containers. Defender for Containers now provides not only hardening assessment for Kubernetes clusters running on Azure Kubernetes Services (AKS), Kubernetes on-premises, IaaS, Amazon Elastic Kubernetes Service (EKS), and Google Kubernetes Engine (GKE) but also threat detection.

While these features are considered part of your security hygiene, Defender for Containers also has the capability to trigger alerts for different scenarios, which provides another level of threat detection for nodes and clusters. To generate alerts, Defender for Containers analyzes data coming from the following sources:

- Audit logs and security events from the API server
- Cluster configuration information from the control plane
- Workload configuration from Azure Policy
- Security signals and events from the node level

The architecture shown in Figure 7-3 represents how Defender for Containers shows recommendations and alerts.

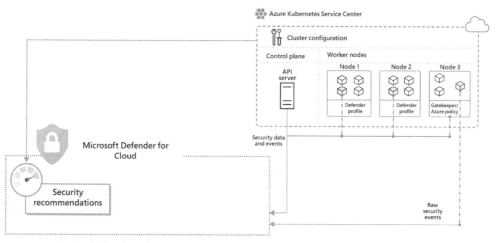

FIGURE 7-3 Defender for Containers

As you can see in Figure 7-3, two major components will communicate with Defender for Cloud via the Defender for Containers plan:

- **Defender profile**   This profile is deployed to each node; it provides runtime protections/collects signals and includes the DaemonSet. For more information on DaemonSet see *https://kubernetes.io/docs/concepts/workloads/controllers/daemonset*.

- **Azure Policy add-on for Kubernetes** This profile is responsible for collecting cluster and workload configuration for admission control policies. It also includes Gatekeeper. For more information about Gatekeeper, see *https://github.com/open-policy-agent/ gatekeeper.*

Thought experiment

In this thought experiment, demonstrate your skills and knowledge of the topics covered in this chapter. You can find answers to this thought experiment in the next section.

Design a strategy for securing PaaS and IaaS services at Fabrikam, Inc

You are the Cybersecurity Architect for Fabrikam, an online general store specializing in various home products. Fabrikam has an on-premises environment using Active Directory Domain Services (AD DS) called corp.fabrikam.com. Fabrikam also has a single-tenant Azure AD environment with a single subscription. Fabrikam also has some workloads (EC2 instances) in AWS.

You are working on a project to improve the security of cloud workloads (PaaS and Iaas) used by Fabrikam. The workloads that need better protection include Azure Storage, VMs, Cosmos DB databases, and containers.

Fabrikam CISO required the following:

- The adoption of a single solution to visualize the security posture of these workloads
- Funnel all security alerts generated by the threat detection solution for these workloads to their SOC team
- A vulnerability assessment for containers and threat detection for IoT

Based on this scenario, respond to the following questions:

1. Which solution should be utilized to allow centralized visualization of the security posture and alerts in all these workloads?

2. Which solution should they utilize to enable them to have threat detection for IoT?

3. Which solution will enable them to proactively harden their containers while providing threat detection?

Thought experiment answers

This section contains the solution to the thought experiment. Each answer explains why the answer choice is correct.

1. Microsoft Defender for Cloud

2. Microsoft Defender for IoT

3. Microsoft Defender for Container

Chapter summary

- In an Azure infrastructure using IaaS and PaaS service models, you can utilize Microsoft Defender for Cloud Secure Score to assist you in improving the Azure workloads' security posture.

- When designing a cloud solution that includes IoT workloads, it is imperative to understand the potential threats to these workloads and ensure that you use the defense-in-depth approach as part of your design and architect it.

- How the IoT workloads are distributed in the network is another important security aspect that needs to be considered. You should design your IoT architecture into several components/zones.

- Data workloads will have different security requirements according to the type of data that resides on the workload. Some data workloads might be more critical than others and require more protections.

- Azure Cosmos DB is a fully managed NoSQL database for modern, fast, and flexible app development, capable of having single-digit millisecond response times, automatic and instant scalability, and multiple SDKs and APIs to support a variety of non-relational data models.

- Defender for App Service detects many threats by continuously monitoring the VM instance in which the App Service is running and its management interface. It also monitors the requests and responses sent to and from your App Service apps and the underlying sandboxes and VMs.

- When designing your Azure storage account security strategy, it is important to understand that threat actors targeting cloud storage will initially perform reconnaissance to enumerate storage account names to find active accounts.

- Defender for Containers has this capability by leveraging the built-in integration with Qualys. With Defender for Containers, the vulnerability assessment solution scans all pushed images and shows the vulnerability assessment result in the dashboard.

CHAPTER 8

Specify security requirements for applications

Because applications are often the part of an organization's infrastructure that handles and manages data, it could be argued that they are almost more critical to secure so that sensitive customer or organizational data is kept secure and confidential. As a security architect, you will need to specify security standards for your organization that developers can use when designing and building applications. Also, you'll need to make sure secure coding practices are used and applications have sufficient security controls to reduce the likelihood of a breach.

Skills covered in this chapter:

- Skill 8-1: Specify priorities for mitigating threats to applications
- Skill 8-2: Specify a security standard for onboarding a new application
- Skill 8-3: Specify a security strategy for applications and APIs

Skill 8-1: Specify priorities for mitigating threats to applications

Just like all parts of an IT environment, applications have threats that need to be mitigated as part of a comprehensive security strategy, and just like the rest of the IT environment, not all threats can be mitigated. This might be from a lack of budget or expertise, or the business might decide a particular threat is not worth mitigating versus the cost and operational impact. To understand application threats in the business context, we recommend that an analysis takes place to identify the threats, attacks, vulnerabilities, and mitigations and/or countermeasures to protect each application. This analysis needs to be performed for each application because a high-priority threat for one application might not be considered high for another. Context is king!

This section covers the skills necessary to specify priorities for mitigating threats to applications according to the Exam SC-100 outline.

Classifying applications

Most organizations have many applications of varying importance. It's important to understand which applications are critical to an organization's key operations and must be prioritized
for threat modeling activities and implementing security controls because (sadly) no organization has unlimited funds, resources, and time to implement every security control.

For example, if an e-commerce company makes all its revenue through its customer-facing
website, this would be considered a high-priority/critical application. If the website were
breached or unavailable, the company would make no revenue, and its operations could not
continue until the website was up and running again. Conversely, if a website for a local dog
trainer was unavailable, it would be inconvenient and might mean the trainer might miss out
on a few new customers searching the web for a dog trainer. However, it wouldn't impede the
trainer's ability to train dogs. In these circumstances, the website would not be considered a
business-critical application.

Context really matters for classification: one organization's critical application is a low priority for another. In general, the principles of a critical/high-priority application are something
like this:

- **Applications that would have a significant impact on the organization's mission
  if they were compromised**   Typically, the impact would be in terms of operations,
  revenue, reputation—or all three!

- **Applications that handle highly sensitive and/or regulated data**   This could be HR
  systems with personal information, national security, or top secret information (to name
  just a few examples).

- **Applications with a high level of access to the rest of the IT environment**   If the
  identity store were compromised, a much wider swathe of IT could be damaged.

- **Applications with high attack exposure**   Most Internet-facing applications belong
  in this category.

Application threat modeling

But how do you determine which applications have the highest attack exposure? If you have
worked in security for any length of time, you are likely already aware of the general concepts
of threat modeling.

EXAM TIP   Several different methodologies can be used to perform threat modeling.
While the SC-100 Exam outline does not specify a particular methodology, we will look in
more depth at the Microsoft Security Development Lifecycle (SDL) based on the STRIDE
methodology.

Microsoft Security Development Lifecycle (SDL)

Microsoft started using the SDL more than 20 years ago, and although the threats have evolved and changed, the fundamental steps and principles remain the same. You can see the five major threat-modeling steps in Figure 8-1.

FIGURE 8-1 The SDL's five major threat-modeling steps

- **Define security requirements** At a high level, the organization and/or business unit that owns the application should have security requirements the application needs to adhere to maintain the organization's risk posture. Depending on the organization's maturity and the application specifics, the security requirements might be overarching organizational ones or ones specifically for that application.

- **Create an application diagram** An application diagram should show all the components of an application, their connections, and their relationships with other applications and components in your IT environment. Getting these diagrams accurate is crucial to effective threat modeling.

- **Identify threats** In this stage, an application's potential threats should be listed. They can be external or internal and may be specific to that application or a broader threat to the organization. For example, a government intelligence agency may have an overarching organizational threat that state-sponsored hacking may be attempted against any of their systems to expose top-secret data. In contrast, an organization's payroll system may have a payroll-specific threat regarding a rogue insider paying themselves a bigger salary by manipulating the payroll. Threat intelligence should be used to enrich threat modeling. Threats should be categorized by severity: critical, high, medium, and low.

- **Mitigate threats** Threats identified in the previous step should be mitigated, or countermeasures put in place. The business may choose not to mitigate some threats, accepting the risk that comes with not mitigating a threat. This should be documented and signed off at an appropriate management level. (Typically, the higher the threat severity, the higher the level of sign-off required to accept the risk.)

- **Validate threats have been mitigated** Threat mitigations should be tested to validate they've been implemented correctly.

Microsoft has made the Microsoft Threat Modeling Tool that can assist in threat modeling and creating application diagrams. See Figure 8-2.

> **NOTE** You can read more about the Microsoft Threat Modeling Tool (and download it) at *https://www.microsoft.com/en-us/securityengineering/sdl/threatmodeling.*

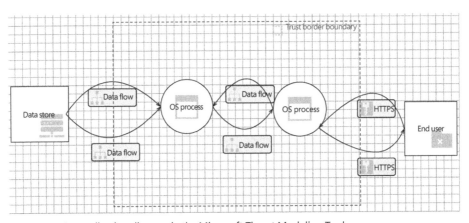

FIGURE 8-2 An application diagram in the Microsoft Threat Modeling Tool

As mentioned earlier in this section, the Microsoft SDL is based on the STRIDE methodology:

- **Spoofing** Pretending to be someone else, often through compromised credentials
- **Tampering** Modifying data held within a system
- **Repudiation** Allowing users to deny that they took action within a system (meaning, the system doesn't record certain actions)
- **Information disclosure** Discloses nonpublic information held within a system to audiences that should not have access to it (often the whole public Internet)

- **Denial of service**   Compromises the system availability of a system
- **Elevation of privilege**   When a user account with less privilege gains additional privilege it shouldn't have and then accesses it to change or destroy the system

Mitigating threats

After you've established the application threats (or maybe the threat modeling tool has told you—either way is fine), then you need to start looking at mitigations that can be put in place to prevent this threat from occurring. Multiple mitigations can often be implemented. This is what we call defense-in-depth.

Defense-in-depth is the idea that if one security control fails to prevent a threat, other controls will also help prevent a threat. Of course, it's possible that applying security controls could go on ad infinitum, so each time a security control is implemented, an assessment needs to determine how likely it is that this control will fail. Also, it is worthwhile for the organization to implement further controls to prevent this threat from occurring. All organizations won't make the same choices here. The organization's security posture and risk tolerance will ultimately determine how many security controls are considered adequate to mitigate a threat.

The mitigation categories listed in the Microsoft Threat Modeling Tool are as follows:

- Auditing and Logging
- Authentication
- Authorization
- Communication Security
- Configuration Management
- Cryptography
- Exception Management
- Input Validation
- Sensitive Data
- Session Management

NOTE   These categories are based on the Web Application Security Framework.

As a security architect, the final decision on how many security controls are implemented to mitigate threats likely will not be made by the security group. However, you must articulate why one or more controls are needed and why other controls could fail so stakeholders can use your expertise to make a call regarding how many controls and layers of protection are appropriate for the business.

Skill 8-2: Specify a security standard for onboarding a new application

Applications hold more risk than other parts of an organization's IT infrastructure for a couple of reasons:

- They are responsible for executing and/or supporting business processes.
- They process and store high-value business data and will require high levels of confidentiality, integrity, and availability.

Therefore, it's critically important that strong application security strategies are in place at an organization, starting with onboarding a new application into an organization's IT environment. This section covers the skills necessary to specify a security standard for onboarding a new application according to the Exam SC-100 outline.

Old versus new

When applications are built from scratch or migrated into a cloud environment, this application transformation can happen in one of several ways:

- **Legacy** These applications will undergo a lift-and-shift, where the application is moved from running on an on-premises VM to running on a cloud VM (IaaS). As far as the application is concerned, absolutely everything is the same as it was, and no reworking of the code or platforms it runs on has taken place; it has simply shifted into the cloud.
- **Hybrid/transitional** These are legacy applications beginning their journey to become modern applications. Refactoring a legacy application can be an extensive amount of work that has to be undertaken in stages. Therefore, it is common to see these hybrid/transitional applications in an environment with some modern aspects but still using legacy components (such as an on-premises database).
- **Modern** Also known as Platform as a Service (PaaS) applications, these applications are often fully serverless and don't require the application owner to manage and secure the underlying infrastructure (as would have been the case in legacy applications). Because of the complexity of migrating legacy applications into modern applications, most organizations' modern applications will be brand-new applications that have been "born in the cloud," and no migration from on-premises has had to take place. As time passes and an organization moves along in its cloud transformation journey, you would expect to see fewer legacy and hybrid applications and more modern ones.

Three different types of an application's components are required to be covered by a security standard:

- **The application's code** The actual code of the application that contains the logic to enable business processes. This includes the code written by the developer and the code's dependencies on third-party libraries and packages.

- **The services the application uses**   Some would not consider this as part of the application, but application services refer to the shared components in the IT environment that applications use within an organization (such as databases, identity providers, and so on).

- **The application hosting platform**   This is where the application actually runs. It's not as easy as saying "on-premises" or "cloud," either. The application-hosting platform can vary even within one vendor's cloud platform. Two applications running in Azure—depending on what services they are using and where they are running—may not have the same security considerations. Also, the kind of application running (see the breakdown earlier in this section) will change the security considerations.

Security standards for onboarding applications

A common theme that you'll have noticed throughout this book is that many recommendations and best practices can be implemented from a security perspective. Still, all organizations are constrained by time, budget, and resources to implement, so it can be challenging to distill down which ones are the most important for your organization (this is where threat modeling comes into play, as described earlier in the chapter).

However, it is still critically important to specify some standards that must be adhered to when either moving or building applications in the cloud. There can be challenges, and as a security architect, you can almost certainly expect a degree of pushback from the business because specifying security standards for onboarding applications can increase costs and timelines, which isn't what a business wants to take on. This is usually worse when migrating a legacy application because it likely has associated technical debt (meaning it uses legacy protocols). It is critically important to develop solid onboarding standards for applications understood by any projects or initiatives to minimize pushback from the business. Doing so allows the business to account for any potential changes or additional work that will be required to bring the application up to an appropriate security standard during the project's planning phase.

> **NOTE**   Security issues in code are technical debt, but not all technical debt is a security issue!

Use cloud-native services where possible

Utilize your cloud provider's services when they are available. Most cloud providers will have mature, well-maintained services available for the following:

- Authentication (see the next section for more detail)
- Encryption
- Key/secret storage
- Databases
- Logging
- Network security controls (firewalls, WAF, network segmentation)

The benefits of using built-in services from your cloud provider are many: firstly, some of the responsibility for maintaining and securing that service will be given to your cloud provider, which reduces the workload on your developers, security, and operational teams.

> **NOTE** Using cloud-native services doesn't mean all security controls and maintenance responsibility has been transferred to your cloud provider. Ensure that you, as a security architect, and developers and operational teams are clear on whether your organization or your cloud provider is responsible for a particular control when using a cloud service. You can read more about the shared responsibility model here: *https://docs.microsoft.com/en-us/azure/ security/fundamentals/shared-responsibility*

Additionally, writing custom versions of these services can be time-consuming and costly, and they are unlikely to have the same robust security controls as an in-built service. If the service isn't an offering from a cloud provider, it may also be harder to perform management at scale. For example, Azure Policy allows an organization to specify "guardrails" and how things can be configured in an Azure tenant. A common, simple example of Azure Policy use is to prevent Azure resources from being deployed in a region where an organization chooses not to operate or isn't allowed to operate due to industry standards or local legislation. Using non-native services in an application may limit the use of such tooling.

Use a modern, centralized identity provider

Identity services have come a long way. In days gone by, it wasn't always possible to integrate an application with an identity provider because of proprietary protocols, architecture, and a multitude of other complications. This led to developers making their own identity stores that lacked adequate security controls and decentralized the management of identity stores, thus making it challenging for the security and identity teams within an organization to ensure that those credentials were properly managed and has led to breaches in the past, with attackers targeting these less secure credential stores.

Nowadays, the identity provider landscape has changed and matured, with modern identity providers such as Azure AD using industry-standard, modern protocols such as SAML 2.0, OpenID Connect, and OAuth 2.0 to authenticate identities. Few (if any) applications cannot be integrated with a modern identity provider—and this is what allows centralized identity management. In Chapter 2, we discussed how identity is the new perimeter in modern hybrid IT environments, but this can only be enforced if all applications and resources within an IT environment use the same identity provider. Modern identity providers also have stronger controls to protect credentials stored within them (able to support multifactor authentication). It's also important to train developers to use identity services rather than cryptographic keys or strings where possible, as the security controls for authentication built into identity providers are vastly superior to the controls around a key stored in a credential store. In Figure 8-3, you can see an application being registered in Azure AD.

Register an application

* Name

The user-facing display name for this application (this can be changed later).

Contoso Accounting

Supported account types

Who can use this application or access this API?

(●) Accounts in this organizational directory only (Default Directory only - Single tenant)

( ) Accounts in any organizational directory (Any Azure AD directory - Multitenant)

( ) Accounts in any organizational directory (Any Azure AD directory - Multitenant) and personal Microsoft accounts (e.g. Skype, Xbox)

( ) Personal Microsoft accounts only

Help me choose...

Redirect URI (optional)

We'll return the authentication response to this URI after successfully authenticating the user. Providing this now is optional and it can be changed later, but a value is required for most authentication scenarios.

| Select a platform | ∨ | e.g. https://example.com/auth |

FIGURE 8-3 Registering an application in Azure AD

Deploy a WAF in front of Internet-facing applications

Any Internet-facing application must have a WAF deployed in front of it to mitigate the risk of common web vulnerabilities being exploited in the application. Even if you have strong, secure coding best practices, even the best developers can make mistakes, or new web vulnerabilities can be discovered and exploited more quickly than you can update your code. Azure offers a native WAF capability, as seen in Figure 8-4.

FIGURE 8-4 Configuring firewall rules in Azure WAF

Use container-specific security tooling and best practices

Containers are structurally different from more traditional infrastructure architectures, and not all security tooling can detect container-specific threats. Make sure that if your application is containerized, appropriate tooling is used to detect threats at both the container and the orchestrator (such as Kubernetes) level. Figure 8-5 shows Microsoft Defender for Cloud being used to scan container images for vulnerabilities.

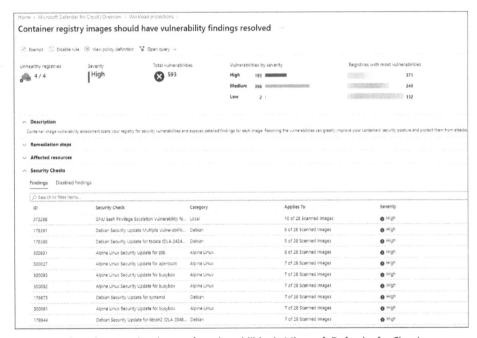

FIGURE 8-5 Scanning container images for vulnerabilities in Microsoft Defender for Cloud

Other best practices for container security include:

- Using trusted container images.
- Storing container images in a private image repository. (Azure has its own service for this: Azure Container Registry.)
- Not "baking in" credentials and secrets into container images.
- Not running containers as root.
- Hardening the orchestrator running the containers.

Use threat modeling to identify additional risks

The importance of threat modeling was covered extensively earlier in this chapter, but it's also important to require teams to undertake threat modeling as part of their application onboarding process to understand the potential risks to an application.

Skill 8-3: Specify a security strategy for applications and APIs

DevOps (also known as the *agile methodology*) isn't a new phrase; doubtless, you've heard it before and may already be using it in your organization. This is Microsoft's definition of DevOps:

> *"DevOps combines development (Dev) and operations (Ops) to unite people, process, and technology in application planning, development, delivery, and operations. DevOps lets formerly siloed roles like development, IT operations, quality engineering, and security coordinate and collaborate."*

Using DevOps culture and practices helps organizations create a modern approach to securing applications and APIs. This section covers the skills necessary to specify a security strategy for applications and APIs according to the Exam SC-100 outline.

Waterfall to Agile/DevOps

A waterfall is the "traditional" application development lifecycle where each methodology stage is linear, and projects do not progress until a stage is completed. Roles within the waterfall methodology are generally static, and a defined team implements each stage. If you have used this methodology in the past (and let's face it, you probably have!) you might be familiar with a diagram like the one in Figure 8-6.

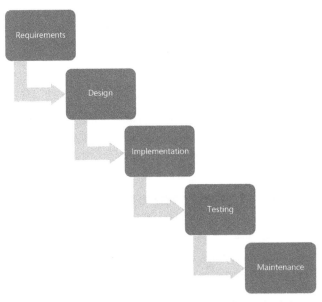

FIGURE 8-6 An example of the stages of the waterfall methodology

Across the industry, the waterfall methodology is widely acknowledged not to be the optimal way to develop and run applications in modern IT environments. DevOps provides greater flexibility and responsiveness to build and manage applications. However, each organization will be at different stages of its transition to DevOps.

Conversely, DevOps is a cyclical process, and each phase relies on the others. Each phase can be repeated as many times as necessary. In fact, it is expected that an application developed and maintained in an organization that uses DevOps will constantly be going through the DevOps cycle to adapt and improve the application. The core tenet of the agile methodology is that changes can be made to an application much more quickly to keep it as useful and relevant to users as possible. A typical DevOps process is shown in Figure 8-7.

FIGURE 8-7 An example of the stages of a DevOps methodology

Let's break down the main stages of a DevOps methodology:

- **Plan** Teams define and describe what kind of application they're going to be building, the application's components, and how those tasks will be broken down and/or grouped. Importantly from a security perspective, this is where threat modeling would take place (covered earlier in this chapter). DevOps teams will use some manner of tracking for these tasks that can be assigned to individuals or groups of people. This might be a backlog for tasks or bugs, a kanban board, and so on.

- **Develop** The stage at which team members write code. Because more than one person will likely be working on code simultaneously, using a code repository such as GitHub allows for versioning and storing different versions of that code in a controlled, recorded manner before it is reviewed. A decision is made about whether to merge the code into the master version of your repository or if further work must occur first. Using modern versioning tools allows small code changes to be iterated quickly and tedious and manual checks to be automated (such as automated code checks in GitHub). From the security side of the house, this is where secure coding best practices and automated security code checks may take place.

- **Deliver** This is the process where an application is deployed into a production environment to start doing the task it was created to do. In a true DevOps environment, the deployment should happen through a CI/CD (continuous integration/continuous delivery) pipeline where the entire deployment is "pushed" into production as a package through the pipeline rather than someone logging in manually editing the code. Even smaller code iterations will be deployed in this manner. More automated security checks should happen here as part of the CI/CD pipeline.

- **Operate** This is what would have been traditionally known as the "maintenance" lifecycle phase of the application in the waterfall methodology; in fact, it isn't dissimilar. This is where teams focus on the smooth running of the application. Still, unlike traditional on-premises systems where downtime was almost inevitable, modern operating practices aim for zero downtime (something possible with distributed cloud computing platforms). In terms of security, in this phase, teams should focus on monitoring the application for any security issues that may affect confidentiality, integrity, and availability. While the other DevOps phases are more focused on preventative actions (to reduce the likelihood of a security issue happening in the first place), this phase is more reactive and focused on identifying and responding to security issues.

Security in DevOps (DevSecOps)

From a security perspective, moving to an agile methodology can be challenging. Traditional waterfall processes allowed for fixed periods within the project timeline that security would perform comprehensive security testing before the project could move to the next stage. When DevOps is being used, comprehensive security testing can't necessarily be completed every time a small code change is made. Doing so is both time-consuming and expensive (either in terms of internal people hours, external consultants, or both).

Moving to DevSecOps requires not only a technological change but also a significant mindset shift, where the security function in an organization cedes a degree of responsibility and control to developers. For those used to security being able to review every bit of code, this can be a challenging shift. It also requires developers to "step up" and upskill themselves in aspects of application security. Organizations with mature waterfall processes should expect a degree of resistance to this change. In Chapter 11, we will explore how you should recommend a DevSecOps process.

Thought experiment

In this thought experiment, demonstrate your skills and knowledge of the topics covered in this chapter. You can find answers to this thought experiment in the next section.

Application migration and modernization at Fabrikam, Inc.

You are the new security architect for Fabrikam, Inc., an organization that is migrating all of its applications onto a cloud platform as part of a larger digital transformation. The CISO has also asked that you modernize the organization's approach to application security as part of this migration and review the decisions already made.

Below is a summary of the current application environment and decisions made about the migration:

- Applications are not classified by their criticality for supporting key business processes.
- There is no formal, ongoing threat modeling process in place for new applications or applications in the current environment.
- The organization has decided it will lift-and-shift all its applications into the cloud environment, even if some of the applications in the environment could run on PaaS/serverless.
- The application onboarding security standard is outdated and refers to only on-premises services and tools, but it has been deemed out of scope to update this.
- The organization has a mature waterfall process. Most security teams want to keep using waterfall because they understand it and can have full visibility and control of the changes made.

With this information in mind, answer the following questions:

1. What threat modeling methodologies could you suggest that the organization investigates that it could use for application threat modeling?

2. What improvements could you suggest to the Fabrikam CISO regarding some of the decisions already made about the application migration?

3. What reasons could you use to persuade the security teams that they should not use the waterfall methodology?

Thought experiment answers

This section contains the solution to the thought experiment. Each answer explains why the answer choice is correct.

1. Several different threat modeling methodologies are available; the Microsoft SDLC uses STRIDE as its foundation. OWASP also provides a threat modeling methodology. Note that threat modeling is much easier if application classification has taken place, so you should also recommend to the CISO that this is undertaken.

2. There are a few decisions that may not be optimal for Fabrikam, Inc.:

   - Deciding to "lift and shift" all their applications rather than look to optimize them and run them on modern platforms may lead to increased running costs in the cloud and sub-optimal performance.

   - The application security standard should be updated as part of the application migration program because applications moving to the cloud may not be taking advantage of stronger security controls offered by native services and identity providers unless the standards specify they must.

3. The strongest reason for using DevOps / Agile methodology is that applications can be tuned and changed more quickly and responsively to meet customer demand. The same applies to security updates, patches, and changes to improve security posture. However, this fact alone may not be enough to convince security professionals; shifting to an agile methodology can be challenging.

Chapter summary

- Applications need to be classified according to their potential business impact, which, in turn, feeds into threat modeling activities.

- Several threat modeling methodologies exist (such as STRIDE and the OWASP threat modeling process): which one to use is less important than using one consistently in your application security strategy.

- Multiple mitigations will be required to reduce the risk of an application breach. This is known as defense-in-depth.

- Applications can be migrated into a modern cloud environment in several ways legacy (lift-and-shift), hybrid, or modern.

- Key security standards for onboarding applications should address identity, cloud-native services, a WAF for Internet-facing applications, and performing threat modeling.

- Moving from a waterfall methodology to an Agile/DevOps can be challenging from both a technical and process perspective, but it allows an organization to respond to customer demand much faster.

CHAPTER 9

Design a strategy for securing data

When designing your strategy for securing data, you need to identify the data you have, understand where this data resides, and understand the options available to protect, monitor, and detect attempts to compromise that data. Understanding your data landscape is critical because you can't protect what you don't know exists. Also, consider whether the data is at rest or in transit (also known as in motion). This also will dictate which security controls should be in place to secure the data.

Skills covered in this chapter:

- Skill 9-1: Specify priorities for mitigating threats to data
- Skill 9-2: Design a strategy to identify and protect sensitive data
- Skill 9-3: Specify an encryption standard for data at rest and in motion

Skill 9-1: Specify priorities for mitigating threats to data

According to the Cybersecurity & Infrastructure Security Agency (CISA) Alert Report (AA22-040A) issued in February 2022, ransomware attacks tactics and techniques evolved in 2021. This report noted that cybercriminals were highly successful using old attack methods. These attacks included accessing network infrastructure via phishing emails, stealing credentials via Remote Desktop Protocol (RDP) brute-force attacks, and exploiting known and unpatched vulnerabilities.

The new threat landscape increases the likelihood of data getting compromised. Because protecting your entire data state might be challenging, you need to ensure your design strategy to secure your data prioritizes the most important threats. This section covers the skills necessary to specify priorities for mitigating threats to data according to the Exam SC-100 outline.

Common threats

A threat that grew exponentially, mainly during the peak of COVID-19, was ransomware. According to the Microsoft Digital Defense Report of September 2020, 70 percent of human-operated ransomware attacks originated from Remote Desktop Protocol (RDP) brute-force attacks. This is an alarming number for a problem that can be easily fixed using technologies such as Just-in-time VM access in Defender for Servers.

Threat actors also use existing attack methods against new workloads, such as Kubernetes. The Defender for Cloud research team started mapping the security landscape of Kubernetes and noticed that although the attack techniques are different than those that target single hosts running Linux or Windows, the tactics are similar. When the Kubernetes cluster is deployed in a public cloud, threat actors who can compromise cloud credentials can take over a cluster. Again, the attack's impact changes because the whole cluster can be compromised, but the tactic is similar to the one used to compromise a single host.

According to the Verizon Data Breach Report of 2021, phishing attacks are still the predominant malware delivery method. This makes total sense since the end user is almost always the target because they are the weakest link. With the proliferation of mobile devices, bring-your-own-device (BYOD) models, and cloud-based apps, users are installing more and more apps. All too often, these apps are merely malware masquerading as valid apps. It is important to have good endpoint protection in place and a detection system that can look across different sources to intelligently identify unknown threats by leveraging cutting-edge technologies such as analytics and machine learning.

The likelihood that a threat actor can exploit the system based on the attacks mentioned above is higher nowadays because of the lack of security hygiene. According to the Verizon Data Breach Report from 2020, misconfiguration accounted for 40 percent of the root cause of compromised systems. The simple fact that users often provision a storage account and leave it open for an Internet connection is enough to increase the attack vector. That's why it is so important to have a tool such as Microsoft Defender for Cloud that will bring visibility and control over different cloud workloads.

Data breaches can occur for different reasons, such as the system being compromised by malware that extracted the data. Also, a data breach could happen because a user inadvertently granted access to a broad group of users, and one member of that group had their credentials compromised. But data breach scenarios also occurred because a device was lost. In this scenario, some of the outcomes are:

- Unauthorized users access data from a lost or stolen removable drive
- Data leakage arises from a lost or stolen laptop or removable media that contains confidential information
- Data leakage arises from user emails with sensitive content inadvertently being sent to unintended recipient(s)

Threat actors actively scan public storage to find sensitive content, and they usually leverage the Azure Storage API to list content available within a public storage container. Usually, this process takes place in the following phases:

- **Finding storage accounts** During this phase, threat actors will try to find Azure storage accounts using this Blob storage URL pattern:

  `<storage-account>.blob.core.windows.net.`

- **Finding containers**   The next step is to find any publicly accessible container by guessing the container's name. This can be done using an API call to List blobs or any other read operation.
- **Finding sensitive data**   In this phase, threat actors can leverage online tools that search through large volumes of data, looking for keywords and secrets to find sensitive information.

When you enable Defender for Storage, you have a series of analytics created for different scenarios, and the anonymous scan of public storage containers is one of those.

Cloud weaponization is happening, and current data exposed in the Microsoft Security Intelligent Report Volume 22 shows the global outreach of these attacks. According to these reports, more than two-thirds of incoming attacks on Azure services in the first quarter of 2017 came from IP addresses in these locations:

- China (35.1 percent)
- United States (32.5 percent)
- Korea (3.1 percent)

The remaining attacks were distributed in 116 other countries and regions. Sometimes, threat actors will weaponize the cloud to send an attack to a targeted system. (Figure 1-4 shows an example of this scenario.) Other times, they will simply hijack the targeted system's resources. For example, let's say a cloud admin misconfigured a Kubernetes or Docker registry, exposing the system by allowing free public access to it. Attackers could deploy containers that mine crypto.

Ransomeware is another rising threat to data and can be fatal for many organizations because they might not have data backups and can't even pay the ransom. The strategy for dealing with ransomware is to

- Ensure that you implement preventative security controls to reduce the likelihood of being compromised
- Establish a strategy to prevent a ransomware attack from causing too much damage
- Establish a recovery plan to restore the compromised data

It is also important to mention that some attacks or attack campaigns might use multiple techniques to accomplish their mission. On March 13, 2020, the Brno University Hospital in the city of Brno, Czech Republic, was hit by a ransomware attack in the middle of the pandemic.

The hospital was forced to shut down the entire network. As a result, doctors could not access patient data, some data was lost, and surgeries had to be postponed. The attack most likely started with a spearphishing email, followed by ransomware deployment.

Ransomware is a type of malware that encrypts files and folders, preventing access to important files. Cybercriminals deploy ransomware to extort money from victims (usually in the form of cryptocurrencies) in exchange for the decryption key. Unfortunately, cybercriminals won't always follow through and unlock the encrypted files.

One of the most challenging aspects of defending your systems against cybercriminals is recognizing when those systems are being used for some sort of criminal activity in the first place—especially when they are part of a botnet. A botnet is a network of compromised devices that an attacker controls without their owners' knowledge. Botnets are not new. A 2012 Microsoft study found that cybercriminals infiltrated insecure supply chains using the Nitol botnet, which introduced counterfeit software embedded with malware to secretly infect computers even before they were purchased.

Prioritization

To prioritize which threats will be remediated first and which workloads are affected, you need to ensure you have a well-established vulnerability management system that can identify threats across different workloads. It's important always to prioritize vulnerabilities based on the threat landscape and your organization's detections.

Vulnerability assessment solutions such as Microsoft threat and vulnerability management (TVM), which is part of Microsoft Defender for Endpoint, will already prioritize the vulnerabilities according to their criticality. Defender Vulnerability Management also has the *Exposure Score*, which reflects your organization's vulnerability to cybersecurity threats. A low exposure score means your devices are less vulnerable to exploitation. To improve your exposure score, you need to remediate security recommendations continuously. These recommendations are threat mitigations that have already been prioritized according to the criticality level.

Defender for Cloud is the most recommended option to provide a centralized security posture management solution where you can see your Secure Score for each cloud provider, such as Azure, AWS, and GCP. Recommendations are natively prioritized based on the level of criticality of the recommendation and the workload.

Skill 9-2: Design a strategy to identify and protect sensitive data

Data protection starts with identifying the type of data you have because, without this step, you can't really prioritize what needs to be protected and how it should be protected. To identify the data, you need to have a mechanism to discover your data across your workloads.

After discovery, you need to classify the data according to the data type and risk. Now that you have the data classified, you understand which data is considered sensitive. With this information at hand, you can start designing a data protection strategy for sensitive data. This entire process is summarized in Figure 9-1.

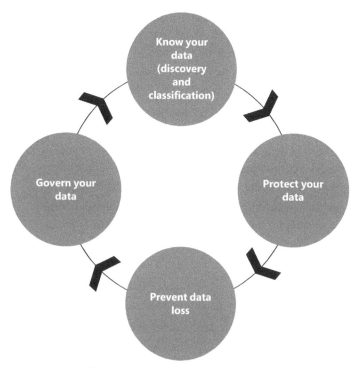

FIGURE 9-1 Data lifecycle management

This section covers the skills necessary to design a strategy to identify and protect sensitive data according to the Exam SC-100 outline.

Know your data

One of the major challenges faced by today's organizations is identifying what kind of, and how much, data exists in their environment. Without a deep understanding of your data, you can't define how much sensitive data exists and where it is stored before it can be protected and governed. As part of the strategy to identify your data, you need to answer at least the following questions:

- What type of data do I have?
- Where is my data located?
- Is my data at risk?

To answer these questions, you need a solution that can look across your data state and provide a comprehensive view of your data. You can use Microsoft Purview to automate the data discovery. Microsoft Purview has data scanning and classification as a service that checks metadata and descriptions of discovered data assets. You can also discover and classify data in Microsoft 365 apps and services, which include Exchange email, SharePoint sites, OneDrive accounts, and Team messages/chats. Also, you can discover and classify SQL Databases using native SQL Database features.

After discovering your data, you need to classify your data. Classification is the process of labeling the data that you identified to get a better understanding of your data landscape. This process will apply one or more of the following to your data:

- **Sensitive information types** Defined by a pattern that a regular expression or function can identify. An example of that would be a credit card number.

- **Trainable classifiers** Use artificial intelligence and machine learning to classify your data intelligently.

- **Labeling** This is like a stamp for your data; you can create these labels according to your organization's needs. For example, your company might create a label named "Top Secret" to indicate data that should not be shared outside of a specific group.

After classifying your data, you can create policies using the above capabilities as inputs. Your policy defines behaviors, for example, if there will be a default label, if labeling is mandatory, what locations the label will be applied to, and under what conditions.

Protect your data

Now that you know your data, you can apply the adequate level of protection according to the sensitivity level of the data. The type of protection will also vary according to the organization and technical requirements. Table 9-1 shows common scenarios and the suggested solution to protect the data:

TABLE 9-1 Common scenarios for data protection

Requirement	Type of protection	Product(s) that can fulfill this requirement
A single labeling solution across apps, services, and devices ensures that the data is protected as it travels inside and outside your organization.	Sensitivity labels	Microsoft Purview
Only your organization can decrypt protected content, and you must hold encryption keys within a geographical boundary.	Double key encryption	Microsoft Purview Azure Information Protection
Extend labeling to File Explorer and PowerShell on Windows computers.	Labeling client	Azure Information Protection
Encrypts email messages and attached documents sent to any user on any device while allowing only recipients to read emailed information.	Message Encryption	Microsoft Purview
Protect against viewing of data by unauthorized systems or personnel.	Service encryption with Customer Key	Microsoft 365

Requirement	Type of protection	Product(s) that can fulfill this requirement
Protects SharePoint lists and libraries so that the downloaded file is protected when a user checks out a document. Only authorized people can view and use the file according to your specified policies.	Information Rights Management	SharePoint Information Rights Management (IRM)
Protection-only for existing on-premises deployments that use Exchange or SharePoint Server or file servers that run Windows Server.	Rights management	Microsoft Rights Management connector

As you can see in this table, different requirements might lead to different solutions and products. When designing your data protection strategy, you need the flexibility to apply a different level of protection according to the level of data confidentiality and the requirements you must comply with.

While all the scenario requirements presented in the table are important, scenarios involving sensitive labels are more prevalent because they allow you to classify and protect your organization's data while ensuring that user productivity and their ability to collaborate aren't compromised. You can use sensitive labels in the following scenarios:

- Addition of encryption and watermark in Office apps across different platforms and devices
- Protection of content in third-party apps and services
- Protection of data on Teams, Microsoft 365 Groups, and SharePoint sites
- Apply and view labels in Power BI, and protect data when it's saved outside the service
- Apply your sensitivity labels to files and schematized data assets in Microsoft Purview Data Map

EXAM TIP Because labels can be applied in different scenarios, you will need to determine the scope in which you want to apply the label. On the SC-100 exam, you might have drag-and-drop scenarios where you must select the appropriate scope.

There are three types of scope available, as shown below:

- **Items (which used to be known as files and emails)** This scope includes protection settings for labeled emails, Office files, and PowerBI items.
- **Groups and sites** This scope includes privacy, access control, and other settings for protected labels in Teams, Microsoft 365 Groups, and SharePoint sites.
- **Schematized data assets** This scope includes labels for files and schematized data assets in Microsoft Purview Data Map, SQL, Azure SQL, Azure Cosmos, Azure Synapse, AWS, RDS, and more.

Prevent data loss

It is very important to establish clear guidelines for data prevention exclusive to this scenario, mainly because some organizations wrongly believe that by implementing data protection mechanisms, they are also preventing data loss. However, this is not necessarily true. To prevent data loss, companies must ensure that they have a data loss prevention (DLP) technology that can help prevent accidental oversharing in and outside the organization. Some organizations might choose to implement DLP to comply with various governmental or industry regulations, such as the European Union's General Data Protection Regulation (GDPR), the Health Insurance Portability and Accountability Act (HIPAA), or the California Consumer Privacy Act (CCPA).

The DLP solution must consider the data source. In other words, it needs to evaluate whether the user is actually allowed to share the data and, if so, share it securely. Another important variable is the destination; the source might be legitimate, but the destination is suspicious.

While source and destination are important variables to analyze, you also need to be aware of the amount of data that is being shared. It might be acceptable if the approved source shares one credit card number with an allowed destination. However, if the same source shares 200 credit card numbers to the same destination, it won't be allowed and should be blocked.

DLP capability in Microsoft Purview detects sensitive items by using deep content analysis. This is not simply done by using a text scan. Instead, it is done by evaluating regular expressions, internal function validation, and secondary data matches in proximity to the primary data match. In addition, DLP also uses machine learning algorithms and other methods to detect content that matches your DLP policies. DLP policies can be applied to data at rest, data in use, and data in transit in locations such as:

- Exchange Online email
- SharePoint Online sites
- OneDrive accounts
- Teams chat and channel messages
- Microsoft Defender for Cloud Apps
- Windows 10, Windows 11, and macOS (Catalina 10.15 and higher) devices
- On-premises repositories
- PowerBI sites

Microsoft Purview DLP includes ready-to-use policy templates that address common compliance requirements, such as U.S. Health Insurance Act (HIPAA), U.S. Gramm-Leach-Bliley Act (GLBA), or U.S. Patriot Act. While these templates follow strict guidelines, DLP policies can be configured to allow override. In other words, users can add justification to override items. You can use the built-in reports available to review those exceptions and the provided justification.

Once you are ready to deploy the DLP policies, you should consider rolling them out gradually to assess their impact and make sure you are testing their effectiveness before fully enforcing them. If you foresee a large potential impact with the policies that you are creating, make sure to:

- Start in Test mode and use DLP reports to assess the impact.

- Transition to Test mode with notifications and Policy Tips so you can begin to educate users about your company's compliance policies and prepare them for the policies that will be applied.

- Use full enforcement on the policies so the actions in the rules are applied and the content is protected.

 EXAM TIP On the SC-100 exam, make sure to carefully read the scenario requirements for keywords such as "prevention." For example, you must recommend a solution to prevent Personally Identifiable Information (PII) from being shared. In this case, the solution is DLP.

Govern your data

Establishing what data you need to keep and what data can be discarded is the foundation of data governance. You need to identify your workloads that need a retention policy and whether you need to create retention labels for exceptions. While data retention and deletion are often necessary for compliance and regulatory requirements, there is business value in deleting content that is no longer needed. Also, data retention and deletion help you to manage risk and liability.

Deciding what is important for your organization to keep (and for how long) needs to be defined upfront, even before implementing any technology to manage data retention. Business, legal, and compliance requirements might impact your strategy. Those responsible for making these decisions in your organization should identify the content to retain or discard for business and legal requirements. The governance team will also need to identify the regulations that apply to your organization, many of which include data retention requirements.

Microsoft Purview Data Lifecycle Management (formerly Microsoft Information Governance) and Microsoft Purview Records Management can be leveraged for this purpose. These solutions will address scenarios such as:

- Contoso needs to create an organization-wide retention policy to delete all Microsoft Teams communications older than ten days.

- Contoso needs to implement a solution for its five-year retention policy requirement, where automatically labeled content will be kept for five years and then automatically deleted.

- Contoso needs to implement a solution that enables them to review documents stored in a SharePoint document library before they are deleted due to the retention policy expiration.

Two terms are always used in the scenarios above: retention and deletion. It is important to understand what will happen with potential conflict. For example, let's use a scenario where there is one retention policy configured to delete Exchange email after three years. Another retention policy is configured to retain Exchange email for five years and then delete it. In this type of scenario, any content that reaches three years old will be deleted and hidden from the user. However, it will remain in the Recoverable Items folder until the content reaches the five-year retention period. After this, it will be permanently deleted.

Content being retained by one policy cannot be permanently deleted by another policy. In other words, retention takes precedence over deletion. Additionally, the longest retention takes precedence if multiple retention policies exist for the same content. When there are multiple deletion policies without retention for the same content, the shortest deletion period takes precedence over the longest.

 EXAM TIP On the SC-100 exam, you might have questions about where to select the best option based on the scenario's requirements. Table 9-2 shows common scenarios and the suggested solution to govern your data.

TABLE 9-2 Common scenarios for retention and deletion

Scenario	Capability	Feature that can fulfill this requirement
Retain or delete content with policy management for email, documents, and Teams and Yammer messages	Retention policies for Microsoft 365 workloads, with retention labels for exceptions	Microsoft Purview Data Lifecycle Management
Retain mailbox content after employees leave the organization so that this content remains accessible to administrators, compliance officers, and records managers	Inactive mailboxes	Microsoft Purview Data Lifecycle Management
Provides additional mailbox storage space for users	Archive mailboxes	Microsoft Purview Data Lifecycle Management
Create retention labels interactively and label support additional administrative information (optional) to help identify and track business or regulatory requirements	File plan	Microsoft Purview Records Management
Support flexible retention and deletion schedules that can be applied manually or automatically, with records declaration when needed	Retention labels for individual items, retention policies if needed for baseline retention	Microsoft Purview Records Management
Review content before it's permanently deleted, with proof of disposition	Disposition review and proof of disposition	Microsoft Purview Records Management

Skill 9-3: Specify an encryption standard for data at rest and in motion

When migrating to the cloud, you should ensure that the data is secure, no matter where this data is located. That's why it is important to specify encryption methods for data at rest (in the endpoint or server) and data in motion (also called in transit), when the data flows from end-to-end. This section of the chapter covers the skills necessary to specify an encryption standard for data at rest and in motion according to the Exam SC-100 outline.

Encryption at rest

Encryption at rest in Azure uses symmetric encryption to encrypt and decrypt large amounts of data quickly. A symmetric encryption key is used to encrypt data as it is written to storage, and the same encryption key is used to decrypt that data as it is readied for use in memory.

While encryption at rest is primarily used to prevent threat actors from accessing unencrypted data by ensuring on-disk data is encrypted, it can also be required by an organization's need for data governance and compliance efforts. Industry and government regulations, such as HIPAA, PCI, and FedRAMP, lay out specific safeguards regarding data protection and encryption requirements. This makes encryption at rest a mandatory measure required for compliance.

An important aspect to consider is the location where the encryption keys will be stored. The keys must be highly secured but manageable by specified users and available to specific services. For Azure services, Azure Key Vault is the recommended key storage solution and provides a common management experience across services.

Since you can use encryption in all three cloud models (SaaS, IaaS, and PaaS), it is important to understand how each model leverages encryption by reviewing Table 9-3:

TABLE 9-3 Cloud model and encryption technologies

Model	Platform	Encryption technologies
SaaS	Office 365	■ Office 365 message encryption (OME) ■ Service encryption with Microsoft Purview Customer Key ■ Mobile Device Management for Office 365
IaaS	Azure	■ Azure Disk Encryption (ADE)
PaaS	Azure	■ Server-side encryption using Service-Managed keys ■ Server-side encryption using customer-managed keys in Azure Key Vault ■ Server-side encryption using customer-managed keys on customer-controlled hardware

The Microsoft Cloud service for SaaS is Office 365, and the encryption at rest includes

- Files uploaded to a SharePoint library
- Project Online data
- Documents uploaded in a Skype for Business meeting
- Email messages and attachments stored in folders in a mailbox
- Files uploaded to OneDrive for Business

Some organizations might need to control the encryption keys used to encrypt their data in Microsoft's data centers, where the SaaS services will be running. In this case, you can control your organization's encryption keys and then configure Office 365 to use them to encrypt your data at rest in Microsoft's data centers, which in this scenario will leverage customer keys. Using a customer key enhances the ability of your organization to meet the demands of compliance requirements that specify key arrangements with the cloud service provider. With a customer key, you provide and control the root encryption keys for your Microsoft 365 data at-rest at the application level. As a result, you exercise control over your organization's keys.

For scenarios where you need to encrypt files saved on mobile devices, you can use mobile device encryption features, such as Mobile Device Management for Office 365. You can set policies that determine whether to allow mobile devices to access data in Office 365. A common policy is to allow only devices that encrypt content to access Office 365 data.

When it comes to IaaS, data encryption at rest is an extremely important part of your overall VM security strategy. Defender for Cloud will even trigger a security recommendation when a VM is missing disk encryption. You can encrypt your Windows and Linux virtual machines' disks using Azure Disk Encryption (ADE). For Windows OS, you need Windows 8 or later (client) and Windows Server 2008 R2 or later (servers).

ADE provides operating system and data disk encryption. For Windows, it uses BitLocker Device Encryption; for Linux, it uses the DM-Crypt system. ADE is not available in the following scenarios:

- Basic A-series VMs
- VMs with less than 2 GB of memory
- Generation 2 VMs and Lsv2-series VMs
- Unmounted volumes

ADE requires that your Windows VM has connectivity with Azure AD to get a token to connect with Key Vault. At that point, the VM needs access to the Key Vault endpoint to write the encryption keys, and the VM also needs access to an Azure storage endpoint. This storage endpoint will host the Azure extension repository and the Azure storage account that hosts the VHD files.

Group policy is another important consideration when implementing ADE. If the VMs for which you are implementing ADE are domain-joined, make sure not to push any group policy that enforces Trusted Platform Module (TPM) protectors. In this case, you will need to make sure that the Allow BitLocker Without A Compatible TPM policy is configured. Also, BitLocker policy for domain-joined VMs with custom group policy must include the following setting:

`Configure User Storage Of BitLocker Recovery Information / Allow 256-Bit Recovery Key.`

Because ADE uses Azure Key Vault to control and manage disk encryption keys and secrets, you need to make sure Azure Key Vault has the proper configuration for this implementation. One important consideration when configuring your Azure Key Vault for ADE is that they (VM and Key Vault) both need to be part of the same subscription. Also, make sure that encryption secrets are not crossing regional boundaries; ADE requires that the Key Vault and the VMs are collocated in the same region.

While these are the main considerations for encrypting Windows VM, Linux VMs have some additional requirements. When you need to encrypt both data and OS volumes where the root (/) file system usage is 4 GB or less, you will need to have at least 8 GB of memory. However, if you need to encrypt only the data volume, the requirement drops to 2 GB of memory. The requirement doubles if Linux systems use a root (/) file system greater than 4 GB, meaning that the minimum memory requirement is twice the root file system usage.

Understanding those considerations before implementing ADE is very important, mainly when reading a scenario in the SC-100 exam. The scenario description will give you the requirements and the constraints, which means that in some scenarios, it won't be possible to implement ADE unless some other tasks are executed before the ADE implementation.

> **IMPORTANT** PaaS services such as Azure Storage services (blob, queue, and table storage and Azure Files) support server-side encryption at rest.

Encryption in motion

Encryption in motion should always be an essential part of your data protection strategy. Data in motion is the data that is moving back and forth from many locations, which is always recommended to be encrypted using SSL/TLS protocols. In some circumstances, you might want to isolate the entire communication channel between your on-premises and cloud infrastructures by using a Virtual Private Network (VPN).

For data moving between your on-premises infrastructure and Azure, consider using safeguards such as HTTPS or VPN. When sending encrypted traffic between an Azure virtual network and an on-premises location over the public Internet, use Azure VPN Gateway. TLS provides strong authentication, message privacy, integrity, interoperability, algorithm flexibility, and ease of deployment and use. You can also use Perfect Forward Secrecy (PFS) to protect the connection between customers' client systems and Microsoft cloud services. Connections also use RSA-based 2,048-bit encryption key lengths. This combination makes it difficult for someone to intercept and access data that is in motion.

When you interact with PaaS services such as Azure Storage through the Azure portal, all transactions take place over HTTPS. If you need to customize your access beyond the portal, you can also use the Storage REST API over HTTPS to interact with Azure Storage. You can enforce the use of HTTPS when you call the REST APIs to access objects in storage accounts by enabling the secure transfer required for the storage account.

Additional capabilities for different services when it comes to data encryption in motion include

- You can make data transfers secure by encrypting data in transit over Azure Virtual Networks using SMB 3.0 for IaaS VMs that are running Windows Server 2012 or later.

- Azure Files shares use SMB 3.0 to support encryption, and it can be leveraged by Windows Server 2012 R2, Windows 8, Windows 8.1, and Windows 10.

- Data in transit over the network in Remote Desktop Protocol (RDP) sessions can be protected by TLS. RDP can be utilized to remote access Windows VMs.

- For remote management of Linux VMs, you can use Secure Shell (SSH). SSH is an encrypted connection protocol that allows secure sign-ins over unsecured connections.

- Other PaaS services, such as Azure App Services, can also use an SSL/TLS certificate. To create a TLS bind of your certificate to your app or enable client certificates for your App Service app, your App Service plan must be configured to the Basic, Standard, Premium, or Isolated tiers. The App Service enables different scenarios to handle certificates, including

  - Buying a certificate
  - Importing an existing certificate from the App Service
  - Uploading an existing certificate
  - Importing a certificate from Key Vault (from any subscription on the same tenant)
  - Creating a free App Service custom certificate

Many organizations will also keep part of their resources on-premises while using cloud computing to host different services, creating a hybrid environment. While this is one common scenario, there are many other scenarios where a VPN can be used. You can use Azure VPN to connect two different Azure regions or different subscriptions.

Azure natively offers a service called VPN gateway, a specific type of virtual network gateway used to send encrypted traffic between an Azure virtual network and on-premises resources. You can also use a VPN gateway to send encrypted traffic between Azure virtual networks. When planning your VPN Gateway implementation, be aware that each virtual network can have only one VPN gateway, and you can create multiple connections to the same VPN gateway. When deploying a hybrid network that needs to create a cross-premises connection, you can select from different types of VPN connectivity. The available options are:

- **Site-to-Site (S2S) VPN** This type of VPN is used in scenarios where you need to connect on-premises resources to Azure. The encrypted connection tunnel uses IPsec/IKE (IKEv1 or IKEv2).

- **Point-to-Site (P2S) VPN** This type of VPN is used in scenarios where you need to connect to your Azure VNet from a remote location. For example, you would use P2S when working remotely (hotel, home, conference, and the like), and you need to access resources in your VNet. This VPN uses SSTP (Secure Socket Tunneling Protocol) or IKE v2 and does not require a VPN device.

- **VNet-to-VNet** As the name states, this VPN is used in scenarios where you need to encrypt connectivity between VNets. This type of connection uses IPsec (IKE v1 and IKE v2).
- **Multi-Site VPN** This type of VPN is used when you need to expand your site-to-site configuration to allow multiple on-premises sites to access a virtual network.

ExpressRoute is another option that allows connectivity from your on-premises resources to Azure. This option uses a private connection to Azure from your WAN instead of a VPN connection over the Internet.

The Azure VPN connection is authenticated when the tunnel is created. Azure generates a pre-shared key (PSK), which is used for authentication. This pre-shared key is an ASCII string character no longer than 128 characters. This authentication happens for policy-based (static routing) or routing-based VPN (dynamic routing).

For point-to-site (P2S) VPN scenarios, you can use native Azure certificate authentication, RADIUS server, or Azure AD authentication. For native Azure certificate authentication, a client certificate is presented on the device, which is used to authenticate the connecting users. The certificate can be issued by an enterprise certificate authority (CA) or a self-signed root certificate. For native Azure AD, you can use the native Azure AD credentials. Keep in mind that native Azure AD is only supported for the OpenVPN protocol and Windows 10 (Windows 10 requires the Azure VPN Client).

If your scenario requires the enforcement of a second authentication factor before access to the resource is granted, you can use Azure Multi-Factor Authentication (MFA) with conditional access. Even if you don't want to implement MFA across your entire company, you can scope the MFA to be employed only for VPN users using conditional access capability.

If your connectivity scenario requires a higher level of reliability, faster speeds, consistent latencies, and higher security than typical connections over the Internet, you should use ExpressRoute, which provides layer three connectivity between your on-premises network and the Microsoft Cloud.

ExpressRoute supports two different encryption technologies to ensure the confidentiality and integrity of the data that is traversing from on-premises to Microsoft's network. The options are

- Point-to-point encryption by MACsec
- End-to-end encryption by IPSec

MACsec encrypts the data at the media access control (MAC) level or network layer 2. When you enable MACsec, all network control traffic is encrypted, including the border gateway protocol (BGP) and your (customer) data traffic. This means that you can't encrypt only some of your ExpressRoute circuits.

If you need to encrypt the physical links between your network devices and Microsoft's network devices when you connect to Microsoft via ExpressRoute Direct, MACsec is preferred. MACsec also allows you to bring your own MACsec key for encryption and store it in Azure Key Vault. If this is the design choice, remember that you will need to decide when to rotate the key.

The other option is to use end-to-end encryption with IPsec, which encrypts data at the Internet protocol (IP) level or at network layer 3. A common scenario is using IPsec to encrypt the end-to-end connection between on-premises resources and your Azure VNet. If you need to encrypt layers 2 and 3, you can enable MACsec and IPsec. Use Table 9-4 to evaluate each protocol's advantages and limitations.

TABLE 9-4 Advantages and limitations

Protocol	Advantages	Limitations
OpenVPN Protocol	This TLS VPN-based solution can traverse most firewalls on the market. Can be used to connect from various operating systems, including Android, iOS (versions 11.0 and above), Windows, Linux, and Mac devices (OSX versions 10.13 and above).	Basic SKU is not supported. Not available for the classic deployment model.
Secure Socket Tunneling Protocol (SSTP)	Can traverse most firewalls because it uses TCP port 443.	Only supported on Windows devices. Supports up to 128 concurrent connections, regardless of the gateway SKU.
IKEv2	Standard-based IPsec VPN solution. Can be used to connect to Mac devices (OSX versions 10.11 and above).	Basic SKU is not supported. Not available for the classic deployment model. Uses nonstandard UDP ports, so you need to ensure that these ports are not blocked on the user's firewall. The ports in use are UDP 500 and 4500.

 EXAM TIP   For the SC-100 exam, make sure to carefully read the scenarios because there will be indications of what the company wants to accomplish. Those indications will be used to decide which protocol to implement or which is not an option for the specified scenario.

Thought experiment

In this thought experiment, demonstrate your skills and knowledge of the topics covered in this chapter. You can find answers to this thought experiment in the next section.

Design a strategy for securing data

You are the Cybersecurity Architect for Tailwind Traders, an online general store specializing in various home improvement products. Tailwind Traders management is concerned with threat actors scanning public storage accounts and wants to ensure their incident response team can quickly identify potential attempts to access publicly exposed storage accounts.

As part of the data protection strategy, Tailwind Traders must adopt a single labeling solution across apps, services, and devices to ensure that the data is protected as it travels inside and outside their organization. They also need protection for existing on-premises deployments that use Exchange, SharePoint Server, and file servers running Windows Server.

Based on this scenario, respond to the following questions:

1. Which solution should be utilized to detect threat actors scanning public storage accounts?

2. Which solution should they utilize for single labeling across apps, services, and devices?

3. Which solution should they utilize to protect existing on-premises resources?

Thought experiment answers

This section contains the solutions to the thought experiment.

1. Microsoft Defender for Storage

2. Microsoft Purview

3. Microsoft Rights Management connector

Chapter summary

- When you enable Defender for Storage, you have a series of analytics created for different scenarios, and the anonymous scan of public storage containers is one of those.

- A rising threat for data is ransomware, which can be fatal for many organizations as they might not have a backup of the data and can't even pay the ransom.

- How the IoT workloads are distributed in the network is another important security aspect that needs to be considered. You should design your IoT architecture into several components/zones.

- To prioritize which threats will be remediated first and which workloads are affected, you need to ensure you have a well-established vulnerability management system that can identify threats across different workloads.

- After discovering your data, you need to classify your data. Classification is the process of labeling the data that you identified to get a better understanding of your data landscape.

- Since labels can be applied in different scenarios, you will need to determine the scope in which you want to apply the label.

- To prevent data loss, companies must ensure that they have data loss prevention (DLP) technology that can help prevent accidental oversharing in and outside the organization.

- Microsoft Purview DLP includes ready-to-use policy templates that address common compliance requirements, such as U.S. Health Insurance Act (HIPAA), U.S. Gramm-Leach-Bliley Act (GLBA), or U.S. Patriot Act.

- Establishing what data you need to keep and what data can be discarded is the foundation of data governance. You need to identify your workloads that need a retention policy and whether you need to create retention labels for exceptions.

- Encryption at rest in Azure uses symmetric encryption to encrypt and decrypt large amounts of data quickly. A symmetric encryption key is used to encrypt data as it is written to storage, and the same encryption key is used to decrypt that data as it is readied for use in memory.

- Encryption in motion (also known as in transit) should always be an essential part of your data protection strategy. Data in motion is the data that is moving back and forth from many locations, which we recommend always be encrypted using SSL/TLS protocols.

Microsoft Cybersecurity Reference Architectures and Microsoft cloud security benchmark best practices

Best practices are recommended ways to approach problems, typically because they have been found to work well in similar situations or because they represent how the product or technology is intended to be used. Microsoft publishes best practices to help organizations solve security problems that combine the technology's design intent and lessons learned in practice.

This chapter covers two key sources of best practices:

- **Microsoft Cybersecurity Reference Architectures (MCRA)** These detailed technical architecture diagrams and slide sequences describe Microsoft's cybersecurity capabilities and
  - How to integrate them with Microsoft and third-party platforms
  - Best practices for Zero Trust, security operations, attack chain coverage, cloud-native security controls, security organizational functions, and more
- **Microsoft cloud security benchmark (MCSB)** Formerly the Azure Security Benchmark (ASB), these specific best practices and recommendations help you secure the services your organization uses in Azure, hybrid, and multi-cloud environments. The MCSB includes security controls and specific baselines for Azure services that apply these controls.

Cybersecurity architects should be familiar with these two pieces of guidance and the best practices in them.

Skills covered in this chapter:

- Skill 10-1: Recommend best practices for cybersecurity capabilities and controls
- Skill 10-2: Recommend best practices for protecting from insider and external attacks
- Skill 10-3: Recommend best practices for Zero Trust security
- Skill 10-4: Recommend best practices for the Zero Trust Rapid Modernization Plan

What are best practices?

Best practices are recommended practices that are the most effective or efficient way to address a particular discipline or problem. Best practices help you avoid mistakes and ensure your resources and effort aren't wasted.

Best practices come in many forms. Sometimes, they are prescriptive and explicit instructions with clear definitions of what to do, why to do it, who should do it, and how to do it. Sometimes, they are high-level principles guiding different decisions and actions. Sometimes, they are part of a reference architecture that describes components that should be included in a solution and how to integrate them.

Microsoft has embedded best practices in various forms of guidance, including the Microsoft Cybersecurity Reference Architectures, Microsoft cloud security benchmark, and other guidance, such as the Cloud Adoption Framework (CAF), Microsoft Azure Well-Architected Framework, and Microsoft security best practices.

Antipatterns are the opposites of best practices

Antipatterns are common mistakes that lead to negative outcomes, effectively the opposite of a best practice. Many best practices are designed explicitly to help you avoid one or more antipatterns. For example, going beyond VPN for remote access helps you avoid the "use VPN for all remote access" antipattern that causes user frustration and security issues caused by weak authentication. Also, this causes users to work around security to get their work done.

Regularly applying security patches is an example of a best practice that helps you overcome numerous antipatterns. Microsoft has observed multiple antipatterns that get in the way of regularly applying this basic and critically important security best practice:

- **We don't patch (unless it's critical)**   Avoiding patch installations because of an implicit assumption that patches aren't important—"if it ain't broke, don't touch it." Another version of this antipattern is, "It won't happen to us," a belief that unpatched vulnerabilities won't be exploited because they haven't been exploited before (or haven't been detected).

- **Waiting for patch perfection instead of building resilience**   Avoiding patching because something could go wrong with the patches (which then increases the likelihood of downtime from attackers).

- **Broken accountability model**   Holding security accountable for negative outcomes of patches leads to other teams deprioritizing security maintenance.

- **Over-customizing patch selection**   Using unique criteria for patching instead of applying all manufacturer-recommended patches. This effectively creates unique custom builds of Windows, Linux, and applications that have never been tested in that configuration.

- **Focusing only on operating systems**   Patching only servers and workstations without also addressing containers, applications, firmware, and IoT/OT devices.

How architects use best practices

Like any guidance or advice, best practices only have value if they are applied in practice. Security best practices must be integrated into people's skills and habits, repeatable processes of your organization, and technology architecture and implementation.

- Cybersecurity architects help integrate security best practices and make them actionable via

    - Integrating best practices into security architecture and policy

    - Advising security leaders on how to integrate best practices into business processes, technical processes, culture, and more

    - Advising technical teams on implementing best practices, which technology capabilities help make doing so easier and more effective, and more

    - Advising others in the organization (such as enterprise architects, IT architects, application owners, developers, and more) on how to integrate security best practices into their architecture, processes, and so on

- Architects should follow these two rules regarding the application of best practices:

    - **Follow best practices unless you have a reason not to**   Organizations should follow well-defined and well-reasoned best practices unless there is a specific reason not to. While some organizations should ignore some best practices for good reasons, organizations should be very cautious before ignoring high-quality best practices like those provided by Microsoft. Best practices are not unquestionably perfect and applicable to all situations, but they have been proven to work elsewhere, so you should not ignore or alter them without good reason.

    - **Adapt but don't over-customize**   Best practices are general guidance that works across most organizations, so you must always adapt best practices to the unique circumstances of your organization. You should be careful not to customize them to the point where the original value is lost (for example, adopting passwordless and multifactor authentication but providing exceptions for the highest-impact business and IT accounts that attackers value most).

Adopting best practices will increase your security posture, reduce business process friction, and make everyone's jobs easier by reducing common mistakes and improving security effectiveness and efficiency.

Where do Microsoft's best practices come from?

Microsoft's best practices come from several sources, including the following:

- **Technology intent and design**   Microsoft draws from the experience of building and operating both hyperscale technology platforms and security capabilities. Microsoft combines these two key perspectives on how products and platforms were designed and intended to be used and the perspective of a security provider applying a critical eye to those platforms and other third-party platforms.

- **Effective common practices** Microsoft also draws best practices from what has been observed to work well across many organizations. These validated approaches have been proven to work many times in practice in different circumstances.

- **Bright spots and early adopters** Microsoft also pays close attention to emerging spaces and leading organizations that are early adopters of new technology, business models, and other innovations. These organizations face new problems and solutions before other organizations. These same problems and solutions are likely to be faced by many other organizations that later adopt the new technology, business models, and other innovations.

Microsoft's best practices represent lessons learned from the product design process and other organizations that you can use to improve security and productivity while avoiding common challenges.

Are security best practices permanent, or do they change?

Security best practices can change over time as business models, technology, and attack techniques change (or our understanding of any of these improves). Most security best practices stay valid and stable for years, but it's always worth checking with vendors and other organizations to see if any have changed or new best practices are emerging. Microsoft's security best practices are periodically updated to reflect changes and new learnings.

Following are some illustrative examples of how security best practices have changed over time:

- **Changed from security controls and configurations to secure code and secure operational practices** The security of systems was once exclusively measured by the presence of security controls and their configuration (such as the U.S. Department of Defense Trusted Computer System Evaluation Criteria, better known as "the orange book"). After worms exploited software vulnerabilities and disrupted organizations around the globe in the early 2000s, new best practices for a secure development lifecycle and applying security patches were defined. Security best practices then expanded further into the operational practices for managing systems and using privileged accounts in the early 2010s as credential theft techniques like pass-the-hash were automated in tools like the Pass the Hash Toolkit, Windows Credential Editor, and Mimikatz. See *https://aka.ms/SPA* for more information.

- **Protecting the edge of the technical estate** The dividing line between an organization's valuable assets and potential risks to them was once defined by the edge of the corporate network at the Internet ingress/egress points. Protecting the enterprise consisted mostly of a network perimeter of firewalls and intrusion detection/prevention (IDS/IPS) systems that monitored or intercepted traffic on this border. The advent of mobile devices and cloud services started to define a new "line" that stopped at any devices or cloud service that had a copy of the organization's valuable data and assets. Security best practices shifted to protecting data and other valuable assets wherever they are in a Zero Trust approach using different types of controls. Network controls are still included but no longer the main or only control type.

- **Shifting security to the cloud**   Before the cloud, all assets and all security tools were located in on-premises datacenters and offices. As cloud services became available, organizations shifted IT workloads to the cloud. Later, security vendors began offering Software as a Service (SaaS) versions of existing and SaaS-only security tools. These SaaS-based security tools simplified the installation, maintenance, and operation of security tools, similar to how SaaS apps simplify IT workloads. Security best practices shifted to preferring SaaS delivery where possible (some geographies don't have good connectivity to cloud services) as this shifted the maintenance of security tooling to the vendor, freeing up security experts to focus on other critical tasks. This best practice of preferring cloud capabilities applies to security tools and the IT and management systems that have to be secured. Shifting IT and management to the cloud is particularly useful for highly complex technologies that require rare and hard-to-find skill sets like containers.

- **Cloud Native Controls**   As cloud services matured, they began to integrate security controls into them, like Azure Firewall, Azure Web Application Firewall (WAF), Amazon Web Services (AWS) Security Groups, and Azure Network Security Groups (NSGs). These capabilities are made for cloud technology and can often be automated into infrastructure as code (IaC) capabilities like Azure Resource Manager (ARM), Azure Bicep, and Terraform. Security best practices evolved to prefer these capabilities over traditional security appliances for many scenarios because they can be easily automated and monitored, work well with cloud workloads, and simplify security setup and maintenance to the point that workload teams can implement them without requiring security experts.

- **Require multifactor and passwordless authentication**   Authenticating user accounts with only passwords is no longer sufficient to maintain security assurances. Attackers can efficiently defeat password-only authentication easily at scale with password spray, credential theft, device compromise, and many other means. Organizations should require multifactor authentication (MFA) and ensure they are quickly moving to strong forms of MFA authentication that are difficult for attackers to defeat.

IMPORTANT   **PRIORITIZE CREDENTIAL THEFT OF PRIVILEGED ACCOUNTS**

Stealing and re-using administrative credentials is one of the most common and damaging attack techniques in the history of the cybersecurity industry. This attack technique was first described in a 1997 publication by Paul Ashton on pass-the-hash but only saw limited use until it was popularized by the release of the Pass-the-hash Toolkit for Windows in 2007 (and then subsequently the Windows Credentials Editor and Mimikatz tools).

The best practices to effectively mitigate this attack often don't get to become the top of the priority list for many organizations. While it's difficult to say for certain why this is the case, some likely contributors to this strange and dangerous dynamic are:

- **The attack is difficult to detect**   These attacks abuse identity protocols and involve theft and re-use of legitimate credentials, which is very difficult to detect. It requires specialized sensors and tooling like Microsoft Defender for Identity and/or sophisticated use of event logs and other signals to find the anomalous use of credentials and related artifacts. Most security organizations and professionals started with a strong network security background (or occasionally an application development background). So, understanding the nuances of identity protocols (a complex space) to design detections is very challenging with traditional SIEM-centric and network-centric detections.

- **Effective mitigations are difficult and require significant process change**   While exploiting these attacks is relatively easy and well understood, mitigating these attacks requires a deep investment into changing how both humans and applications/services use all privileged accounts. Changing how IT administrators perform daily tasks (such as what workstations they use for daily work) requires significant effort to change practices, habits, hardware budget, and other assumptions. Changing the usage of service accounts requires understanding and changing how applications and services work. This is no easy task because many applications no longer have active developers /owners who understand the architecture and the permissions required to operate them. Additionally, it takes investment to set up a privileged account lifecycle to prevent new problems.

- **Common misperception that PIM/PAM tools solve the problem**   Some people have a misperception that Privileged Identity/Access Management (PIM/PAM) solutions fully solve the problem, even though these solutions only mitigate part of it. PIM/PAM solutions help immensely with some parts of the mitigation (discovery of accounts, increased visibility, and control over administrative account sessions). Still, they fall short of mitigating scenarios where attackers gain control of the privileged user's device (and some attacks even abuse those PIM/PAM solutions).

- **Mitigations aren't required by regulatory standards**   Most security regulatory standards don't require the measures described above that will effectively mitigate these attacks. Organizations can be fully compliant with regulatory standards while being fully vulnerable to these routine and highly damaging attacks.

Full guidance on securing privileged accounts can be found at *https://aka.ms/spa*.

As you can see, security best practices have evolved over time and will continue to evolve. Microsoft's security best practices reflect the currently known trends and are periodically updated as needed.

Microsoft Cybersecurity Reference Architectures (MCRA)

The MCRA diagrams and sections are a key source of security best practices.

These reference architectures include detailed technical diagrams on Microsoft cybersecurity capabilities, Zero Trust user access, security operations, multi-cloud and cross-platform capabilities, operational technology (OT), attack chains and technical capability coverage,

Azure native security controls, as well as security roles and responsibilities. The MCRA also includes an overview of Zero Trust from Microsoft and The Open Group and the Zero-Trust Rapid Modernization Plan (RaMP).

The MCRA guidance is designed to address the modern, "hybrid of everything" technical estate that includes on-premises datacenters and workloads, Microsoft 365, Microsoft Azure, and third-party apps and platforms like ServiceNow, Salesforce, Box, Dropbox, Amazon Web Services (AWS), Google Cloud Platform (GCP), and more.

Figure 10-1 illustrates the contents of the MCRA.

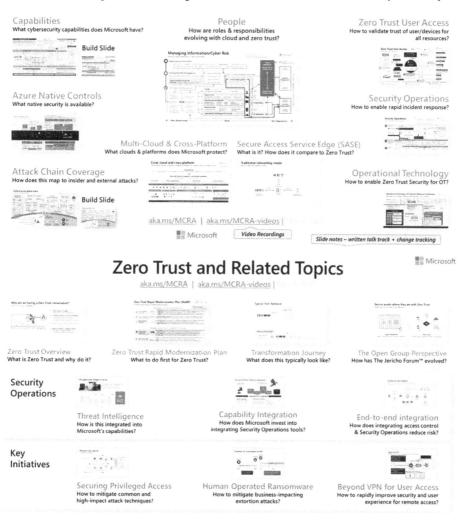

FIGURE 10-1 MCRA Menu slides with Thumbnails of diagrams and sections in it (Figure courtesy of Microsoft)

MCRA's use cases include:

- **Template for a new Security Architecture** To use as a starting point for a new security architecture that can be customized as needed.

- **Comparison of existing security architecture** To evaluate an existing architecture against Microsoft's recommendations to identify how to improve it.

- **Learn what Microsoft capabilities are available** To identify what capabilities are available from Microsoft (which the organization might already own).

- **Learning about Microsoft capabilities** To understand more about capabilities and how they work together. Note that the MCRA includes a ScreenTip with a short summary of each capability and a documentation link for many elements of many slides.

The MCRA includes several types of security best practices, many of which are described later in this chapter.

Microsoft cloud security benchmark (MCSB)

Microsoft cloud security benchmark provides security best practices for infrastructure and development platforms that could include a hybrid of Microsoft Azure, on-premises datacenters, and other cloud providers like AWS and GCP. The MCSB is composed of high-impact security recommendations designed to increase your security. The MCSB includes two types of guidance:

- **Security controls** Recommendations that are generally applicable across an environment

- **Service baselines** A specific interpretation of these security controls to individual Azure services to provide prescriptive recommendations on the service's security configuration

You can find the Microsoft cloud security benchmark at *https://aka.ms/benchmarkdocs*.

Microsoft Defender for Cloud (MDC) uses the MCSB as the default security compliance initiative with more than 200 Azure Policy checks to help customers automatically measure their compliance posture against MCSB. The MCSB security controls are also mapped to other security standards, including Center for Internet Security (CIS) Controls, NIST SP 800-53, and PCI-DSS. MDC includes mappings to additional standards in the regulatory compliance dashboard.

> **NOTE** Azure landing zone is a mature, scaled-out target architecture to help organizations adopt the cloud and drive their business while maintaining best practices for governance and security. The Azure landing zone is aligned to the MCSB and includes automated architecture implementation, drastically simplifying the application of best practices in MCSB. For more information on the Azure Landing Zone, see *https://aka.ms/alz*.

The MCSB is primarily used as a starting point for creating an internal security standard or as a comparison point for an existing internal standard. Organizations typically develop an internal security standard to make it easier to consistently manage the obligations of meeting multiple external regulatory standards. Some organizations also use internal security standards to increase security rigor and consistency across different technical teams and workload teams.

Many organizations also use the MCSB baselines when evaluating the security features and capabilities of Azure services before approving them for use or inclusion in a cloud service catalog.

Figure 10-2 illustrates an example of a security control in the benchmark.

PA-6: Use privileged access workstations

Mapping

CIS Controls v8 ID(s)	NIST SP 800-53 r4 ID(s)	PCI-DSS ID(s) v3.2.1
12.8, 13.5	AC-2, SC-2, SC-7	N/A

Security principle — **Security principle:** Secured, isolated workstations are critically important for the security of sensitive roles like administrator, developer, and critical service operator.

Azure guidance — **Azure guidance:** Use Azure Active Directory, Microsoft Defender, and/or Microsoft Intune to deploy privileged access workstations (PAW) on-premises or in Azure for privileged tasks. The PAW should be centrally managed to enforce secured configuration, including strong authentication, software and hardware baselines, and restricted logical and network access.

You may also use Azure Bastion, which is a fully platform-managed PaaS service that can be provisioned inside your virtual network. Azure Bastion allows RDP/SSH connectivity to your virtual machines directly from the Azure portal using a browser.

implementation and additional context:

- Understand privileged access workstations
- Privileged access workstations deployment

Implementation and context — **AWS guidance:** Use Session Manager in AWS Systems Manager to create an access path (a connection session) to the EC2 instance or a browser session to the AWS resources for privileged tasks. Session Manager allows RDP, SSH, and HTTPS connectivity to your destination hosts through port forwarding.

You may also choose to deploy privileged access workstations (PAW) centrally managed through Azure Active Directory, Microsoft Defender, and/or Microsoft Intune. The central management solution should enforce secured configuration, including strong authentication, software and hardware baselines, and restricted logical and network access.

AWS implementation and additional context:

- AWS Systems Manager Session Manager

Customer security stakeholders (Learn more**):**

Stakeholders —
- Application security and DevSecOps
- Security Operations (SecOps)
- Identity and key management

FIGURE 10-2 A Microsoft cloud security benchmark security control

The composition of each control in the benchmark includes:

- **Mapping**   Maps the security control to controls in other industry security standards.
- **Security Principle**   Provides a clear and simple statement describing the security control. The principle is cloud-neutral and can be applied across resources on any cloud provider and on-premises resources (and often on other security aspects).
- **Azure guidance**   Provides specific implementation guidance to make the security controls prescriptive and actionable for Azure resources.

- **Implementation and additional context**   Provides references to implementation documentation and other context that helps with planning and implementing the security control.

- **Customer security stakeholders**   Provides insights into which security stakeholders typically focus on implementing or monitoring this control.

The Microsoft cloud security benchmark comprises explicitly defined security best practices, several of which are referenced later in this chapter.

MCRA and MCSB include different best practices architects should be familiar with. These include different best practices (explicit recommendations and diagrams with components and relationships) that complement each other and increase clarity.

Now let's take a look at some of the recommendations in this guidance.

Skill 10-1: Recommend best practices for cybersecurity capabilities and controls

Some best practices focus on technical capabilities and controls. While security technology doesn't improve security on its own or replace the need for security experts, technology is critically important to automate processes and empower people to do more.

Capabilities and control best practices can be found throughout the MCRA and MCSB. Some are embedded into MCRA architecture diagrams, others are in other MCRA sections, and still others are explicitly called out in the MCSB. Additionally, various other best-practice sources are referenced in the MCRA, such as the *Azure Security Top 10 Best Practices* (published at *https://aka.ms/azuresecuritytop10*).

Key best practices in the MCRA include:

- **Learn what you have available**   Learn about and utilize all the security capabilities and controls you have access to.

- **Use the right tool for the job**   Use a multi-technology approach to apply the best solution to the problem, rather than relying on the same technology over and over, like a network firewall or Security Information and Event Management (SIEM).

- **Data and management plane security**   Ensure that you include both data plane security controls (available since pre-cloud on-premises datacenters) as well as management plane security controls (embedded into cloud platforms that allow an additional layer of visibility and control).

- **Security for the platform/infrastructure and the workload**   Ensure you have controls to protect the specific workload (such as web application firewalls (WAFs)) as well as the overall infrastructure and development environments.

- **Native cloud controls**   Use native cloud controls that are designed to secure your cloud assets.

- **Consistent tooling**   Use consistent tooling across cloud providers to ensure controls are effectively implemented across all your infrastructure and platforms. This reduces the time and effort to implement and monitor controls, allowing you to accomplish more in security with the resources you have.

- **Approach security holistically**   Securing an asset requires establishing visibility and control over the full lifecycle. For the example of a cloud-hosted resource, this would include

  - People accessing it

  - Accounts and groups they use to access it

  - Devices they log into those accounts with

  - Interface that provides access to the resource (Azure portal, command-line interface, application programming interfaces, and so on)

  - The resource itself

  - Any underlying storage, virtual machines, containers, or other cloud/application services that interact with the resource

  - Any devices and customer accounts that interact with the resources

- **Focus on security and productivity**   Ensure that security enables productivity and reduces risk. Security should provide "healthy friction" that causes people to think critically about risk while designing or operating a system but shouldn't create unhealthy friction that blocks productivity and/or doesn't reduce risk in a meaningful way.

- **Protecting privileged access**   Ensure privileged accounts and systems are protected with elevated security protections, monitoring, and response. Compromises of privileged access enable attackers to shut down business operations across the organization in a ransomware/extortion attack. Attackers frequently target highly privileged accounts because doing this allows rapid and efficient compromise of many systems at once and increases the attacker's return on their illicit investment.

The elevated protections organizations should implement include

- **Protect privileged user accounts**   With strong MFA, threat detection, and tagging accounts to ensure rapid response to anomalous events.

- **Protect workstations and devices**   Protect workstations and devices used by these accounts with Privileged Access Workstations (PAWs) and additional monitoring and response.

- **Protecting intermediaries**   Protect intermediaries that handle privileged accounts and sessions such as virtual private networks (VPNs), PIM/PAM solutions, domain controllers, and more with elevated protections, security policy monitoring, threat detection, and more.

NOTE   More details on securing privileged access can be found at *https://aka.ms/SPA*.

- **Prepare for ransomware and extortion attacks** Ensure that you are mitigating the risk of ransomware attacks, starting with the most impactful controls.

- **Validating BC/DR process** Ensure your business continuity/disaster recovery (BC/DR) process includes all business-critical systems in scope, includes a scenario for a ransomware/extortion attack, and has exercised this scenario recently. Without this, your ability to recover from this type of attack might be much slower, and you might not recover all business-critical systems.

- **Securing backups against sabotage** Ensure that backups are protected against deliberate attacker erasure or encryption, which is a common tactic. Without this, you might find that critical business operations cannot be recovered without paying for the ransom/extortion payment (which is much slower, has no guarantee of success, and incurs potential liability and other risks).

- **Protecting privileged access** Protect privileged access as described earlier in this list.

The MCSB security controls contain many best practices for cybersecurity capabilities and controls, including both technical and non-technical capabilities and controls like processes. Table 10-1 lists several relevant security controls:

TABLE 10-1 MCSB best practices for cybersecurity capabilities and controls

MCSB control domain	Security controls
Data Protection (DP)	DP-1: Discover, classify, and label sensitive data DP-2: Monitor anomalies and threats targeting sensitive data DP-3: Encrypt sensitive data in transit DP-4: Enable data at rest encryption by default DP-5: Use customer-managed key option in data at rest encryption when required DP-6: Use a secure key management process DP-7: Use a secure certificate management process DP-8: Ensure security of key and certificate repository
Asset Management (AM)	AM-1: Track asset inventory and their risks AM-2: Use only approved services AM-3: Ensure security of asset lifecycle management AM-4: Limit access to asset management AM-5: Use only approved applications in virtual machine
Posture and Vulnerability Management (PV)	PV-1: Define and establish secure configurations PV-2: Audit and enforce secure configurations PV-3: Define and establish secure configurations for compute resources PV-4: Audit and enforce secure configurations for compute resources PV-5: Perform vulnerability assessments PV-6: Rapidly and automatically remediate vulnerabilities PV-7: Conduct regular red team operations
Endpoint Security (ES)	ES-1: Use Endpoint Detection and Response (EDR) ES-2: Use modern anti-malware software ES-3: Ensure anti-malware software and signatures are updated
Backup and Recovery (BR)	BR-1: Ensure regular automated backups BR-2: Protect backup and recovery data BR-3: Monitor backups BR-4: Regularly test backup

MCSB control domain	Security controls
DevOps Security (DS)	DS-1: Conduct threat modeling DS-2: Ensure software supply chain security DS-3: Secure DevOps infrastructure DS-4: Integrate static application security testing into DevOps pipeline DS-5: Integrate dynamic application security testing into DevOps pipeline DS-6: Enforce security of workload throughout DevOps lifecycle DS-7: Enable logging and monitoring in DevOps
Governance and Strategy (GS)	GS-1: Align organization roles, responsibilities, and accountabilities GS-2: Define and implement enterprise segmentation/separation of duties strategy GS-3: Define and implement data protection strategy GS-4: Define and implement network security strategy GS-5: Define and implement security posture management strategy GS-6: Define and implement identity and privileged access strategy GS-7: Define and implement logging, threat detection, and incident response strategy GS-8: Define and implement backup and recovery strategy GS-9: Define and implement endpoint security strategy GS-10: Define and implement DevOps security strategy

MORE INFO For more information on the security controls in each area, see *https://aka.ms/ benchmarkdocs*.

These best practices in MCRA and MCSB can help you improve your security capabilities and controls.

Skill 10-2: Recommend best practices for protecting from insider and external attacks

Effective security programs must protect against insider risk and external threat actors' attacks. You can find best practices for protecting from insider and external attacks throughout the MCRA and MCSB. While all security controls should reduce risk in one or both of these scenarios, this section will focus primarily on insider risk aspects and the security operations elements of external attacks.

An attack chain describes insider and external attacks and the typical chain of events during an attack that leads to organizational damage. This includes technical and non-technical steps taken by adversaries or insiders during the attack. It's important to note that there is no single linear path for either insider risk or external attacks. There are many common elements across attacks, but each can take a unique path.

The MCRA includes an attack chain diagram that depicts common techniques related to both external attacks and insider risks, as shown in Figure 10-3.

Defend across attack chains
Insider and external threats

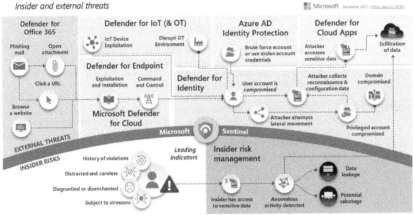

FIGURE 10-3 MCRA Attack Chain Diagram (Figure courtesy of Microsoft)

The top portion of this diagram represents common steps seen in many external attacks and the Microsoft capabilities that map to each area. The bottom portion shows the insider risk leading indicators and how Microsoft Purview Insider Risk Management helps quickly identify, triage, and act on risky user activity.

Most external attacks include common steps and follow common patterns that are depicted in Figure 10-3. Most of the variation in external attacks comes from different entry points used by the attacker(s), such as

- Compromising a user account with password spray or social engineering
- Sending a phishing email with a malicious link
- Compromising an Internet of things (IoT) device
- A watering hole attack where malware is hosted on a site the target user regularly visits
- Implanting malware on a cloud application

Attacks also differ based on the attackers' objectives, such as stealing or encrypting data, disrupting business for either ransomware/extortion, or other means of monetization/benefit.

Most external attacks that result in a major incident include some form of privilege escalation using credential theft, which is mitigated by securing privileged access (covered in the MCRA section of the same name and documented in detail at *https://aka.ms/SPA*).

Lockheed Martin created one of the first adaptations of the "kill chain" military concept to cybersecurity. While this first effort no longer describes current attack patterns well, it helped mature how organizations understand attacks and plan security controls by viewing attacks as a sequential chain of events—an attack chain. Many organizations today use the MITRE ATT&CK framework for detailed control planning, like threat detection coverage.

Figure 10-4 describes how these relate to each other and to a simple Prepare-Enter-Traverse-Execute (PETE) model that Microsoft developed to improve communications with business leaders and non-security professionals.

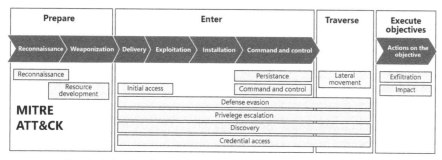

FIGURE 10-4 Attack chain mapping

Attackers can frequently choose from using techniques (phishing, credential theft, or exploiting software vulnerability) to achieve each goal of preparing, entering, traversing, and executing objectives. Attackers might also repeatedly use a combination of techniques or the same technique to achieve their objectives.

All the security best practices in the MCRA and MCSB are intended to reduce the risk of attackers succeeding (either directly or indirectly via effective governance, role organization, and so on). Several MCRA best practices focus directly on the security operations aspects of external attacks—detect, respond, and recover.

These best practices include:

- **Continuous improvement toward complete coverage** Ensure you are always working to continuously improve coverage of the attack chain to remove blind spots with no visibility and highly vulnerable areas with no preventive controls.

- **Balanced control investments** Ensure you are balancing investment into security controls across the full lifecycle of identify, protect, detect, respond, and recover.

- **From SIEM for everything to "XDR + SIEM"** The primary tool for security operations to detect attacks and respond to them has been the Security Information and Event Management (SIEM) capability. Once introduced, extended detection and response (XDR) tools quickly became indispensable for the platforms they monitor (starting with Endpoint Detection and Response (EDR) for endpoints) because they quickly reduce false positives that waste scarce analyst time and attention. These tools do not cover the breadth of sources that the SIEM does, but they greatly simplify and increase the effectiveness of detection and response for technologies covered by XDR. Security best practices then shifted to reflect the strengths of SIEM (broad visibility and correlation across all tools and technology), XDR tooling (simple high-quality threat detection on covered assets), and the collective need for both types of tooling in security operations.

- **SOAR automation and modern analytics** Reduce the amount of manual effort in security operations by integrating the use of security orchestration, automation, and response (SOAR), machine learning (ML), and User Entity Behavioral Analytics (UEBA) technologies.

  - SOAR technology automates manual efforts that distract and tire human analysts during detection, investigation, and other response tasks.

- ML is an artificial intelligence technology that greatly improves detection by allowing computers to extend human expertise over large datasets and spot anomalies that could be attacker activity.

- UEBA improves detection and investigation by profiling the individual user accounts and entities that attackers compromise rather than attempting to find patterns in the full set of raw log data.

- **Adapt processes to Operational Technology (OT)**   As you integrate OT environments into your security program, adjust your tools and processes to adapt to the unique constraints of that environment. These environments prioritize safety and update and often have older systems (which don't have patches available and might crash from an active scan). Focusing on approaches like passive network detections for threats/discovery and isolation of systems is often the best approach.

- **Build appropriate controls for Insider Risk as a distinct focus area**   While some of the objectives and techniques for insider risk attacks are similar to external attacks, reducing insider risk is different than reducing risk from external attacks. Insider risks can include elements like

  - Leaks of sensitive data and data spillage

  - Confidentiality violations

  - Intellectual property (IP) theft

  - Fraud

  - Insider trading

  - Regulatory compliance violations

The MCSB includes many best practices that help protect from insider and external attacks, including the security controls listed in Table 10-2, focused on security operations-related topics:

TABLE 10-2 MCSB best practices for security operations

MCSB control domain	Security controls
Incident Response (IR)	IR-1: Preparation—update incident response plan and handling process IR-2: Preparation—setup incident notification IR-3: Detection and analysis—create incidents based on high-quality alerts IR-4: Detection and analysis—investigate an incident IR-5: Detection and analysis—prioritize incidents IR-6: Containment, eradication, and recovery —automate the incident handling IR-7: Post-incident activity—conduct lessons learned and retain evidence
Logging and Threat Detection (LT)	LT-1: Enable threat detection capabilities LT-2: Enable threat detection for identity and access management LT-3: Enable logging for security investigation LT-4: Enable network logging for security investigation LT-5: Centralize security log management and analysis LT-6: Configure log storage retention LT-7: Use approved time synchronization sources

These best practices in MCRA and MCSB can help you improve your security program effectiveness for both insider risk and attacks by external threat actors.

Skill 10-3: Recommend best practices for Zero Trust security

A Zero Trust approach to security is required to be effective at keeping up with threats, changes to cloud platforms, and changes in business models responding to a rapidly evolving world. You can find best practices for adopting a Zero Trust approach to security throughout the MCRA and MCSB. Nearly all modern security controls support a Zero Trust strategy, so this section will focus primarily on best practices related to the first and most visible priority for Zero Trust – modernizing access control.

Microsoft's Zero Trust approach to security is based on three principles of assume-breach (assume-compromise), verify explicitly, and least-privilege. These principles apply across the whole technical estate and are usually applied to a Zero Trust transformation through a series of modernization initiatives.

Figure 10-5 depicts how these Zero Trust principles apply across these initiatives.

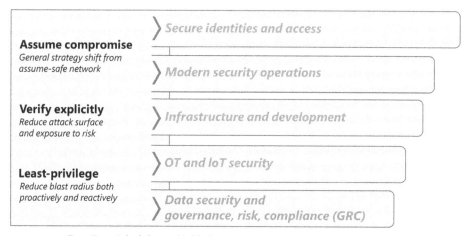

FIGURE 10-5 Zero Trust Principles and Initiatives

The initiatives include:

- **Secure identities and access** This initiative focuses on modernizing access control, ensuring that users can access the resources they need securely from anywhere. This focuses heavily on explicit validation of trust signals on users and devices, rather than on traditional reliance on network location for trust. This also applies the general mindset of assuming breach/compromise, and implementing least-privilege to limit who has access to resources (limiting permissions, just-in-time permissions, and more).

- **Modern security operations** This initiative focuses on reducing organizational risk by reducing attacker dwell time, which is how much time attackers have access to resources before they are detected and removed. This heavily focuses on the assume breach/compromise principle to build modern detection for attackers that try to stay hidden and ensure the organization can quickly kick them out.

- **Infrastructure and development security** This initiative focuses on integrating security into new and existing infrastructure, platforms, and applications. The main focus is to integrate security into existing initiatives like migrating existing workloads to the cloud, developing new workloads using DevOps/DevSecOps and other processes, or a security modernization initiative. All three Zero Trust principles are applicable across many aspects of these processes and environments.

- **Operational technology (OT) and Internet of Things (IoT) security** This initiative focuses on modernizing the security of OT and IoT devices and adapting Zero Trust principles within the constraints of the older technologies that are hard to maintain and have limited processing power and connectivity, stringent regulations and safety concerns, and operational uptime requirements.

- **Data security and governance, risk, compliance (GRC)** These focus on key aspects of security that have technical components but are primarily about business processes and outcomes.

- **Data security** This focuses on enabling organizations to discover, classify, protect, and monitor business-critical data wherever it is and goes.

- **Governance, risk, and compliance** This focuses on the modernization of these functions that ensure the organization is consistently meeting the various security and compliance requirements. These functions embed Zero Trust principles in processes, practices, and policies.

The MCRA includes many best practices related to the access control modernization initiative:

- **Prioritize privileged access** Ensure you are following security best practices to protect privileged resources with elevated protections (described more in Skill 10-1).

- **Apply Zero Trust principles to modernizing access control** Ensure you are assuming breach/compromise, explicitly validating telemetry and signals during access requests and authorized sessions, and applying the least-privilege principle to how much access accounts get (and for how long). This can be done with Azure Active Directory (Azure AD) Conditional Access and should include the following:

- **Explicitly validate multifactor authentication (MFA)**   Ensure that user account authentication combines multiple types of validation that the user is who they claim to be.

- **Explicitly validate user trust signals**   Measure risk on the user and their session, including behavior patterns, timing, location, and other indicators. This can be implemented with Azure AD Identity Protection and Azure AD Conditional Access.

- **Explicitly validate device trust signals**   Measure whether the user's device is configured properly and patched and whether the device is known to be compromised by an attacker. This can be implemented with Azure AD Conditional Access, Microsoft Intune, and Microsoft Defender for Endpoint.

- **Continually improve signal coverage and fidelity**   Keep up with attackers as they find new ways to evade existing controls.

- **Consistent application across the technical estate**   Ensure that authentication policies are consistently enforced across all access requests, including direct-to-cloud applications, remote network access through VPNs, remote access of legacy and on-premises applications through application proxies, and local wireless and wired network access. This allows people to work securely from anywhere.

- **Integrated security operations signals with access decisions**   Access decisions should integrate current information on compromised devices, users, and other assets. Access should be blocked to and from compromised assets while security operations are cleaning them up, and then access should be restored after the asset integrity has been restored.

- **Simplify Identity and Access management architecture**   Complexity is the enemy of security as it causes human errors in manual tasks and in designing/implementing automation. These errors open up gaps and inconsistencies that attackers can exploit. While identity and access technology across a complex technical estate will always be complicated, the user experience of users and IT and security roles (architects, engineers, administrators, developers, and operations) should be simplified as much as possible to reduce human error. For example, using a single identity and implementing single sign-on will simplify the user experience and reduce friction and complexity in security operations workflows, administrator workflows, and more. Using a single directory (or fewer directories) will simplify architecture, operations, security operations, and more.

- **Go beyond VPN**   Modernize access to existing legacy and on-premises applications. This enables people to work from home without slowdowns and extra steps that VPN introduces while increasing security assurances. This is an implicit message in adopting secure access service edge (SASE) architectures that focus heavily on identity-enabled network access technologies.

Many Zero Trust best practices can be found throughout the MCSB security controls, including those listed in Table 10-3 that focus on modernizing access control:

TABLE 10-3 MCSB best practices for access control

MCSB control domain	Security controls
Identity Management (IM)	IM-1: Use a centralized identity and authentication system IM-2: Protect identity and authentication systems IM-3: Manage application identities securely and automatically IM-4: Authenticate server and services IM-5: Use single sign-on (SSO) for application access IM-6: Use strong authentication controls IM-7: Restrict resource access based on conditions IM-8: Restrict the exposure of credentials and secrets IM-9: Secure user access to existing applications
Privileged Access (PA)	PA-1: Separate and limit highly privileged/administrative users PA-2: Avoid standing access for user accounts and permissions PA-3: Manage the lifecycle of identities and entitlements PA-4: Review and reconcile user access regularly PA-5: Set up emergency access PA-6: Use privileged access workstations PA-7: Follow just enough administration (least-privilege) principle PA-8: Determine access process for cloud provider support
Network security (NS)	NS-1: Establish network segmentation boundaries NS-2: Secure cloud services with network controls NS-3: Deploy firewall at the edge of enterprise network NS-4: Deploy intrusion detection/intrusion prevention systems (IDS/IPS) NS-5: Deploy DDoS protection NS-6: Deploy web application firewall NS-7: Simplify network security configuration NS-8: Detect and disable insecure services and protocols NS-9: Connect on-premises or cloud network privately NS-10: Ensure Domain Name System (DNS) security

MORE INFO For more information on the security controls in each area, see *https://aka.ms/benchmarkdocs*.

These best practices in MCRA and MCSB can help you with your Zero Trust security transformation.

Skill 10-4: Recommend best practices for the Zero Trust Rapid Modernization Plan

Zero Trust is a major transformation of a security program, so it's critical to focus on quick wins and incremental progress that prioritize the items that get you the most security and productivity increases with the least amount of time and resources.

The Zero Trust Rapid Modernization Plan (RaMP) is included in the MCRA and is focused on providing best practices that help you prioritize your security modernization. This RaMP identifies the most effective controls for the most relevant and common attacks that require the least amount of investment of time, effort, and resources.

Figure 10-6 is a screenshot of the Zero Trust RaMP in the MCRA.

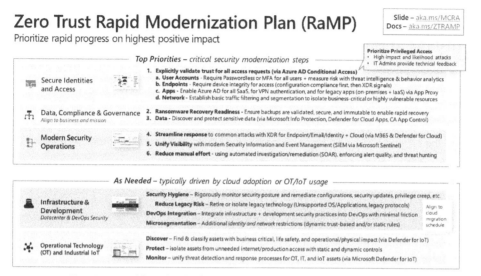

FIGURE 10-6 Zero Trust Rapid Modernization Plan (RaMP) (Figure courtesy of Microsoft)

The Zero Trust RaMP aligns to the recommended security modernization initiatives:

- **Secure identities and access** These quick wins focus on using cloud-based security capabilities like Azure AD, Intune, Microsoft Defender for Endpoints, and Azure AD App Proxy to rapidly modernize access control to increase productivity and security assurances.

- **Data security and governance, risk, compliance (GRC)** These quick wins focus on ensuring the organization can rapidly recover from a ransomware/extortion attack without paying attackers and protecting the most valuable business-critical data.

- **Modern security operations** These quick wins focus on streamlining responses to common attacks, getting end-to-end visibility across the enterprise, and automating manual tasks that slow down analysts and cause exhaustion/burnout.

- **Infrastructure and development security** These quick wins focus on security hygiene, reducing legacy risk, integrating security into DevOps and development processes, and applying the micro-segmentation concepts to identity and network access control.

- **Operational technology (OT) and Internet of Things (IoT) security** These quick wins focus on quickly discovering, protecting, and monitoring these systems for attacks.

These best practices in the Zero Trust RaMP can help you accelerate your journey of Zero Trust security transformation.

Thought experiment

In this thought experiment, demonstrate your skills and knowledge of the topics covered in this chapter. You can find answers to this thought experiment in the next section.

Identifying applicable best practices

Contoso is undergoing a Zero Trust modernization initiative to support the digital transformation and cloud transformations already in progress. The Chief Information Officer (CIO) and Chief Information Security Officer (CISO) have decided on three key priorities and created formal initiatives to structure the modernization around those areas.

You are the cybersecurity architect at Contoso and have been asked to support each of these by providing:

- A security architecture to help integrate and coordinate the technical work of these initiatives
- Applicable best practices for each modernization initiative
- Three to five security best practices from the MCRA and MCSB that are most applicable to these initiatives:
  1. Enabling and securing remote work to support hybrid and work-from-home scenarios
  2. Modernizing Security Operations to protect cloud assets and challenges with efficiency, effectiveness, and staff burnout/attrition
  3. Migrating business-critical workloads from on-premises to Azure and securing existing cloud workloads on AWS and GCP
  4. Prepare the organization for ransomware/extortion attacks

Thought experiment answers

This section contains the solution to the thought experiment. Each answer explains why the answer choice is correct.

1. **Enabling and securing remote work to support hybrid and work-from-home scenarios** The best practices for this could include:

   - **Apply Zero Trust principles to modernizing access control** This enables Contoso to access from anywhere with consistent strong assurances that apply to all resource access. Contoso will use Azure AD Conditional access to increase security by including policy requirements that do the following:

     - **Require multifactor authentication (MFA)** Require MFA to ensure that user account authentication combines multiple types of validation that the user is who they claim to be.

     - **Explicitly validate user trust signals** Do this on the user and their session, including behavior patterns, timing, location, and other indicators.

- **Explicitly validate device trust signals**   Measure whether the user's device is configured properly and patched and whether the device is known to be compromised by an attacker. This will help Contoso reduce risk by ensuring that vulnerable and compromised devices aren't accessing business-critical resources. Integrating near real-time security operations signals significantly reduces risk and improves the user experience. Attackers who compromise devices are rapidly cut off from accessing further resources from those devices. As Security Operations cleans them up (automatically with SOAR or with a manual human investigation and remediation), access is quickly restored. This helps quickly close the net around an attack and contain the damage while restoring access to users as soon as it is safe to do so.

> **NOTE**   The adoption of Zero Trust access control also benefits security operations (aka the security operations center or SOC). This reduces the number and severity of incidents the SOC must deal with, enabling them to focus more resources on proactive threat hunting and other valuable tasks that would normally not get done when there is a flood of avoidable incidents.

- **Moving Beyond VPN**   Contoso will first increase the security of VPN by using Azure AD to quickly take advantage of Azure AD Conditional Access. Contoso will then publish legacy and on-premises applications using Azure AD App Proxy, giving users less reason to use the VPN. This will help Contoso move beyond VPN for (remote) application access.

- **Simplify Identity and Access management architecture**   Contoso will also consolidate its identity infrastructure by consolidating several directories and identity management systems into the main corporate directory and identity management architecture. This will reduce the organization's attack surface, which has to be maintained and monitored by IT and security teams, while simplifying the user experience and training.

- **All MCSB Controls related to Identity Management, Privileged Access, and Network security**   These outline an approach that spans the major focus areas for each topic.

2. **Modernizing Security Operations to protect cloud assets and challenges with efficiency, effectiveness, and staff burnout/attrition**   The best practices for this could include:

- **Move from a SIEM only to an XDR+SIEM tooling strategy**   Adopting Microsoft 365 Defender XDR tooling will help Contoso address challenges with effectiveness and efficiency in their Security Operations Center (SOC) that is increasing burnout and staff turnover. They plan to replace noisy SIEM alerts based on homegrown queries with higher-quality alerts in XDR tooling that Microsoft maintains. This will reduce the number of false positive events that security analysts have to deal with and reduce their mean time to remediate (MTTR) incidents by informing their investigation workflows with context and threat intelligence. This will also help Contoso cover more asset types because their analysts don't have to build custom queries for each application and system. These tools are provided in a Software as a Service (SaaS) model, reducing the time and effort required to implement and operate them.

- **Migrate to cloud-native SIEM**   Contoso also plans to migrate to Microsoft Sentinel to reduce the engineering and operations overhead of maintaining their legacy on-premises SIEM. This will enable Contoso's SOC to redirect these teams into proactive hunting activities and other security automation. This will also simplify analyst workflows between SIEM and XDR tooling.

- **Adopt SOAR automation and modern analytics**   Contoso plans to prioritize adopting automation technologies and modern analytics, including the use of SOAR, ML, and UEBA technologies in Microsoft 365 Defender and Microsoft Sentinel. This will help Contoso improve detection quality and automate manual tasks that are highly disruptive and tiring for human analysts during investigation and remediation workflows.

- **All Incident Response and Logging and Threat Detection security controls in the MCSB**   These outline an approach that spans the major focus areas for each topic.

3. **Migrating business-critical workloads from on-premises to Azure and securing existing cloud workloads on AWS and GCP**   The best practices for this should be based on the full set of Microsoft cloud security benchmarks. This provides a consistent security configuration across all workloads, establishing core security assurances. These can be applied to an existing cloud environment or by migrating workloads to a new environment using Azure landing zone automation that already has many MCSB security controls implemented. Top MCSB control domains to focus on should include:

- **Backup and recovery**   These ensure you can recover in the event of a ransomware/extortion attack.

- **Privileged access**   This mitigates the risk of major compromises of multiple workloads or the larger technical estate (including ransomware/extortion attacks).

- **Logging and threat detection**   This ensures that malicious activity can be detected and investigated via XDR tooling and logs via centralized SIEM.

- **Posture and vulnerability management**   This reduces the ability of attackers to use well-known vulnerabilities and configuration errors to compromise resources and assets.

- **Network security**   Ensure basic networking controls are applied to protect workloads from well-known existing attacks.

- **DevOps security**   This ensures that security is built into new capabilities and updates to capabilities to reduce the likelihood of compromise of those applications (and use of that foothold for a larger compromise).

4. **Prepare the organization for ransomware/extortion attacks** The best practices for this should include:

- **Validating BC/DR process** Ensure your business continuity/disaster recovery (BC/DR) process includes all business-critical systems in scope, includes a scenario for a ransomware/extortion attack, and has exercised this scenario recently. This will enable Contoso to recover from an attack reliably without avoidable delays in the process.

- **Securing backups against sabotage** Ensure that backups are protected against deliberate attacker erasure or encryption, which is a common attacker tactic. This ensures that Contoso can recover without paying a ransom/extortion payment (which is much slower, has no guarantee of success, and incurs potential liability and other risks).

- **Protecting privileged access** Contoso should ensure that privileged accounts and systems are protected with elevated security protections, monitoring, and response. This will limit the ability of attackers to access and disrupt business operations across the organization without investing significant effort into individual compromises (which will make them easier to detect and evict). Blocking opportunistic attackers (like ransomware gangs) from easily getting this access might even deter them from attacking your organization and cause them to choose other targets.

The elevated protections organizations should implement include:

- **Protect Privileged User Accounts** With strong MFA, threat detection, and tagging accounts to ensure rapid response to anomalous events.

- **Protect workstations and devices** Protect workstations and devices used by these accounts with Privileged Access Workstations (PAWs) and additional monitoring and response.

- **Protect Intermediaries** Protect intermediaries that handle privileged accounts and sessions such as Virtual Private Networks (VPNs), PIM/PAM solutions, domain controllers, and more with elevated protections, security policy monitoring, threat detection, and more.

Chapter summary

- **Best practices** Best practices are recommended practices that are the most effective or efficient way to address a particular discipline or problem. Best practices help you avoid mistakes and ensure your resources and effort aren't wasted.

- **Follow best practices unless you have a reason not to** Organizations should follow well-defined and well-reasoned best practices unless there is a specific reason not to. Best practices are not unquestionably perfect and applicable to all situations, but they have been proven to work elsewhere so you should not ignore them without good reason.

- **Apply and integrate best practices** Like any guidance or advice, best practices only have value if they are applied in practice. Security best practices must be integrated into people's skills and habits, repeatable processes of your organization, and technology architecture and implementation.

- **Key Microsoft security best practice sources** Microsoft has embedded best practices in various guidance forms, including the Microsoft Cybersecurity Reference Architectures, Microsoft cloud security benchmark, the Cloud Adoption Framework (CAF), and Microsoft security best practices. These best practices come from several sources, including these:

  - **Technology intent and design** From Microsoft building and operating both hyperscale technology platforms and security capabilities.

  - **Effective common practices** From what Microsoft observed to work well across a large variety of organizations.

  - **Bright spots and early adopters** From learnings at organizations that are early adopters of new and emerging technology.

  - **Security best practices evolve over time** Microsoft security best practices reflect the current reality of the world; Microsoft updates them regularly.

  - **The Microsoft Cybersecurity Reference Architecture (MCRA)** These detailed technical architecture diagrams and slide sequences describe Microsoft's cybersecurity capabilities and are a key source of security best practices for many topics, including Zero Trust user access, security operations, multi-cloud and cross-platform capabilities, operational technology (OT), attack chains and technical capability coverage, Azure native security controls, and security roles and responsibilities.

  - **Microsoft cloud security benchmark (MCSB)** MCSB provides security best practices for infrastructure and development platforms across a hybrid of Microsoft Azure, on-premises datacenters, and other cloud providers like AWS and GCP. The MCSB includes two types of guidance:

    - **Security controls** Security recommendations that are generally applicable across the environment.

    - **Service baselines** Specific interpretation of these security controls to individual Azure services to provide prescriptive recommendations on the service's security configuration.

  - **Security best practices for capabilities and controls** These best practices focus on capabilities and controls to ensure that security has the necessary tools to be effective and efficient. While security technology doesn't improve security on its own or replace the need for security experts, technology automates processes and empowers people to do more.

  - **Security best practices for insider risk and external attacks** Effective security programs must protect against both insider risk as well as attacks by external threat actors. You can find best practices for protecting from insider and external attacks throughout the MCRA and MCSB. You should understand the attack chain concept that adapts the kill chain concept from military conflict to cybersecurity. This helps you understand attacks and plan security controls by viewing them as a sequential chain of events.

- **Security best practices for Zero Trust**   These best practices are critical to success today. A Zero Trust approach to security helps security become agile to keep up with changing threats, changes to cloud platforms, and changes in business models (which are responding to a rapidly evolving world). You can find best practices for adopting a Zero Trust approach to security throughout the MCRA and MCSB.

- **Zero Trust Rapid Modernization Plan (RaMP)**   RaMP outlines quick wins across different initiatives in the Zero Trust transformation of a security program, strategy, and architecture. This guidance provides quick wins and incremental progress to help you prioritize items with the most security and productivity increases from the least amount of time and resources. The Zero Trust Rapid Modernization Plan (RaMP) is included in the MCRA.

Recommend a secure methodology by using the Cloud Adoption Framework (CAF)

The Cloud Adoption Framework (CAF) is an all-encompassing framework that helps anyone looking to migrate into the cloud to accomplish this task. It has cloud adoption best practices collected and gathered into one place, taking experiences and lessons learned from Microsoft employees, partners, and customers. As one might expect, the CAF contains guidance on cloud adoption best practices, but it also provides narratives and tools that can be used to achieve the most effective cloud adoption and best business outcomes possible for an organization. Note that the CAF is not security-specific and covers the entirety of cloud adoption, but for the SC-100 exam outline, we will only be focusing on the security aspects of the CAF.

EXAM TIP Although not specifically required for the SC-100 Exam, we strongly recommend you explore and read as much of the CAF as possible. The CAF is an extremely useful reference for any security architect. You can read the CAF at *https://docs.microsoft.com/ en-us/azure/cloud-adoption-framework/*.

Skills covered in this chapter:

- Skill 11-1: Recommend a DevSecOps process
- Skill 11-2: Recommend a methodology for asset protection
- Skill 11-3: Recommend strategies for managing and minimizing risk

Skill 11-1: Recommend a DevSecOps process

We already outlined what DevSecOps is and how it differs from traditional engineering approaches earlier in this book, so if you need a refresher, go back and look at Chapter 8. In a nutshell, DevSecOps integrates security processes and tools into the DevOps development process.

It's still a relatively new discipline, so approaches to DevOps and DevSecOps vary from organization to organization, and there is no industry standard yet. However, Microsoft has its own recommendations for DevSecOps in the CAF. This section covers the skills necessary to recommend a DevSecOps process according to the Exam SC-100 outline.

DevSecOps Controls

Microsoft provides recommended controls that can be inserted at every stage of the DevOps process that every organization should consider. Not all controls will be applicable or relevant to every organization, but they should all be considered and reviewed for relevancy. Figure 11-1 shows a breakdown of these controls.

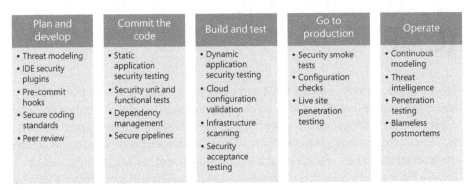

FIGURE 11-1 Microsoft's recommended DevSecOps controls

Plan and develop

The very first stage in any development process (even before DevOps existed) was planning—and this is still the case. Security often used to be left out of these early stages of development, but the reality is that the earlier in development that security issues are found, the easier and less costly they are to fix. For this reason, it's important to have security controls in the planning phases of any DevOps process. Below is a list of the security controls you should consider in the planning phases of a DevOps process.

> **NOTE** If you need to refresh your knowledge of threat modeling and the various methodologies used, see Chapter 8.

- **Threat modeling** This allows the developers to understand how a potential attacker would view their application and the most likely attack vectors.
- **IDE security plugins and pre-commit hooks** Integrated development environment (IDE) plugins look at a developer's code while it is being written in their own environment. Some plugins can look for vulnerabilities in the libraries and packages the

developers are using, and others can alert to potential security vulnerabilities written in the code as it is being developed. Pre-commit frameworks allow scripts to be run before code is committed to a repo to help alert reviewers and developers to security issues. All these tools allow developers to get speedy feedback on their code regarding security issues so they can be fixed early in the development process. Figure 11-2 shows an example pull request (PR) in GitHub with several pre-commit checks to help reviewers decide whether to commit the code.

FIGURE 11-2 Pre-commit Git hook scripts running against a PR submitted for review

■ **Peer review and secure coding standards**   Although automated checks can take some of the burdens of peer reviews away from individual team members, it is recommended that the code is peer-reviewed by another team member, ideally a security champion within the development team. These security champions will use their knowledge and secure coding best practices (such as the OWASP Top 10) to assess the code for security issues.

Commit the code

Nowadays, most development teams use repositories to store and version their code centrally. However, having a central repository of code that a whole dev team is working off can lead to security issues inadvertently being introduced into the code. A common mistake is forgetting to remove credentials in the code before committing it to a repository; this is such a frequent occurrence that attackers constantly scan public repositories looking for usable credentials, keys, and strings to try and use to access IT environments. Development teams need to have controls to analyze and scan code to look for security issues that can be introduced into code repositories. Below is a list of the security controls you should consider in the commit code phase of a DevOps process:

■ **Dependency management**   Arguably, this is one of the trickiest parts of development to put security controls around because about 90 percent of application code comes from or is based on external packages and libraries. These packages and libraries also need to be kept up to date as they are updated to address security vulnerabilities. Not only can developers download packages and libraries with security vulnerabilities, but failing to keep their dependencies up-to-date can lead to code vulnerabilities over time. Both open-source and commercial tools can assist with dependency management and scan code to identify if out-of-date or compromised libraries or packages are being used in code.

- **Static application security testing (SAST)**   In prior years, this would have simply been called the "code scan" part of the waterfall development process. Many SAST tools will scan code and look for vulnerabilities. Traditional code scanning could take days if the code were big enough, but modern SAST tools can analyze the code delta as it is committed to a repository, which is likely to be a much smaller, incremental change and will be able to give rapid feedback to a developer if there are issues in the code.

- **Secure pipelines**   If your development teams use a CI/CD pipeline to deploy code to your production environments, controls must be implemented to ensure that attackers can't manipulate the pipeline to run or deploy malicious code or steal credentials.

> **NOTE**   You can read more about the controls required for securing CI/CD pipelines at *https://docs.microsoft.com/en-us/azure/devops/pipelines/security/overview?view=azure-devops*.

Build and test

As code is being built and tested, security controls should also test the built application and how it responds to inputs. As with everything in DevOps, ideally, these tests should be automated to reduce friction in the development process.

- **Dynamic application security testing (DAST)**   DAST tools are also known as web application vulnerability scanners. They test how an application responds to requests specially crafted to mimic the malicious requests an attacker might use to breach a web application. Many DAST tools available in the market provide this functionality: OWASP ZAP, Rapid7, BurpSuite, and Qualys are just a few of the many tools that can provide this testing capability. In a DevOps environment, it is recommended that the DAST tool should be run as part of the pipeline because this is quicker than manual penetration testing and/or running the DAST tool completely separately from the rest of the process.

- **Cloud configuration validation and infrastructure scanning**   The application's infrastructure can also make it vulnerable if it has been misconfigured or not set up according to the organization's security standards. In Azure, you can use Azure Policy to set up guardrails to prevent certain configurations from being deployed (such as preventing deployment to a certain region or configuration of external access to a resource with a public IP address). Using infrastructure as code (IaC) allows infrastructure to be deployed consistently from a centralized repository (just like application code). Thus, it generates the same pattern every time it is used. A repeatable and consistent infrastructure is possible as long as templates generating the IaC are good. Of course, the templates should be scanned for vulnerabilities, just like code, before they are deployed. Specialized tools can scan for IaC vulnerabilities before they are deployed.

Go to production and operate

Applications must continue to be protected and managed from a security perspective, even when deployed and live. At this stage, the security controls and monitoring focus on the whole application rather than just the code.

- **Configuration and infrastructure scanning**   Tools should be used to scan and monitor the application's environment for misconfigurations and anomalous behaviors. Cloud security posture management (CPSM) and cloud workload protection (CWP) tools such as Microsoft Defender for Cloud can detect misconfigurations and unusual events in both IaaS and PaaS. A SIEM can consume alerts to correlate them across the entire IT environment with other logs and alerts.

- **Penetration testing**   When professional "white hat" hackers attempt to break in and/or manipulate the application, penetration testers are trying to simulate what a real attacker might attempt to do to breach your application. Typically you will receive a report at the end of the testing with a list of vulnerabilities discovered, their severity, and recommended remediations.

> **NOTE**   Penetration testing in cloud environments is slightly different from penetration testing on-premises. Attempting to test your cloud provider's base infrastructure might be considered a breach of your terms and conditions with that provider. Make sure you have read your cloud provider's guidance on what parts of their cloud infrastructure can and cannot be penetration tested. You can read the Azure penetration testing guidelines at *https://docs.microsoft.com/en-us/azure/security/fundamentals/pen-testing*.

- **Actionable intelligence**   Alerts and incidents should be integrated into an IT service management (ITSM) platform so that both the security teams can learn from the rest of the IT organization and vice versa.

- **Feedback loops**   Throughout this section, we've discussed the controls that can identify issues in a DevSecOps process. Still, there also needs to be a consistent pattern to feed these issues back to the development team so they can be fixed. The very worst scenario is that a security issue is flagged by some of the DevSecOps controls but is never acted upon because the feedback loop to the team that could fix the issue failed. This has happened with some serious public breaches in the past. There should be a consistent feedback process at every stage of the DevOps process. This feedback should be picked up and used by the development team to address support system tickets, issues on the developer's backlog, and so on.

Skill 11-2: Recommend a methodology for asset protection

IT Assets can be any number of things. Often when we think of assets, we think of laptops and desktops, but the reality is that an IT asset can be files, virtual machines, databases, storage accounts, and any number of things that can exist in an IT environment. Asset protection is the process whereby security controls and configuration standards are applied consistently to each type of asset. A simple example of asset protection is that every Windows laptop within an organization will have Defender for Endpoint installed on it. This section of the chapter covers the skills necessary to recommend a methodology for asset protection according to the Exam SC-100 outline.

Getting secure

When most organizations start an asset protection program, they will have two aspects of asset protection to address:

- **Brownfield assets**   These are existing assets within the organization that might not have been configured to security standards when they were onboarded into the environment. This is also known as "technical debt," "legacy code," or other similar monikers. Although it can be challenging to find the budget and resources to apply security controls to these assets retrospectively, it's critically important this isn't overlooked because any insecure asset is a potential attack vector. Depending on the type of asset, the kinds of activities required to bring brownfield assets up to standard might be software updates, updating or applying encryption protocols, applying good security configuration best practices, etc.

- **Greenfield assets**   When new assets are brought into an organization, they must be configured to security standards when introduced; otherwise, they immediately become brownfield/technical debt and increase the risk of a breach. This asset protection process needs to be baked into the organization's project methodology so that it is not overlooked during the introduction of new assets. Security standards for each type of asset must be clearly defined so that they are easy to adopt.

Staying secure

The security landscape changes frequently, new vulnerabilities are found, new technologies are developed, and attackers find new techniques to exploit IT environments. Hence, the security standards of an organization (and the assets that should align with those standards) need to be continually updated to align with industry and technological developments to keep an organization's security posture as high as possible.

These changes happen much more quickly in today's digital and cloud-enabled landscape than in prior years. Fifteen years ago, it was probably sufficient to make sure that a piece of software got an annual patch and upgrade once a year; in today's environment, these changes and updates must happen much more frequently, powered by the agile/DevOps way of working. Trying to keep abreast of these changes is onerous and a challenge for even the more well-resourced of organizations, so it is recommended that a key focus for ongoing asset protection should address the following areas:

- **Continuous cloud improvement tooling**   Where possible, use in-built cloud capabilities where some (if not all) of the responsibility for security controls rests with your cloud provider, who will adapt and update features over time on your organization's behalf.

- **Retiring end-of-life assets**   End-of-life software, operating systems, and any other asset where the vendor no longer provides security patches and updates must be retired or upgraded as soon as possible. Out-of-date, unpatched systems are an easy and cheap vector for attackers to exploit, and it can and will happen. Ideally, end-of-life assets should be migrated to a SaaS or PaaS provider where much of the subsequent update maintenance falls to the cloud provider rather than your organization. Remove old container images from your container registry and remove old versions of artifacts from build environments.

- **Patching strategy**   Every organization should have a well-defined and adhered to patching strategy that allows patches to be applied in a timely manner as advised by the vendor. There are inherent business conflicts with patching. If an update goes wrong, this can cause downtime and affect business processes. However, if an attacker exploits an unpatched environment, it could lead to significant downtime. This is a tricky situation for all IT functions to navigate but can be made easier by designing processes and IT architectures that lower the risk of downtime due to maintenance and have clear communication channels with the business.

- **Network isolation for older assets**   For older assets that cannot be retired or upgraded in the short term, network isolation might be a valid option to consider, but the controls that isolate the system from the rest of the production network must be strong to prevent attackers from compromising the isolated system and then "hopping" into production. Network isolation is commonly seen in operational technology (OT) environments.

Key recommendations for an asset protection program

Microsoft's recommendations for an asset protection program are as follows:

- **Use vendor/industry baselines**   Many vendors—Microsoft included—provide security best practices and baselines steeped in their experience with multiple customers. These baselines are a wonderful way to kick off your asset protection program; there are many proven ones out there. Microsoft has the Microsoft security baselines, and another well-known set of industry best practices are the Center for Internet Security (CIS) benchmarks.

- **Create security controls collaboratively** The controls that will form an asset protection program should be sourced from different subject matter experts (SMEs) in your organization. Also, security, governance, business owners, and SMEs for different types of assets should be involved.

- **Define accountable and responsible teams** Critical for the success of any business program, clear lines of accountability and responsibility should be defined. Ultimately, the accountability for security resides with the business resource owner, who also owns the other risks for that resource. Security teams and SMEs are there to advise those owners on risks and mitigation. The actual implementation of asset protection might fall to one of several teams—typically, IT operations, DepOps, and DevSecOps teams. If an asset is running on SaaS or PaaS, the responsibility for asset protection might fall to the cloud provider; make sure you have checked your shared responsibility model to be sure!

- **Adapt processes for cloud elasticity** Cloud assets can be spun up and removed quickly, so an organization needs to have good, dynamic inventories to have an effective asset protection program. (In other words, an organization needs to have an accurate list of what is in the environment at any time.) This will also affect how security controls are implemented to ensure consistent baselines.

- **Automate controls where possible** As mentioned in the previous bullet, the elasticity of the cloud and the ease with which new assets can be created can make it hard to apply manual controls consistently. It is critical to automate this process where possible. As already described earlier in this book, Azure Policy allows security teams to specify configurations that are not allowed in a tenant, subscription, or even an individual resource group. This granularity allows for flexibility and consistency in enforcing configuration baselines across an organization. Figure 11-3 shows Azure Policy configured to make all resources in a defined subscription stream their logs to a particular Log Analytics workspace.

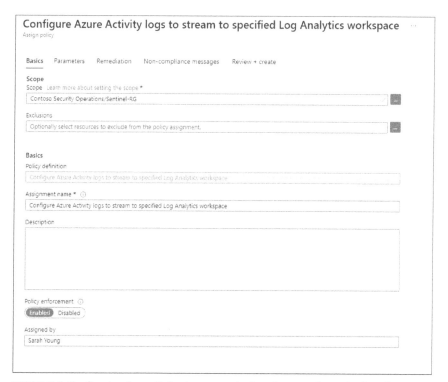

FIGURE 11-3 Configuring Azure Policy to automatically enforce configuration baselines

- **Have a defined exception management process** In any real-life IT environment, there will always be exceptions to standards. It might be that a software asset cannot be upgraded until a specific project is complete or a workstation running on an old operating system (OS) provides critical functionality that cannot be moved to a newer OS. Exceptions should always be considered temporary and have expiration dates. They should be reassessed and evaluated at the expiration time for whether the exception can be resolved now. There should be a well-defined process for recording and evaluating exceptions so asset owners can review them.

Skill 11-3: Recommend strategies for managing and minimizing risk

Risk exists in every facet of life: there is risk in walking across the road, you might get run over by a car; there is a risk that your favorite ice cream flavor will not be in stock at the supermarket. However, how severe a risk is can vary hugely. In technology terms, operating any IT system or asset comes with security risks (there are other types of risks too, but that's not for the SC-100 exam!), and managing these risks effectively should be a key component of any organization's goals. This section of the chapter covers the skills necessary to recommend strategies for managing and minimizing risk according to the Exam SC-100 outline.

Measuring risk

Security risks are usually measured in terms of two things:

- **Probability**   How likely is the risk to occur?
- **Impact**   How much impact would the risk have on the organization if it were to occur? Factors considered when thinking about impact include monetary consequences, reputational damage, impact to business operations, danger to life, and so on.

Most organizations will have their own criteria for how probability and impact are rated. (For example, if a risk could involve loss of life, that risk might automatically be rated as having a very high impact.) It's important to have consistent criteria for measuring risks rather than allowing each individual taking part in risk rating to make arbitrary judgments. Many organizations will plot security risks on a risk matrix, as seen in Figure 11-4.

Impact		Probability				
Very high (5)	5	10	15	20	25
High (4)	4	8	12	16	20
Medium (3)	3	6	9	12	15
Moderate (2)	2	4	6	8	10
Minor (1)	1	2	3	4	5
	Very unlikely (1)	Unlikely (2)	Likely (3)	Very likely (4)	Certain (5)

Probability

FIGURE 11-4 A typical risk matrix chart enables users to score a risk's severity

Using a risk matrix allows both technical and non-technical stakeholders to understand where a particular risk sits in the bigger picture for that organization's overall risk posture and helps decision-makers prioritize mitigations and controls for those risks.

Managing security risk

Many organizations still treat security risks as technical problems that can be solved. All seasoned security professionals know security can never be 100 percent and that security risks cannot be entirely eradicated. Both organizational leadership and security need to understand how the other team thinks and considers risk, so security can advise leadership appropriately and be aligned in their approach. There are a few key initiatives to ensure are taking place in this space:

- **Explain security threats in the appropriate language to the rest of the business** In other words, use plain English. Security personnel might find it extremely interesting to talk about a cross-site scripting (XSS) vulnerability in a web application that generates all of an organization's income, but this might mean very little to a non-technical person in corporate.

- **Security should understand the wider business context of the technology they secure** Security should take the time to meet with non-technical stakeholders and understand how the technology assets they secure relates to key business processes: a key IT asset going down doesn't necessarily mean that the business is severely impacted, and vice versa. Security must understand as much of this business context as possible.

- **Translate business risks into real-world actions** Don't let security risk discussions just become a "talking shop." If both the business and security agree a risk is high enough to require mitigation and controls, then action must be taken. Whether addressing technical debt, applying data classifications to assets, applying additional security controls to critical assets, or creating a zero-trust strategy for the organization, concrete actions must be taken to reduce risk.

- **Establish a healthy security culture** Encourage everyone in the organization to take part in security. After all, security is a team sport! In particular, focus on collaboration between the business, IT, and security and removing silos and the "us vs. them" culture that often accompanies siloed ways of working within organizations. Organization teams that communicate and collaborate have a much better chance of successfully reducing security risks.

Thought experiment

In this thought experiment, demonstrate your skills and knowledge of the topics covered in this chapter. You can find answers to this thought experiment in the next section.

Using the CAF for secure methodologies at Tailwind Traders

You are the security architect for Tailwind Traders, a startup with staff spread across several jurisdictions. The organization was "born in the cloud" and only has cloud-based IT assets, but it lacks security processes and methodologies as it continues along its digital transformation journey. You have been hired to help introduce stronger and more effective security processes.

Some of the current challenges at Tailwind Traders are as follows:

- Developers complain about security slowing their development process.
- The security team insists on fully reviewing every incremental code change.
- Although Tailwind Traders is a relatively young company, they have significant technical debt from IT assets onboarded into the environment with no asset security considerations.

- Regarding IT asset security, there are still many types of assets with no baselines.
- Security risk ratings are done arbitrarily, with no guidance about how to rate impact and probability. This leads to different risk ratings depending on who is carrying out the assessment.
- Some business stakeholders dismiss security risks as "technobabble by the computer nerds in security."

With this information in mind, answer the following questions:

1. What suggestions could you make for security controls that would not slow the developers' work?
2. What resources could you use to start internal security baselines for the IT assets that don't currently have any?
3. How could you standardize the security risk rating process?
4. What could you do to help business stakeholders understand how security risks translate into business risks for the organization?

Thought experiment answers

This section contains the solution to the thought experiment. Each answer explains why the answer choice is correct.

1. Security controls need to be integrated into the developers' processes at every stage of the DevOps process, but they also need to be as frictionless as possible. Some tools that could be used in this space are
   - IDE security plugins and pre-commit hooks
   - SAST
   - DAST
   - Dependency management
   - Automated configuration
   - Infrastructure scanning
2. Many vendors (Microsoft included) provide their own baselines for the products and tools they create based on the experience they have using their products with many customers. If you don't have any baselines in your organization, it's a good idea to start with these. Industry and not-for-profit bodies also provide baselines that you can use (such as CIS).
3. It is recommended that criteria are established so that risk ratings happen consistently. This will need to be created in dialogue with the business. For probability, it might be decided that "very unlikely" is something that is expected to happen every five years; "unlikely" is every three years; "likely" is every year, and so on. It might be decided that a "very high" impact is when lives are at risk, monetary damages exceed $1 million, or

significant media coverage of the event leads to extreme reputational damage. "High" is when people might be injured, monetary damages exceed $500,000, and there is severe reputational damage. Every organization will need to determine the criteria that work for them in the context of their operations. Having these criteria means that risks are rated consistently and improves the decision-making around risk management.

4. To help business (often non-technical) stakeholders understand security risk, security teams need to explain security problems in plain English, using language and concepts that non-technical people can understand. Talking about a severe misconfiguration in the organization's WAFs might concern someone who works in security, but it has no meaning to a non-technical stakeholder. However, explaining that there is a misconfiguration in the device that protects the organization's main website that could allow an attacker to potentially take down the website and affect revenue explains the security risk in business terms. It's a real skill that takes time to develop, but it is key for improving business and security communication flows.

Chapter summary

- Security controls should be added into every stage of the DevOps process but in a frictionless manner.
- When addressing asset security, there are two types of assets to consider—brownfield and greenfield assets.
- One of the biggest challenges with asset security is staying secure over time.

Key initiatives for keeping secure in an IT asset security program are

- Using cloud provider tooling (when available)
- Retiring end-of-life assets
- Defining and implementing a patching schedule
- Considering total network isolation for assets that cannot be upgraded or retired

- Risk is measured against two factors—probability and impact.
- Mapping security risks on a risk matrix can help stakeholders and security professionals understand all security risks in a wider context.
- Security risk can never be 100 percent eradicated from an organization; it can only be managed and reduced.
- Explaining security risk to business stakeholders in simple, non-technical terms is essential for good communication channels and securing business support to mitigate security risks.

CHAPTER 12

Recommend a ransomware strategy by using Microsoft Security Best Practices

The Verizon 2022 Data Breach Investigations Report revealed that ransomware attacks increased 13 percent in a single year, representing a jump greater than the past 5 years combined. Ransomware is an attack that destroys or encrypts files and folders to prevent the affected resource's owner from accessing their data until a ransom is paid. Microsoft has been tracking the growth of Ransomware as a Service (RaaS), also called *human-operated ransomware*, which has become the most impactful threat to organizations. In this chapter, you learn how to improve your security strategy to defend against ransomware attacks using Microsoft security best practices.

Skills covered in this chapter:

- Skill 12-1: Plan for ransomware protection and extortion-based attacks
- Skill 12-2: Protect assets from ransomware attacks
- Skill 12-3: Recommend Microsoft ransomware best practices

Skill 12-1: Plan for ransomware protection and extortion-based attacks

According to the Cybersecurity & Infrastructure Security Agency (CISA) Alert Report (AA22-040A) issued in February 2022, ransomware attack tactics and techniques evolved in 2021. Also, cybercriminals were still using old methods of attack with a high success rate, such as accessing network infrastructure via phishing emails, stealing credentials via Remote Desktop Protocol (RDP) brute-force attacks, and exploiting known vulnerabilities that weren't patched. There are two main types of ransomware:

- **Commodity ransomware** This type of malware spreads using techniques such as phishing and encrypts files before demanding a ransom.
- **Human-operated ransomware** This kind of malware has a bigger scope, including well-planned operations coordinated by cybercriminals who employ multiple attack methods.

The new threat landscape increases the likelihood of data getting compromised. Because protecting your entire data state can be challenging, you must ensure your design strategy to secure your data is prioritizing the most important threats. This section of the chapter covers the skills necessary to specify priorities for mitigating threats to data according to the Exam SC-100 outline.

Preparation

While planning for ransomware protection, you must ensure that you have security controls in place to make it much harder for a threat actor to access and disrupt your systems. At the same time, you also need to ensure that it is relatively easy for your organization to recover from an attack without paying the ransom in case the threat actor can access and encrypt your data. The impact of a ransomware attack on any organization is difficult to accurately quantify because it depends on the scope of the attack. However, the impact can include the following:

- Loss of data access
- Business operation disruption
- Financial loss
- Intellectual property theft
- Customer trust
- Legal actions

> **IMPORTANT**   Consider adding ransomware to your Enterprise Risk Management (ERM) system as a high-likelihood and high-impact scenario and track mitigation status via your ERM assessment cycle.

Threat actors using ransomware attacks against an organization are looking for financial gains. However, their approach to pressure an organization to pay the ransom to have their data back can vary. Threat actors may demand payment under the threat that they won't give you back access to your data or in exchange for not releasing sensitive or embarrassing data to the public. Whatever the approach is, the best remedy is to ensure that your organization can restore the hijacked data to a location where the threat actor can't access or modify it.

It is important to understand the scope of a ransomware attack and which data can be potentially compromised. That's why it is so important to know your data and have a good data classification system that allows you to make strategic decisions regarding the data that needs to be restored. Once the critical systems and their data are backed up, you also must ensure that backups are protected against deliberate erasure or encryption by threat actors. This is an important step because attacks on your backups are normal, and the goal is to deprive your organization's ability to respond without paying.

Ransomware extortion and destructive attacks are only considered successful when all legitimate access to data is lost. This means that part of preparation needs to ensure that threat actors cannot remove your ability to resume operations without paying the ransom. To improve your defense, you need to protect your data. Data protection comprises multiple actions and layers, from change management to security awareness across the entire workforce. The list below has some important tasks that you need to take into consideration:

- Consider migrating your data to the cloud to leverage cloud solutions such as OneDrive/SharePoint to take advantage of versioning and recycle bin capabilities

- Create internal campaigns to educate users on how to recover their files by themselves to reduce delays and the cost of recovery

- Review your current data set to ensure permissions are applied using the concept of least privilege. During this exercise, you can reduce the broad permissions for critical data locations while meeting business collaboration requirements

Security hygiene and damage control

Continuous improvement of your security posture is another vital aspect of your plan for ransomware protection. Since threat actors will usually use well-known vulnerabilities that have not yet been patched as attack vectors, the proactive approach of improving your security posture helps to reduce the attack surface and focus on vulnerability management of your workloads.

As security posture management is a continuous process, you should leverage tools such as Microsoft Secure Score to track your progress over time. Secure Score in Defender for Cloud has a series of recommendations that can assist you in prioritizing the most critical ones for your environment and use capabilities, such as the Quick Fix, to deploy mitigations to remediate the recommendations rapidly.

Security hygiene improvement is not only about elevating the secure state of each resource but also ensuring that you have secure access to workloads. If your organization provides remote access to your workloads, you also need a well-established remote access strategy that enforces Zero Trust for user authentication and device validation.

If the threat actor can access your system and gain access to some data, you need to ensure that you can limit the scope of the damage by protecting your privileged roles. The rationale is that the threat actors will always try to escalate privileges to gain access to privileged accounts (mainly IT administrators). And with that, they try to access more sensitive information only available to privileged users. For this reason, you need to implement a comprehensive strategy to reduce the risk of privileged access compromise.

During this phase, using a zero-trust strategy is imperative since it allows you to explicitly validate the trust of users and devices before allowing access to administrative interfaces. Protecting and monitoring identity systems is also recommended to prevent privilege escalation attacks.

Another strategy used by threat actors trying to access privileged accounts is moving laterally to other systems. Security controls must be in place to ensure that compromising a single device does not immediately lead to control of many or all other devices. The diagram shown in Figure 12-1 has an example of a normal pattern for a human-operated ransomware.

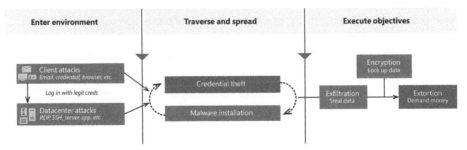

FIGURE 12-1 Typical ransomware attack pattern

In Figure 12-1, you can see that everything starts with client access using legitimate credentials. This happens because threat actors, particularly those launching ransomware attacks, sometimes buy access to target organizations from other attackers in dark markets. By leveraging this method, they gain access to the organization's infrastructure and start performing their actions to traverse and spread. This could take multiple cycles because a potential callback to command and control can also happen to download malware and continue the operation. If the attacker gains administrative access to the organization, they can perform further options to increase the scope of the attack, which can include sabotaging the backup and establishing persistence.

If you identify this type of operation, you need to respond quickly to this incident and contain the spread (ideally, right at the beginning of the operation). However, to respond quickly, you need threat detection built specifically for the workload. For example, suppose you need visibility of potential attacks against your Azure storage account. In that case, you need to use Defender for Storage, which contains threat detections developed based on the Azure storage account threat landscape. Your organization needs responsive threat detection and remediation across all workloads that can be exploited, including endpoints, email, and identities.

> **IMPORTANT** If you are in the United States, contact the FBI to report a ransomware breach using the IC3 Complaint Referral Form at *ransomware.ic3.gov*.

Skill 12-2: Protect assets from ransomware attacks

Protecting your assets from ransomware attacks comprises multiple layers of protection and understanding that threat actors are like water; they take the path of least resistance to achieve their objectives. Having this in mind is important to not only prioritize what needs to be protected but also the protection that you need to use for each asset type. This section covers the skills necessary to protect assets from ransomware attacks according to the Exam SC-100 outline.

Enter environment

As shown previously in Figure 12-1, the usual pattern of behavior for threat actors operating a ransomware attack is to gain initial access through an endpoint technology, which could be an email or even a browser. In this first stage, you should include security controls to protect:

- Email and collaboration
- Endpoints
- Remote access
- Accounts

Email

Threat actors usually use macros to provide rich capabilities, which are also executed in a privileged context. Implementing best practices for email and collaboration solutions will make it more difficult for threat actors to abuse these systems while allowing legitimate users to access external content safely. Office 365 client applications integrate with Antimalware Scan Interface (AMSI), which enables antivirus and other security solutions to scan macros and other scripts at runtime to check for malicious behavior. Microsoft Defender for Endpoint also detects Office macro attacks.

Because email is another common entry point for threat actors, we recommend that you use a solution that can provide advanced safeguards against malicious threats posed by email messages. Microsoft Defender for Office 365 provides threat-protection policies, real-time threat detection, threat investigation, and response capabilities. Also, Defender for Office 365 includes

- **Safe Attachments**   Uses detonation based on a virtual environment that checks attachments in email messages before they're delivered to recipients.
- **Safe Links**   Provides URL scanning capability and rewriting of inbound email messages in mail flow, time-of-click verification of URLs and links in email messages.
- **Anti-phishing protection in Defender for Office 365**   Provides spoof protection and mailbox intelligence for all recipients.

Also, make sure to deploy attack surface reduction (ASR) rules to block common attack techniques such as weaponizing Office documents with macros, executable content, process creation, and process injection initiated by Office applications.

Endpoint

Internet-exposed endpoints are a common entry point for threat actors to access other organizations' assets. Make sure to prioritize blocking common OS and application vulnerabilities with preventive controls to slow or stop them from executing the next stages. It is important to harden these endpoints with security baselines to make sure you are protecting new endpoints from the moment they are provisioned.

As part of this hardening process, you should also isolate, disable, or retire insecure systems and protocols, including unsupported operating systems and legacy protocols. Because threat actors might leverage malware relying on unsolicited inbound traffic to initiate the connection with the endpoint, you should also consider using built-in operating system capabilities to filter network traffic, such as a host firewall.

Threat actors may also try to disable security features on your endpoints, such as antimalware protection. The intent is to get easier access to your data, install malware, or otherwise exploit your data, identity, and devices. Microsoft Defender for Endpoint Tamper Protection capability helps prevent this type of action. Ensure auditing features are enabled to monitor and identify deviations from baseline.

Remote access

After the COVID-19 pandemic, the number of remote users grew exponentially, and these users continuously need to gain access to your organization's resources through a remote access connection. Remote access is an attack vector for a ransomware attack. Once an on-premises user account is compromised, an attacker is free to roam on the corporate network and perform reconnaissance to gather the necessary information to launch the attack.

As part of your remote access strategy, make sure to use Azure AD Conditional Access. With conditional access, you can control many remote access scenarios, including:

- Requiring MFA for users with administrative roles
- Blocking sign-ins for users attempting to use legacy authentication protocols
- Blocking or granting access from specific locations
- Requiring organization-managed devices for specific applications

While conditional access will control the initial authentication and connection, you need to enable tunnel encryption once the connection is established. You can select from different types of VPN connectivity when deploying a network that needs to create a cross-premises connection. The available options are as follows:

- **Site-to-Site (S2S) VPN** This type of VPN is used in scenarios where you need to connect on-premises resources to Azure. The encrypted connection tunnel uses IPsec/IKE (IKEv1 or IKEv2).
- **Point-to-Site (P2S) VPN** This type of VPN is used in scenarios where you need to connect to your Azure VNet from a remote location. For example, you would use P2S when working remotely (hotel, home, conference, and the like), and you need to access resources in your VNet. This VPN uses SSTP (Secure Socket Tunneling Protocol) or IKE v2 and does not require a VPN device.
- **VNet-to-VNet** As the name states, this VPN is used in scenarios where you need to encrypt connectivity between VNets. This type of connection uses IPsec (IKE v1 and IKE v2).
- **Multi-Site VPN** This type of VPN is used when you need to expand your site-to-site configuration to allow multiple on-premises sites to access a virtual network.

ExpressRoute is another option that allows connectivity from your on-premises resources to Azure. This option uses a private connection to Azure from your WAN instead of a VPN connection over the Internet.

TIP Using Azure Bastion is another option providing secure and seamless access to your Azure virtual machines over SSL.

Account

If a user's account is compromised, the likelihood that the threat actor will successfully enter the environment is higher, mainly because it is a legitimate account. For this reason, you should start enumerating critical impact admins and rigorously follow best practices for account security, including enabling MFA. In addition, you should consider using Azure AD Identity Protection to prevent and detect attacks.

Another strategy is to use passwordless sign-in with the Microsoft Authenticator App. Microsoft Authenticator uses key-based authentication to enable a user credential tied to a device, where the device uses a PIN or biometric.

Traverse and spread

If the threat actor enters this phase, you need to increase the threat actor costs with the least resource investment. To accomplish that, you should implement a comprehensive strategy to reduce the risk of privileged access compromise. To help you build a multi-part strategy, visit *https://aka.ms/SPA*.

Part of the strategy to mitigate lateral traversal includes ensuring that a single compromised device will not immediately lead to control of many or all other devices using local account passwords, service account passwords, or other secrets.

Execute objective

Ransomware extortion and destructive attacks are only considered successful when all legitimate access to the data is lost. With that in mind, your goal is to disrupt the attacker by ensuring attackers cannot remove the organization's ability to continue its operations without paying the ransom.

Implementing data protection is part of the strategy to prevent threat actors from accomplishing this objective. You need to ensure that your organization can rapidly and reliably recover from a ransomware attack. In addition, you need to ensure that critical systems are backed up and the backups are protected against malicious operations such as erasure and encryption.

Skill 12-3: Recommend Microsoft ransomware best practices

When evaluating your overall ransomware strategy, you must implement proactive security posture management and reactive measures, including incident response and recovery. This section covers the skills necessary to recommend Microsoft ransomware best practices according to the Exam SC-100 outline.

Best practices

Using the assume-breach principle, which is part of the zero-trust strategy, you must prioritize mitigation. This prioritization is critical because you could face a worst-case scenario with ransomware. While you want to avoid that, the reality is that you must be prepared in case it occurs. To reduce the likelihood of compromise, you need to improve your security hygiene by focusing on attack surface reduction and threat and vulnerability management for your workloads.

Remediating the recommendations triggered by your security posture management tool, such as Defender for Cloud, will allow you to reduce the attack surface across your different workloads and significantly reduce organizational risk. The same applies to vulnerability management, which is integrated with Defender for Cloud. Additionally, you can turn on attack surface reduction rules in Microsoft 365 Defender to prevent common ransomware attack techniques.

Attack surface reduction can be used to identify suspicious behaviors, such as

- Launching executable files and scripts that attempt to download or run files
- Running obfuscated or otherwise suspicious scripts
- Identifying behaviors that aren't usually initiated by apps during normal day-to-day operations

Table 12-1 has a summary of the main rules that are applicable for ransomware attacks and which stage this rule can help to prevent:

TABLE 12-1 Attack surface reduction rules per ransomware stage

Ransomware stage	ASR rule
Enter environment	■ Block all Office applications from creating child processes ■ Block Office communication application from creating child processes ■ Block Office applications from creating executable content ■ Block Office applications from injecting code into other processes ■ Block execution of potentially obfuscated scripts ■ Block JavaScript or VBScript from launching downloaded executable content
Traverse and spread	■ Block executable files from running unless they meet a prevalence, age, or trusted list criterion ■ Block credential stealing from the Windows local security authority subsystem (lsass.exe) ■ Block process creations originating from PsExec and WMI commands ■ Use advanced protection against ransomware

> **IMPORTANT** ASR is also available for Microsoft Defender Antivirus, though it must run with real-time protection in Active mode.

While adding security controls based on features available in different products is an important step to prevent ransomware attacks, it is imperative to promote awareness and ensure there is no knowledge gap among end users. Because most ransomware relies on the end user clicking something that will trigger a series of actions to install the ransomware or connect to compromised websites to download more malware, all end users should be educated about the dangers. Make sure to include ransomware-related topics in your security awareness training and ensure all users are taking this training.

The education doesn't stop with end users. You also need to educate security operations center (SOC) analysts and other privileged users on responding to ransomware incidents. They need to be aware of major ransomware variants, how ransomware behaves, and its typical characteristics. This will help the analyst to identify a ransomware attack and verify if it represents a new incident or whether it may be related to an existing one.

Applying security best practices across all assets you are protecting is important. Table 12-2 summarizes the security best practices according to the different assets.

TABLE 12-2 Security best practices for ransomware

Work item	Best practice
Email/collaboration	<ul><li>Implement advanced email security capabilities.</li><li>Enable ASR.</li><li>Audit and monitor your email.</li></ul>
Endpoint	<ul><li>Use features such as ASR and tamper protection to block known threats.</li><li>Use Microsoft security baselines to harden your workloads.</li><li>Maintain software up to date.</li><li>Block unexpected traffic using a host-based firewall or other network protection.</li><li>Audit and monitor your endpoints.</li></ul>
Detection and response	<ul><li>Prioritize common endpoints and use integrated Extended Detection and Response (XDR) tools such as Microsoft 365 Defender to have high-quality alerts and minimize friction during the response.</li><li>Make sure you are monitoring brute-force attack attempts such as password spray.</li><li>Ensure that you have monitoring systems that can detect attempts to disable security controls or logging, such as event log clearing and PowerShell operational logs.</li><li>Make sure your endpoint protection solution can rapidly isolate compromised computers.</li></ul>
Backup and recovery	<ul><li>Create a regular schedule to back up all critical data automatically.</li><li>Validate your backup.</li><li>Regularly validate your business continuity/disaster recovery (BC/DR) plan.</li><li>Secure access to your backups with strong authentication mechanisms, including multifactor authentication (MFA).</li><li>Require PIN for critical operations.</li><li>Protect supporting documents required for recovery, such as restoration procedure documents.</li><li>Store backups in offline or off-site storage.</li><li>Use a Recovery Services vault, a storage entity in Azure that houses data. You can use Recovery Services vaults to hold backup data for various Azure services, such as IaaS VMs (Linux or Windows), Azure SQL databases, and on-premises assets.</li></ul>

Thought experiment

In this thought experiment, demonstrate your skills and knowledge of the topics covered in this chapter. You can find answers to this thought experiment in the next section.

Developing a strategy to protect against ransomware

You are the cybersecurity architect for Contoso Inc., an online retail store specializing in various products for office improvements. Contoso management is concerned about the rise of ransomware and wants you to create a strategy to mitigate ransomware attacks. The CISO told the Contoso CEO that despite all security controls in place, the company should always be ready for the worst and expand this strategy to deal with a scenario in which they need to recover the data.

Contoso has workloads in Azure (storage accounts, VMs, and the Key Vault) and AWS (VMs). Contoso uses Microsoft Defender for Endpoint on all Windows 10 machines and wants to ensure they use the same EDR solution for their servers (Windows and Linux).

Based on this scenario, respond to the following questions:

1. Which solution should they utilize to help them improve their security hygiene across Azure and AWS?

2. As part of the strategy against ransomware, they need to leverage security best practices for backup and restore. What are the two security best practices they can use for this scenario?

3. Which capability should they utilize to decrease the likelihood that a threat actor will be able to exploit Office applications and create child processes as part of the attack?

Thought experiment answers

This section contains the solution to the thought experiment. Each answer explains why the answer choice is correct.

1. Microsoft Defender for Cloud is the platform that allows centralized posture management across multiple cloud providers.

2. Secure access to your backups with strong authentication mechanisms, including multifactor authentication (MFA) and requiring a PIN for critical operations. These options will increase the overall security of your backup by adding authentication capabilities that align with the Zero Trust strategy.

3. Attack surface reduction rules in Microsoft 365 Defender will help narrow down the attack surface, which decreases the likelihood of compromise.

Chapter summary

- While planning for ransomware protection, you must ensure that you have security controls to make it much harder for a threat actor to access and disrupt your systems.

- Threat actors using ransomware attacks against an organization are looking for financial gains by pressuring an organization to pay the ransom to have their data back can vary.

- It is important to understand the scope of a ransomware attack and which data can be potentially compromised. That's why it is so important to know your data and have a good data classification system that allows you to make strategic decisions regarding the data that needs to be restored.

- Because security posture management is a continuous process, you should leverage tools such as Microsoft Secure Score to track your progress over time.

- Threat actors will use lateral movement techniques to access privileged accounts. You need to have security controls in place to ensure that compromising a single device does not immediately lead to control of many or all other devices.

- Protecting your assets from ransomware attacks comprises multiple layers of protection, and because threat actors are like water, they take the path of least resistance to achieve their objectives.

- Usually, threat actors use macros because they provide rich capabilities, which are also executed in a privileged context. Implementing best practices for email and collaboration solutions will make it more difficult for threat actors to abuse these systems while allowing legitimate users to access external content safely.

- As part of this hardening process, you should also isolate, disable, or retire insecure systems and protocols, including unsupported operating systems and legacy protocols.

- While conditional access will control the initial authentication and connection, you must ensure tunnel encryption once the connection is established.

- Microsoft Authenticator uses key-based authentication to enable a user credential tied to a device, where the device uses a PIN or biometric.

- The implementation of data protection is part of the strategy to prevent threat actors from accomplishing their objectives.

- Using the assume-breach principle, which is part of the zero-trust strategy, you must prioritize mitigation. This prioritization is critical because you could face a worst-case scenario with ransomware.

- Attack surface reduction can be used to identify suspicious behaviors, such as launching executable files and scripts that attempt to download or run files.

- While adding security controls based on features available in different products is an important step to prevent ransomware attacks, it is imperative to promote awareness and ensure there is no knowledge gap among end users.

Index

A

AAD (Azure Active Directory). *See also* AD DS (Active Directory Domain Services); AD FS (Active Directory Federation Services)

    Access Reviews, 69

    Application Proxy, 87, 200–201

    B2B (Business to Business), 66, 67–68, 202

    B2C (Business to Consumer), 66, 67–68

    Conditional Access, 308

    Connect Health for AD FS, 191

    Connect Sync, 70

    Dynamic Group Membership, 69, 87

    Entitlement Management, 69, 86, 87

    Identity Protection, 70

    Provisioning, 65

access management, 126. *See also* authentication; authorization; privileged-role access

    ACLs (access control lists), 86

    ACR (Azure Container Registry), 221–222

    Azure Storage, 219–220

    cloud resources, 56–64

    conditional access , 78–79, 90–93, 177–178

    data workloads, 212–213

    identity stores, 64–69

    overview of, 55

    remote access, 196–203

    roles, 94–99, 103–104. *See also* privileged-role access

    secrets, keys, and certificates, 191–196

    thought experiment, 106–107

Access Reviews, Azure AD, 69

accounts, 265–266, 271, 285, 309

ACLs (access control lists), 86

ACR (Azure Container Registry), 221–222

Active assignments, 101

Active Directory. *See* AAD (Azure Active Directory)

Activity Log, 98

AD DS (Active Directory Domain Services), 160, 183–191

AD FS (Active Directory Federation Services), 71–73, 190–191

addresses, IP, 221

ADE (Azure Disk Encryption), 253–255

ADLS (Azure Data Lake Storage), 218

agile methodology, 237–239. *See also* DevOps controls

AIR (automated investigation and response), 45

air-gapped environments, 36, 211

AKS (Azure Kubernetes Services), 223

alerts, 102, 220

All Users And Groups scope, 102

Allow BitLocker Without A Compatible TPM policy, 254

Allow Log On Locally, 172, 179, 184

Allow Log On Through Remote Desktop Services, 172, 179

AM (Asset Management), 272

AMA (Azure Monitor Agent), 33

AMSI (Antimalware Scan Interface), 307

Analytics dashboard, 103

Android, 162

antipatterns, best practices versus, 262

anti-phishing protection, 307

Antivirus, 182–183

APIs (application programming interfaces), REST, 166, 255

app gallery, Azure AD, 68

App Service, Azure, 215–217

Append effect, 122

Application Control, 87, 166

application diagrams, 229

Application Guard, 99

Application IDs, 77

Application Proxy, Azure AD, 87, 172, 200–201

applications

    classification of, 228

    hybrid/transitional, 232

    legacy, 232

    mitigating threats to, 227–240

    modern, 232

D

N

O

P

Q-R

W

X-Y-Z

Plug into learning at

MicrosoftPressStore.com

The Microsoft Press Store by Pearson offers:

- Free U.S. shipping

- Buy an eBook, get three formats – Includes PDF, EPUB, and MOBI to use with your computer, tablet, and mobile devices

- Print & eBook Best Value Packs

- eBook Deal of the Week – Save up to 50% on featured title

- Newsletter – Be the first to hear about new releases, announcements, special offers, and more

- Register your book – Find companion files, errata, and product updates, plus receive a special coupon* to save on your next purchase

Discounts are applied to the list price of a product. Some products are not eligible to receive additional discounts, so your discount code may not be applied to all items in your cart. Discount codes cannot be applied to products that are already discounted, such as eBook Deal of the Week, eBooks that are part of a book + eBook pack, and products with special discounts applied as part of a promotional offering. Only one coupon can be used per order.

 Pearson